Netspionage: The Global Threat to Information

Other Butterworth–Heinemann Books by William C. Boni and Dr. Gerald L. Kovacich:[1]

I-Way Robbery: Crime on the Internet

High-Technology Crime Investigator's Handbook: Working in the Global Information Environment

Information Systems Security Officer's Guide: Establishing and Managing an Information Protection Program (Kovacich)

---

[1]Excerpts from these books and their other writings can be viewed at http://www.shockwavewriters.com

Netspionage: The Global Threat to Information

William Boni, MBA, CISA

Dr. Gerald L. Kovacich, CFE, CPP, CISSP

BUTTERWORTH
HEINEMANN

Boston   Oxford   Auckland   Johannesburg   Melbourne   New Delhi

Library of Congress Cataloging-in-Publication Data
Boni, William C.
      Netspionage : the global threat to information / William Boni, Gerald L. Kovacich.
      p. cm.
      Includes index.
      ISBN 0-7506-7257-9 (paper : alk. paper)
      1. Computer crimes. 2. Computer security. 3. Internet (Computer network) I. Kovacich, Gerald L. II. Title.
HV6773 .B665 2000
364.16'8—dc21
      00-039832

British Library Cataloguing-in-Publication Data
A catalogue record for this book is available from the British Library.

The publisher offers special discounts on bulk orders of this book.
For information, please contact:
Manager of Special Sales
Butterworth–Heinemann
225 Wildwood Avenue
Woburn, MA 01801-2041
Tel: 781-904-2500
Fax: 781-904-2620

For information on all Butterworth–Heinemann publications available, contact our World Wide Web home page at: http://www.bh.com

10 9 8 7 6 5 4 3 2 1

Printed in the United States of America

Dedication

This book is dedicated to my family, especially my wife Charunee and my children, Aisha and AJ. They provide the support, encouragement, and love that have been the true measure of a fulfilling life. Also, to my parents, for fostering an early love of books, reading, and learning that has persisted to the present.

William C. Boni
Bartlett, Illinois

This book is dedicated to the memory of Colonel Oleg Penkovsky and all the other global freedom fighters that died so that we may all enjoy the freedom of the human spirit.

Dr. Gerald L. Kovacich
Whidbey Island, Washington

The Art of War

Advance knowledge can not be gained from ghosts and spirits, inferred from phenomena, or projected from the measures of heaven, but must be gained from men for it is the knowledge of the enemy's true situation. . . . Thus there are five types of spies to be employed: Local spies employed from the local district; internal spies employ their people who hold government office; double agents who employ the enemy's spies; expendable spies who are employed to spread disinformation with false information and have them leak it to the enemy; and living spies who return with their reports. . . . Unless one is subtle and perspicacious, one cannot perceive the substance in intelligence reports. It is subtle, subtle! There are no areas in which one does not employ spies. . . .[2]

Sun-tzu

It would be normal to spy on the United States in political matters or military matters. But in economic competition, in technical competition, we are competitors. We are not allied.

Pierre Marion,
former director of France's Direction Generale
de la Securite Exterieure (DGSE)

---

[2]Summary taken from Sun-tzu's *The Art of War*, New Translation by Ralph D. Sawyer, Barnes & Noble Books, New York, pp. 229–233, 1994.

Table of Contents

Foreword

It's 10 A.M. Do You Know Where Your Information Is?

Chances are it's in places you never dreamed. Economic and industrial espionage is an ever-increasing threat. The Central Intelligence Agency (CIA), with the National Communications System (NCS), reported 13 countries have industrial espionage and/or offensive information warfare (IW) capabilities, and most of these countries were major U.S. Y2K fix providers. The United States Federal Bureau of Investigation (FBI) warned that 23 countries conduct economic espionage against the United States. It's unreasonable to believe only 11 percent of the world's countries conduct economic espionage against the United States. No doubt this list of 23 countries only includes the names of the countries that the FBI can publicly release.

In France, the School of Economic Warfare, a private concern, developed a list of courses that sounds as if it came from the CIA. Courses are on military strategy, intelligence, subversion, martial arts, psychological operations, and information and situation manipulation, all of which are centered on the modern battleground of computers and the Internet. IW, computer attacks, and the "info-destabilization of companies" are discussion, homework, and essay topics. Christian Harbulot, director of the two-year-old institute, said, "Our main weapon is not poison or a revolver, but an operation of encirclement and intrusion by knowledge."

Don't think France is alone. Idaho State University is one of 13 schools in the nation teaching students a special kind of spying. The students study competitive intelligence (CI). One student said, "If you take any sort of marketing position, you'll be doing this sort of thing."

Of course CI is important, but that's just one area within business and government that is affected. Low-tech theft aided by a computer must not be overlooked. For example, Egyptian police are investigating a crime at Cairo University involving the theft of floppy disks containing classified data about Egypt's oil, gas, and uranium reserves as well as the location of gold and copper deposits.

Dr. Dorothy Denning, a professor at Georgetown University, was part of a three-person panel that met on December 15, 1999, to discuss information warfare and cyber-terrorism at the Carnegie Endowment for International Peace. "Having the best information and denying that to your opponent is the number one goal. I think the only thing that's changed is the technology. To make it all the more interesting, to hack in for espionage purposes—there's nothing wrong with that. This is what countries do." Espionage is, in fact, sanctioned under international law. Using the Internet can lower the cost and shorten the time of collection, and may even improve the quality of what's collected.

Of course, you reap what you sow. Novell conducted a study in the United Kingdom (U.K.) called "Project Trawler." One finding was over a third of U.K. businesses on the Internet are unprotected against Internet crime. The survey, which questioned 150 U.K.-based information technology (IT) managers and directors who use the Internet as a business tool, found that 37 percent of U.K. companies on the net have no firewall and 44 percent do not make use of authentication. Open doors, no matter if they are physical or virtual, are like having a target painted with the caption, "Steal here."

The 1999 American Society for Industrial Security (ASIS) and PricewaterhouseCoopers (PwC) "Trends in Proprietary Information Loss" Survey Report cited the following key findings:

Fortune 1000 companies sustained losses of more than $45 billion from theft of their proprietary information.

Forty-four companies of the 97 that responded reported over 1,000 incidents of theft. Of these, 579 incidents were valued with a total estimated loss of nearly $1 billion.

The average company response was 2.45 incidents with estimated losses per incident of over $500,000.

The study stated the greatest known losses to American companies are in manufacturing processes and research and development (R&D) information.

Although manufacturing reported only 96 incidents, the acknowledged losses of manufacturing companies accounted for the majority of losses reported in the survey, and averaged almost $50 million per incident.

The *Wall Street Journal* reported that the United States government and private spending on R&D is expected to rise a combined 7.8 percent increase in 2000 to a total of $266.2 billion. It's cheaper to steal and copy than to develop from scratch.

The Collaborative Electronic Notebook Systems Association research report entitled "Titanic 2020" concluded the world would soon begin to experience trillion-dollar losses of critical data and legal records due to inadequate software infrastructure.

The PwC/ASIS study also pointed out that on-site contractor employees and original equipment manufacturers (OEMs) are now perceived by companies responding to the survey as the greatest threat to corporate proprietary information. The Department of Defense (DoD) identified the trusted insider as its greatest threat. Why these groups of people? Because they have access to the infrastructure, processes, documentation, and people to get the needed "gold nuggets." They can steal information that they are authorized, or even not authorized, because they know, or are in a position to easily find out, the controls and information protection mechanisms of the organization.

Trust is relative for some people. This reminds me of the son who asked his father about how long people held off before they gave in. The father replied, "Son, every man has his price. You'll be proud to know your father's was very, very high." Trust is a good thing, but verification doesn't hurt.

The value of e-commerce between businesses is expected to rise to $1.5 trillion in 2004 from $114 billion in 1999, according to a forecast by brokerage Goldman Sachs. Although that's an order of magnitude increase in only five years, more explosive growth has been in corporate espionage. Conducted mostly by insiders, their task has been made easier by the networked computer systems that are replacing standalone systems. An International Chamber of Commerce (ICC) survey cited reports from organizations that the hacking attempts into their networks had tripled between 1997 and 1998. Other surveys by the ICC found half of the systems' managers were unaware of any intrusion. Electronic sabotage, especially through viruses, could lead to significant ransom demands using the threat of system wipeout.

What Can Be Gleaned from All This?

There is no such thing as perfect security. For every move that is made, there is a counter move. The counter can be high- or low-tech from outside the organization or from a trusted insider. The moves and counter moves are becoming more and more complex.

Training, awareness, and education must be the foundation of any security program.

If young teenage hackers can successfully penetrate systems, Netspionage agents and techno-spies can do so much more.

Too much information is available on the Internet. The DoD established the Joint Web Risk Assessment Cell (JWRAC) to review information on DoD Web sites to ensure military operations and national security are not jeopardized.

How much information is available via open sources? A 361-page book written in 1991 by two of China's top military intelligence experts, *Sources and Methods of Obtaining National Defence Science and Technology Intelligence*, caught the public's eye in 1999. The authors define intelligence as "critical knowledge necessary to make breakthroughs on key technologies." About 80 percent of the intelligence needed by China's military can be obtained from open sources, they say, while the remaining 20 percent must be sought from classified or secret sources. The open sources listed include published materials, conferences, and electronic information.

Espionage through electronic information systems are limited only by human creativity. For a while in the late 1980s, a popular means of information gathering was based on a hacker seizing control of a modem. A person could log off, and the monitor and the modem's lights indicated logging off, but the hacker maintained control of the session, and had all the privileges of the user. Today a powerful means of collection is via remotely seizing a computer's microphone and Web camera. Bill Lyons, head of the Internet security company Finjan, said, "Military people in the United States have tested this, and you can be sure, if people in general are aware of it, then computer hackers are aware of it. The frightening thing is, there are tools on the Internet that are able to switch on the computer's microphone, make a recording, and forward it to someone else without the user's knowledge. People can bind this malicious code to simple attachments." Experts have also confirmed what can be done with a microphone can also be done with a Webcam—allowing pictures to be taken of people, equipment, and documents near a computer terminal. So what? Now the computer can take the place of an electronic bug or putting a spy on site. Live audio and video is the ultimate intelligence coup.

Security is a hard sell. It always says what you can't do, and the uninformed believe it doesn't add to the bottom line. A more studied view is security experts are not crying "Wolf!" Weak security practices can be costly. Gary Lynch, a partner at Ernst & Young, said the average online theft totals $250,000 (£154,827), and only 2 percent of the cases are successfully prosecuted. In comparison, he said the average bank robber walks away with only $19,000, and fully 82 percent of bank robbers are caught and convicted. It won't take long to amortize security investments.

On the virtual clock it's still 10 a.m. What are you going to do to ensure you know where your information is? Jerry Kovacich and Bill Boni have done a masterful job to explain this new, still dangerous world we live in, lay out vulnerabilities and threats via the Internet, and offer many sound solutions to minimize risks. As Benjamin Franklin said, "Forewarned is forearmed."

Perry G. Luzwick[3]
Lieutenant Colonel, U.S. Air Force
Washington, D.C.

[3]The views expressed by Lt. Col. Luzwick are his and do not reflect the official policy or position of the U.S. Department of Defense or the U.S. government.

Preface

In this book, we will develop, describe, and present a complete picture of the trend that the U.S. National Counter Intelligence Center (NACIC) has called "the single fastest growing modus operandi for theft of critical information."

This book, an introduction to Netspionage (Net-enabled espionage), is intended to educate and inform every corporate manager, executive, security professional, criminal justice professional, corporate employees, and even individual Internet users of the nature and extent of the new risks to sensitive information created by Internet connectivity. It is intended to explain how the Internet may be exploited to gain or sustain a competitive advantage. This book is designed to provide a foundation of knowledge for protecting critical organizational assets from the new risks of Internet enabled espionage and how the Net may be used by ethical practitioners of business intelligence to help their corporations prosper in the 21st century.

We think of this book as a carefully crafted "virtual boot camp" in Internet-enabled competitive intelligence gathering combined with a threat "awareness briefing" for corporate and security managers and executives. The content will be taken from the front lines of the conflict between those committed to stealing information and those who defend it. You will find that there are some paragraphs that provide basically the same information in a different way. This was planned in order to reinforce some of the major points, using the lecture approach of "tell them what you are going to tell them, then tell them, then tell them what you told them."

This book is based on the nearly 50 years of combined "real world" operational experience of the authors who together have been responsible for implementing Internet protection and business intelligence programs for corporations ranging from United States and foreign military, law enforcement and intelligence services; through United States and foreign international high-technology companies. We have also investigated numerous cases of known or suspected loss of sensitive information via the Internet.

We have conducted years of lectures on Netspionage and related topics at professional conferences for a variety of international associations and businesses in the United States, Asia, and Europe. At many of these seminars, attendees wanted to know if additional information could be provided in a book. They suggested that the seminars provided practical insights that put the technical complexities of Internet enabled espionage and business intelligence gathering into perspective. It also helped them appreciate the variety of threats, design and manage protective measures, and understand how to operate ethically in the new "cyber" world. For that reason, this book has been written.

This book tells the reader how the Internet may become a valuable asset supporting practitioners of ethical business intelligence collection, and how the Internet may be exploited by the "dark side." Through examples and mini-case studies it shows how, why, and when corporations are at risk and recommends specific steps to protect against the devastating attack of the network enabled spy that we call the Netspionage agent and the techno-spy. Unlike many Internet-related books, this one will be written for a nontechnical audience. It should be especially useful for corporate managers or executives as well as managers and staff with formal knowledge management or competitive intelligence responsibility.

What sets this book apart from others is that it provides a foundation for dealing with the complex issues arising from an extremely important and profound issue: How the Internet and allied technologies have forever altered the cost-benefit issues associated with the collection and analysis of all forms of competitive information.

The rapid growth of the Internet and associated instances of high-technology crimes foisted upon the public via the Internet are dramatically increasing. There is need for reliable information concerning the threats posed by Netspionage agents and techno-spies, and on how to protect a corporation's sensitive information against the skillful attack from Netspionage.

Within the United States alone, the number of people who have access and use the Internet on a daily basis has grown dramatically and will continue to climb for the foreseeable future. The estimates for individual users ranges from a low of nine to a high of 60-plus million of Internet users. Others put the number at 500 million worldwide. Whatever the number, we all know that there are millions of Internet surfers, and that number is growing. A concise, nontechnical book on how the Internet contributes to gaining competitive advantage through business intelligence and the risks created by network enabled espionage will be a useful primer, which can be used by a wide range of professionals. It is hoped that this book achieves that objective.

Coverage

This book consists of four sections incorporating 17 chapters.

Section I: How Did We Get Here?

Netspionage. Why does it occur? Who are these 21st century techno-spies? How do they steal? What do they steal? What can be done about it? All important questions. However, in order to understand Netspionage, it is important to understand this fairly new phenomena we call the Information Age or Age of Technology. Therefore, the first five chapters are devoted to providing an overview of this environment in which we all must live, work, and play. For only with this broad-based understanding, can we truly begin to understand Netspionage and its implications.

Chapter 1: Introduction to the New Old World—This chapter introduces the New World environment in which we all must live, work, and play. Things seem to change but do they really? This chapter will discuss the real and perceived changes in our new information- or technology-based world.

Chapter 2: The Driving Force: High-Technology—Technology, especially the microprocessor, its computers and global networks, have been the driving force that has pushed and dragged us at breakneck speeds into the age of information and established knowledge. It is also the major driving force of the world economy. This chapter will discuss the technology revolution and evolution of network enabled business. Technological elements that got us to where we are in business competition are identified and some of the key variables that will drive the 21st century global business environment are described.

Chapter 3: The Internet—The Global I-Way to Netspionage and Techno-Crime—The Internet is the foundation for the global business and communications processes of the world. This chapter provides a short history and overview of the Internet and some of its problems that impact businesses and government agencies.

Chapter 4: The Global Business and Government Revolutions—This chapter will discuss some fundamental changes to the business environment that are setting the stage for an era of wholesale espionage. The transformation of value creation from manufacturing of physical product to the creation of knowledge and intangible intellectual property will be highlighted. This transition and ever decreasing product lifecycles drive the need for more comprehensive forms of intelligence collection, including spying. On a national level, we will explain why the evolution of supra-national corporations developing through mega-mergers will create quasi-political entities that may well act outside the laws of any given nation-state. The logic that will drive mega-corporate entities to engage in Netspionage will be explored.

Chapter 5: A Short History of Espionage: Industrial, Economic, and Military—Espionage is no longer just about spies stealing military secrets, in fact, it never was. This chapter will explain the evolution of espionage and describe how the second oldest profession has already leaped into cyberspace. The evolution of Netspionage (network-enabled espionage) in the new global business environment will be described. The differences between the three types of espionage will be explained as well as to their integration and blurring of differences into

Netspionage as the primary 21st century tool for gaining a competitive advantage as a nation, business, or military force.

Section II: Who Does What to Whom, Why and How

This section will provide the reader with a description of how effective use of a wide range of technologies has made the efficient collection and dissemination of timely intelligence information an effective tool for savvy managers in both business and government. We will define and describe technology-enabled ethical competitive intelligence, and distinguish this vital element of corporate success from the criminal acts involved in actual spying.

   Chapter 6: Competitive Intelligence and the Networked World—This chapter will discuss the migration of information to the Web as businesses use it to automate their value chain and build tight linkages with customers, suppliers, vendors, employees, and government agencies. It will detail e-business as fundamentally changing the Web and Internet; increased importance of competitive intelligence collection and analysis; as well as the increased temptation to cross the line and commit Netspionage to supplement the publicly available information.

   Chapter 7: Information Collection in the Gray Zone—Netspionage—This chapter discusses what can be accomplished by operating in the ethical and legal "white zone," the unethical and legal "gray zone," and the unethical and illegal "black zone." It will explain that because of today's global networks connected to the Internet, information brokers, hackers, and private investigators are among the groups of people selling information to those with the money to buy.

   Chapter 8: The Black Zone, Who Uses Netspionage, How and Why—This chapter discusses operating in the black zone where principles such as ethics and legal issues no longer apply. Discussions will include techniques and software products that can be used by the Netspionage agents against multiple and vulnerable corporate targets.

   Chapter 9: Case Studies of Netspionage—This chapter identifies and analyzes Netspionage-related cases; as well as discusses their meaning and impact.

Section III: Protecting What You Have from Those Who Want It

   Now that you understand the new information-based environment detailed in Section I and the threats and techniques that may be used against your corporation as stated in Section II, Section III will discuss what you can do to mitigate the risks to your vulnerable sensitive information.

   Chapter 10: Defending Against Netspionage—This chapter will discuss basic, cost-effective and common sense processes that can and should be in place to defend ones' competitive advantage or market share. Both technological enhancements and human-procedural changes that can toughen the organization's perimeter and dramatically increase the potential to deter, detect, and rapidly respond to known or suspected incidents will be presented.

Chapter 11: Operational Security and Risk Management Techniques to Mitigate the Netspionage Threat—This chapter discusses proactive methods to perform a self-assessment that can help determine the level of vulnerability of a corporation to Netspionage.

Chapter 12: The Best Defense May Really Be a Good Offense and Other Issues—There is an increasing belief that corporations can not depend solely on law enforcement or other government agencies to protect them from Netspionage and techno-spies. Some have begun to attack their adversaries in retaliation or even before their adversaries are able to attack them. This new form of vigilantism and ramifications will be discussed as well as the role of the hacker as a business' new hired gun and defender.

Section IV: Based on Where We Have Been and Where We Are Now, Where Are We Going?

This section provides a short overview of the possible things to come based on the trends of the past. Someone once said, "You don't know where you are going, if you don't know where you've been." In this book, we have looked at the past and the present. Hopefully, that view provides some trends to indicate where we are going.

Chapter 13: Future of Technology—Based on today's technology, there are trends that indicate the technology changes that will be taking place and impacting businesses on a global scale in the 21st century. This chapter will look at those trends and make some "best guesses" about what this 21st century technology will look like and how these trends will impact the potential vulnerability of corporations to both legal competitive intelligence as well as Netspionage and other forms of espionage.

Chapter 14: Business, Crime, and Security in the 21st Century Global Marketplace—This chapter will project into the future and envision the early 21st century business environment incorporating technological changes, social changes, and governmental changes.

Chapter 15: Future Netspionage—This chapter will look at the early 21st century drivers for Netspionage, and discuss the new dangers and their impact on businesses, society, national, and global economies. How, why, and where the well-equipped Netspionage operative will exist and their likely contribution to future conflicts between nation-states and businesses will be explored.

Chapter 16: Businesses and Governments Agencies—Shared Responsibilities: This chapter will discuss the adversarial relationships between United States' businesses and government agencies, and how this has hampered our ability to compete globally. We will suggest what must be done in a joint, cooperative effort to help win the global economic war that is already increasingly intense.

Chapter 17: Epilog: We're All In This Together—Final comments by the authors on the entire topic of Netspionage, and the critical importance of an integrated information collection and protection program to survival and success in the next 20 years of business to gain and sustain the competitive edge for corporations.

Closing Comments

We hope that this book will make a significant contribution to the successful and secure use of the Internet by the general populace, businesses, and government agencies. By one estimate, half of the businesses in the United States already own or operate a Web site or other Internet connection. Given the large numbers of companies and organizations who have recently or will soon connect with the Internet, there is a serious need for timely, accurate, and clear advice on how to prudently manage the very real risks of using the Internet.

Spies and spying have fascinated the public for decades, and the explosive growth of Internet stocks shows that the U.S. public has a love affair with the high technology realm. Our intention is to reach a broad segment of the reading public in a way that will be both entertaining and effective in explaining how successful businesses and users in the 21st century must master technology enabled intelligence gathering while safeguarding themselves against the threat of net-enabled espionage—Netspionage.

William C. Boni and Dr. Gerald L. Kovacich

Acknowledgments

As is always the case for us, in order to take on a project such as this, it takes more than just the authors. It takes friends, professional associates, and peers who unselfishly give of their time and effort, as well as invaluable support, to help make this book worth publishing.

We are very grateful to a special group who have helped us over the years and again with this project, to include: Andy Jones, John Quinn, Perry Luzwick, and Motomu Akashi.

We must also acknowledge the staff of Butterworth–Heinemann, especially Laurel A. DeWolf, Jennifer Packard, Cate Barr, Maura Kelly, Janet Bixler, Diane DeMarco, Jacqui Brownstein, and Irv Hershman for their time, effort, and support in making this book a reality. Over the years, their professionalism, expertise, support, and guidance have made this and our other books a reality.

A thanks and tip of the hat to Paul Zavidniak, Chartmaker and Graphics Designer Extraordinaire, for his ability to take text and make a picture worth a thousand words.

A special thanks to Chiang Hsiao-yun, *Shockwave Writers'* Chief of Research and Analyses, for her contributions to this project, and also for her patience, love, and understanding through 25 years of being Mrs. Gerald L. Kovacich.

We must also thank the many readers of our previous books who have contacted us to express their appreciation for providing them with practical, real-world information; and who have encouraged us to continue to write and publish our books. To them, a special thanks for their support!

If you have comments or questions for us, you can contact us through http://www.shockwavewriters.com.

Disclaimer

This book contains information relative to nation-states, companies, and individuals identified in the news media and through other open sources. It contains the experiences of the authors; as well as information about vendors and their products; search engines; and methods that can be used to commit Netspionage, industrial and economic espionage, as well as how to defend against such attacks.

By discussing and identifying the above, neither the authors nor the publishers in any way imply any wrong doing by those noted nor do they endorse any vendor or their products. Furthermore, the objective of providing the information in this book is for educational purposes only in an effort to make corporate management, as well as security and law enforcement professionals, aware of the threats to information in this age of technology and the global marketplace. We do not condone nor encourage the use of any information provided except as information for professionals involved in managing and protecting corporate and government assets, as well as investigating wrongdoing by the world's miscreants.

Section I: How Did We Get Here?

Netspionage. Why does it occur? Who are these 21st century techno-spies? How do they steal? What do they steal? What can be done about it? All are important questions. However, in order to understand Netspionage, it is important to understand this fairly new phenomena we call the Information Age or Age of Technology. Therefore, the first five chapters are devoted to providing an overview of this environment in which we all must live, work, and play. For only with this broad-based understanding, can we truly begin to understand Netspionage and its implications.

Chapter 1: Introduction to the New Old World

This chapter introduces the New World environment in which we all must live, work, and play. Things seem to change, but do they really? This chapter will discuss the real and perceived changes in our new information or technology-based world.

Chapter 2: The Driving Force: High-Technology

Technology, especially the microprocessor, its computers, and global networks, have been the driving force that has pushed and dragged us at breakneck speeds into the age of information and established knowledge. It is also the major driving force of the world economy.

This chapter will discuss the technology revolution and evolution of network enabled business. Technological elements that got us to where we are in business competition are identified and some of the key variables that will drive the 21st century global business environment are described.

Chapter 3: The Internet:
The Global I-Way to Netspionage and Techno-Crime

The Internet is the foundation for the global business and communications processes of the world. This chapter provides a short history and overview of the Internet and some of its problems that impact businesses and government agencies.

Chapter 4: The Global Business
and Government Revolutions

This chapter will discuss some fundamental changes to the business environment that are setting the stage for an era of wholesale espionage. The transformation of value creation from manufacturing of physical product to the creation of knowledge and intangible intellectual property will be highlighted. This transition and ever decreasing product lifecycles drive the need for more comprehensive forms of intelligence collection, including spying. On a national level, we will explain why the evolution of supra-national corporations developing through mega-mergers will create quasi-political entities that may well act outside the laws of any given nation-state. The logic that will drive mega-corporate entities to engage in Netspionage will be explored.

Chapter 5: A Short History of Espionage:
Industrial, Economic, and Military

Espionage is no longer just about spies stealing military secrets, in fact, it never was. This chapter will explain the evolution of espionage and describe how the second oldest profession has already leaped into cyberspace. The evolution of Netspionage (network-enabled espionage) in the new global business environment will be described. The differences between the three types of espionage will be explained as well as to their integration and blurring of differences into Netspionage as the primary 21st century tool for gaining a competitive advantage as a nation, business, or military force.

1

Introduction to the New Old World

Someone once said that the more things change, the more they stay the same. Well, that certainly applies to our current environment. When it comes to technology, yes, there are changes, some dramatic changes in fact. When it comes to we human beings, not much has changed over the years when it comes to our basic instincts, what we want out of life, our inherent drive for personal freedoms, and the like. However, when we combine our human instincts and desires with technology, we find that we keep doing the same old things but in a technology-based environment. And when it comes to stealing sensitive information such as proprietary information, trade secrets, and government secrets, this certainly holds true.

The global Internet has rapidly been transformed from an academic playground into a global mainstream business and communications medium. This transformation is one of the most significant developments in recent history. It has already had a profound impact on all aspects of our civilization, and the changes are continuing. One of the many areas that have changed dramatically is the area of gathering and using information and intelligence. Already reports have begun to circulate of how sophisticated criminals, terrorists, and especially the intelligence agencies of all major nations are exploiting the new "cyber world" to their various ends. These organizational actors and an increasing number of individual "information brokers" are using the Internet to commit the old crime of "espionage" in a revolutionary new way: *Netspionage*: network enabled espionage (see Figure 1–1).

With the end of the Cold War came the breakup of the Soviet Union, Yugoslavia, and other nations. New global alignments have formed; old hostilities once kept in check have exploded into "new" regional conflicts (see Figure 1–2).

As we have seen over the last several years, nations are globally entwined in the marketplace. Such things as electronic commerce (e-commerce), balance of trade deficits, Asian economic crisis, trade-wars, dumping of goods and products, violation of copyright statutes, competitive intelligence collections, thefts of trade secrets, patent lawsuits, and global mergers have brought corporations and nation-states into the realm of business and economic warfare in the global marketplace. This is the new business environment in which today's business and government managers, security professionals, investigators, law enforcement professionals, and criminal justice professionals work.

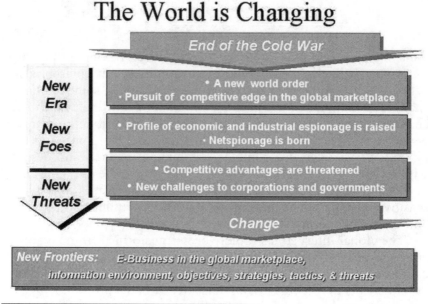

Figure 1–1 World changes leading to Netspionage.

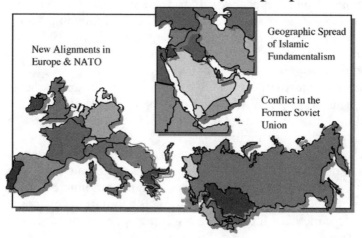

Figure 1–2 Some regional areas of partnership and conflicts.

Espionage activities are proving useful in these battles. Broadly defined, classic espionage, the essential act of spying, has served five major purposes depending essentially on the sponsorship of the activity:

- Defense of a nation
- Assist in defeating an adversary
- Increase economic power of a nation or business
- Expand a business' market share
- Deciding whether to merge or acquire a business

However, as many analysts have noted, military power is now largely, if not wholly dependent on economic strength. This strength is based on the strength of corporations that are increasingly rooted in the world of bits and bytes, and less in the industrial age of mass (physical) production.

In this new information-driven age, the line between the espionage, motivated purely by military advantage and the quest for market dominance is blurred if not completely eliminated. The spy is held in high esteem in many parts of the world, and has been a decisive asset throughout history, as noted by Sun Tzu.[1] The 21st century, which many prognosticators expect to be the "Information Age" or the "Age of Technology," may instead come to be known as the "Age of the Netspionage Agent and Techno-Spy."

This "second oldest profession" thrives upon demand for information. So, in a time when technology and technology-based information equates to power, and the Internet provides unprecedented access to information, we expect the epitome of spying to be the skillful collection of information for every purpose via networks and other computer systems.

The popular media including TV, newspapers, and trade journals have already noted how hackers, governments, and businesses are already using the Internet as a platform that supports a wide range of computer and other crimes. Many criminal schemes depend for their success on efficient gathering and transmission of information.

What's Going On?

Why are groups as disparate as national governments, Federal law enforcement, terrorists, and business associations all investing heavily in the cyber domain? The reason is readily apparent: civilization is experiencing a fundamental transition from a world managed by and

---

[1]Sun Tzu, a general, is credited with writing the *Art of War* for Ho Lu, King of Wu, who reigned in China from 514 to 496 B.C.

devoted to physical "atoms" to the rapidly unfolding world focused on bytes and electronics. Netspionage must inevitably become more common because spies and other criminals live by Willy Sutton's axiom: "Go where the money is!" And the way to the money is down the "yellow brick" information roads called the Internet, the Global Information Infrastructure (GII), and the National Information Infrastructure (NII) of the information-based nation-states.

In the near 21st century, the money is in the information coursing through cyberspace and the global Internet. By some estimates, intangible assets of the enterprise (the knowledge, trade secrets, and sensitive proprietary information utilized by a corporation) already constitute 50 percent or more of the value of a modern business corporation. Such assets are now most commonly found in digital form somewhere in the corporation and often on the corporate Web site. This makes the "crown jewels" ever more accessible to those with motive, opportunity, and capability to work with network enabled tools to capture information, in short perfect targets for Netspionage.

It is believed that Netspionage incidents will become increasingly common in the 21st century as more and more of the world's commerce is enabled or supported by a global Internet. To add to the concern, directors of both the United States Federal Bureau of Investigation (FBI) and the United States Central Intelligence Agency (CIA) have warned that the United States and most modern, information- and technology-dependent states are vulnerable. The United States is at risk to the ravages not only of techno-terrorists and cyber-criminals exploiting the Internet, but also economic espionage. The problem is such a concern to the United States that the Economic Espionage Act was recently passed to establish new and stronger support for the United States Government and its businesses against these new attacks (see Appendix 1). Since the United States is the world's dominant economic power, it is *the* target of other nations and their corporations who must compete in the global marketplace.

The Global Information Age Environment Trends

United States' Vice President Gore once stated:

> We are on the verge of a revolution that is just as profound as the change in the economy that came with the industrial revolution. Soon electronic networks will allow people to transcend the barriers of time and distance and take advantage of global markets and business opportunities not even imaginable today, opening up a new world of economic possibility and progress.

It is very important for today's corporate managers, security professionals, and others to understand this new and growing, global information age environment. Because of the Internet, we all must think differently (see Figure 1–3). What is most important is an understanding of tomorrow's global environment; the trends, which affect nations and corporations, and which will have an impact on their ability to maintain a competitive advantage in the future.

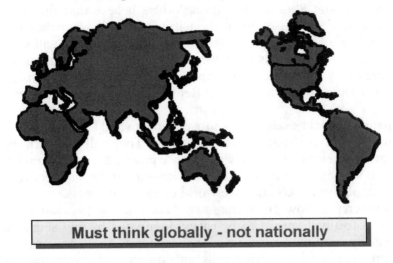

Must think globally - not nationally

Figure 1–3 The global marketplace requires us to think differently.

The corporation or security organization that does not look ahead at the trends in society, technology, business, global competition, criminal justice systems, crime, and any associated rapid changes, will not be able to meet the needs of its customers. This point can not be stressed enough. One must understand this growing and rapidly changing information-driven environment. Understanding it better than the competition gives one a competitive edge in the business warfare arena.

If you do not think today's global competition is a form of business and economic warfare, than you are fooling yourself and are doomed to failure. Your global competitors are on a "war footing" and they aren't taking prisoners. They will use any means at their disposal to gain that competitive advantage and many are doing so with the backing of their government.

The Demise of the Nation-State and the Rise of the Individual

When we look back from the times of the caveman up to today, we often fail to realize that the entity we call the nation-state has a very short history of only 700 years. Some, such as Davidson and Rees-Moog, believe " . . . Something new is coming. Just as farming societies differed in kind from hunting-and-gathering bands, and industrial societies differed radically from feudal or yeoman agricultural systems, so the New World to come will mark a radical departure from anything seen before . . . "[2]

Davidson and Rees-Moog, among others believe that the "sovereign individual" will rise out of the nation-states. If what they say is true, then we all probably can agree that the nation-state will not go quietly. Just as individuals fight for survival, so will the nation-state. There are many rather recent examples such as the former Yugoslavia, the former Union of Soviet Socialist Republics, and Indonesia, to name a few.

There will be those citizens whose patriotism and "love of country" will support the nation-state over its citizens. They will join with those in the government who do not want to lose power, as well as those corporations who find the power of the nation-state to be an effective and important ally in the competitive world of global business.

John Perry Barlow put it this way, "The real issue is control. The Internet is too widespread to be easily dominated by any single government. By creating a seamless global-economic zone, anti-sovereign and unregulative, the Internet calls into question the very idea of a nation-state."[3]

Summary

The new old world is rapidly changing due to technology and yet, the human instincts and spirit remain the same, as does the drive for the businesses' competitive edge. The 21st century is ushering in a vastly new environment than was the case in the beginning of the 20th century. Global competition aided and driven by information and technology-based nations and corporations are rapidly increasing.

Nation-states appear to be waning and the "sovereign individual" is fighting for its place in the world. The nation-state will not go quietly into the night. Whether the nation-state or the sovereign individual prevails, business will survive.

To maintain control, gain power, increase marketshare, and beat the competitors, nations and businesses are using information and technology as the new instruments of business and economic warfare, and Netspionage is their main process.

---

[2]Davidson and Rees-Mogg, *The Sovereign Individual.* New York: Simon & Schuster, 1997.

[3]John Perry Barlow, "Thinking Locally, Acting Globally," *Time* magazine, January 15, 1996, p. 57.

References

Aburdene, Patricia, and John Naisbitt. *Megatrends 2000*. New York: Avon Books, 1990.

Boni, William C., and Gerald L. Kovacich. *Internet Robbery Crime on the Internet*. Boston: Butterworth–Heinemann, 1999.

Davidson, James Dale, and William Lord Rees-Mogg. *The Sovereign Individual*. New York: Simon & Schuster, 1997.

Giles, Lionel. *Sun Tzu on the Art of War*. Taipei: Literature House Ltd., 1964.

Kovacich, Gerald L. *The Information Systems Security Officer's Guide*. Boston: Butterworth–Heinemann, 1998.

Kovacich, Gerald L., and William C. Boni. *High-Technology Crime Investigator's Handbook: Working in the Global Information Environment*. Boston: Butterworth–Heinemann, 1999.

Naisbitt, John. *Megatrends*. New York: Warner Books, 1982.

Naisbitt, John. *Megatrends* Asia. New York: Simon & Schuster, 1996.

Sawyer, Ralph D. *Sun-tzu The Art of War*. New York: Barnes & Noble Books, 1994.

Toffler, Alvin. *Future Shock*. New York: Bantam Books Inc., 1971.

Toffler, Alvin. *The Third Wave*. New York: Bantam Books Inc., 1980.

Toffler, Alvin. *Powershift*. New York: Bantam Books Inc., 1990.

Toffler, Alvin and Heidi. *War and Anti-War*. Boston: Little, Brown and Company, 1993.

Toffler, Alvin and Heidi. *Creating a New World Civilization*. Atlanta: Turner Publishing, Inc., 1994.

2

The Driving Force: High-Technology

Computers are rapidly changing the world. If you are involved in any activity where technology is used as a tool to help you accomplish your work, you are aware of the tremendous and very rapid advances that are being made in that arena. It is something to behold, but what is technology, "high-technology" as some call it?

When we speak of high-technology, we are speaking of computer-based machines, equipment, processing, and communications devices that are used to manage and support personal, business, and government agency processes. Many of today's high-technology devices are used to communicate information on a local, national, and international level. In today's world, the communication of information in information-based societies such as the United States leads to political, economic, and/or military advantages—and disadvantages.

The advantage is the ability to collect and use information that provides a competitive edge over others to assist in meeting government and business objectives. However, high-technology also makes the modern information- and technology-based nations and businesses more vulnerable. This is because the information can be stolen from electronic storage media; multiple copies made and transmitted around the world at the speed of light. Yet, the information is still where we left it the night before. The technology itself has inherent vulnerabilities as anyone running today's systems and Web sites can attest.

We are in the midst of the most rapid technological advances in human history, but this is just the beginning. We are not even close to reaching the potential that technology has to offer, or its impact on all of us—both good and bad.

It is said that there have been more discoveries in the last 50 years than in the entire history of mankind before that time. We have only to read the papers and the trade journals to look at every profession and see what technology is bringing to our world. There are new discoveries in medicine; online and worldwide information systems; the ability to hold teleconferences across the country and around the globe; and hundreds of other examples.

Today's high-technology environment is based on the microprocessor—the computer. Computers have been around for decades; however, they have become more powerful, cheaper, smaller, networked nationally and internationally; and that trend is continuing. Computers have become an integral part—a necessity—in our society. We have entered what some have called "The Information Age." In the United States and in other developed countries of the world, we have become an information- and technology-dependent society.

In the past, computerized information, that information stored on disk drives and tapes, had been supported by hardcopies; however, that is often no longer the case. Therefore, information is more at risk from techno-spies, Netspionage agents, and the like. They can damage, destroy, manipulate, and change information, information that still appears to be the original information. Information that may have no hardcopy backup to compare with. To many, the old adage that "it came from the computer therefore it must be correct," still holds true.

For example, what if someone stole your sales and stock dividend forecast files, and replaced them with files estimating triple the sales and dividend that the corporation actually forecasted, just before that information was released, to include on your Web site? Then, assuming it was eventually noticed to be incorrect, how would you explain it? However you try to explain it, it would not sound like corporate management had control. Would all your information and accounting figures be questioned? What would the U.S. Securities Exchange Commission do? How would the general public, the stockmarket analyst, the stockholders, your customers, suppliers, and the news reporters perceive all this? What would happen to your stock? Your customer base? Remember the old adage that "all is fair in love and war?" This is business warfare and it is supported by the collection of good intelligence through Netspionage. If you think this can't happen, or "can't happen to my corporation," you are naive and only fooling yourself. Then again, that comes as no surprise as it is the same mentality management often has before their systems and Web site are attacked and defaced.

High-technology is the mainstay of our businesses and government agencies. We can no longer function in business or government without them. Pagers, cellular phones, e-mail, credit cards, teleconferences, smart cards, notebook computers, networks, and private branch exchanges (PBX) are all computer-based and are all now common tools for individuals, businesses, public agencies, and government agencies. All these technological wonders store, process, and transmit sensitive, proprietary, national security, and trade secret information on a daily basis, and sadly, *usually without being encrypted*. These devices and their transmission are easy prey for Netspionage agents and techno-spies.

Because the computers are becoming so powerful in terms of speed, storage capacity, memory, size, and their related software and networks, they have become more complex. No one can be a technical expert in all of the various systems, software, etc. However, we must maintain a current, basic understanding of today's technology, how it functions, its threats, its vulnerabilities. We then rely on trusted and experienced specialists in order to understand the problems better so that correct management decisions can be made, and help defend the networks from these modern-day threat agents.

Networking and embedded systems, those integrated into other devices, such as automobiles, microwave ovens, medical equipment, are increasing, and drastically changing how we live, work, and play. According to a study, financed by the United States Advanced Research Projects Agency (ARPA), and published in the book, *Computers at Risk*:

- Computers have become so integrated into the business environments, that computer-related risks cannot be separated from normal business risks, or those of government and other public agencies.
- Increased trust in computers for safety-critical applications, such as medical, that there is increased likelihood attacks or accidents can cause deaths (NOTE: It has already happened).
- Use and abuse of computers is widespread with increased threats of viruses, credit card, PBX, cellular phones, and other frauds.
- Unstable international political environment raises concerns about governments' or terrorists' attacks on information and high-technology dependent nations' computer and telecommunications systems.
- Individual privacy is at risk due to large, vulnerable databases containing personal information, facilitating increases in identity theft and other frauds.

Personal computers have changed our lives dramatically and no end is in sight. The use of modems is now commonplace with all newly purchased microcomputer systems coming with an internal modem already installed and ready for global access through the Internet or other networks. Therefore, the home computers and long distance telephone networks represent some of the potentially most seriously vulnerable and complex environments of the Information Age. This will surely increase as we begin the 21st century.

History of Technology

The history of communication and the technology[1] used to store, process, and transmit information is a relatively short but interesting

---

[1]Some of the information presented was published in *PC World* magazine, December 1999, pp. 136–154.

one. As you read this "short summary of history" (see Figures 2–1 and 2–2), think of the impact the inventions have had on the ability to safeguard proprietary, sensitive, national security, and other information requiring protection from the techno-spies and Netspionage agents.

History of Technology

3000 BC	Abacus was developed (Asia)
876 AD	First use of the symbol for 'zero' (India)
1642	Pascal designed a mechanical calculator
1963	Englebert developed the mouse
1965	Digital Equipment built the first computer
1968	Intel was started
1970	The floppy disk was used
1971	Texas Instruments introduced the pocket calculator
1981	IBM brought the PC and MS-DOS to the public
1984	the CD-ROM was introduced.
1985	Came America Online and Windows 1.0
	Newsgroups and electronic mail were developed in the 1980s Also, the 300-baud modem, cellular phones, 2400-9600 baud modems, 1,000 Internet users, and 100,000 Internet hosts the Macintosh came into being in about 1984. Also during this period came the TCP/IP specification, and GPS satellites.
1991	Personnel at the University of Minnesota created the Gopher
	The 1990's saw the faster modems in the 28K and 56K baud range, over 6,000,000 Internet hosts, Iridium and Globalstar satellites, PCS, digital cell phones; as well as faster, cheaper, smaller and more powerful computers.
1991	World Wide Web: Tim Berners-Lee and others at the Conseil Europeene pour la Recherche Nucleaire (CERN) developed the Web
1993	Came the Personal Digital Assistant (PDA)
1994	Came Netscape, GPS, and Zip drives
1995	Came the flat screen and Windows 95
1996	Web surfing was available through the television, and Palm Pilot was introduced
1997	Came the DVD
1998	Came the e-commerce explosion and portable MP3
1999	The Y2K craze begins
2000	2000, the Y2K fizzles

Figure 2–1 A capsule summary of major technological discoveries.

Fuel for the Fire: Revolution in Technology

Lasers		Fiber Optics			300	2400 9600		28.8K 56K
		Fax			baud	baud baud		baud baud
Copy		Machines						
Machines					1,000	100,000		6,000,000
		Videotape	TCP/IP		Internet	Internet		Internet
		Recorders	Spec		Users	Hosts		Hosts
Satellites								
(Echo I)	Satellites		Satellites	Cellular	Pagers			Satellites
	(Early Bird)		(GPS)	Phones				(Iridium)
Satellites								
(Telstar)			Apple					
			&	IBM	Macintosh			
		Intel	Intel	Microsoft	PC			
		4004	8008	Founded		286	386	486 Pentium

'60	'65	'70	'75	'80	'85	'90	'95
		Development				Refinement	

Figure 2–2 Fuel for the Fire: Revolution in Technology.

Figure 2–2 provides another glimpse of high-technology development. What is interesting to note is the speed at which technology has been invented and improved. Starting slowly at the turn of the century, technology gradually picked up steam and is ending at literally the speed of light as fiber optics replaces twisted pair. Now we have the beginning of fiber being "replaced" by wireless.

With Standardization of Networks Comes Standard Vulnerabilities

Standardization on business, governmental, national, and international levels made for easy communication and information sharing. Like taking a drug to cure some illnesses, there are some serious and bad side effects. The "technology pill" has the same problem. The standardization has brought with it a standardization of vulnerabilities as noted by the many successful attacks on systems and the number of CERT announcements constantly being sent out alerting us about new vulnerabilities and cures for them.

Regardless of whether or not you are in government or business in the United Kingdom, Europe, America, Asia, South America, Mideast, Africa, or some tropical, physically isolated island, if you are using Windows NT, for example, you have automatically inherited its vulnerabilities. Regardless of your configuration, whether you use a LAN, Client-Server, intra-network, or inter-network, you are vulnerable to Netspionage attack.

As vendors compete for market share by trying to be the first to market, they are churning out "buggy" software and software with vulnerabilities. It appears that this attempt of "one-upmanship" as they vie to be the first to market is at the expense of the users. It seems that security continues to play a secondary role to the priority of getting to market with a new or revised product regardless of the security holes. "No problem, we'll fix it on the next release with a patch!" they claim. The Netspionage agents, techno-spies, and the like are becoming more sophisticated at finding the vulnerabilities faster than the vendor can identify and patch them.

Summary

Beginning at the end of the 19th century, through the 20th century and now into the 21st century, we have seen tremendous changes to our working, living, and playing environments. Technology has made the difference. Over the years, we have come to rely more and more on information and technology to the extent we can no longer do without it. Technology has changed our world forever. It has become smaller, accounted for global communications and global business competition, and also made us all more vulnerable.

As technology- and information-based businesses continue to develop their global presence, the global competition—business warfare—will continue to heat up. The demand for information about the business' global marketplace and competitors will drive the need for more information from techno-spies and Netspionage agents.

3

The Internet: The Global I-Way to Netspionage and Techno-Crime[1]

The Internet is the basic field of play for today's Netspionage agents. The Internet is the latest in a series of technological advances that is being used not only by honest people to further their communication, but also by Netspionage agents, techno-spies, miscreants, juvenile delinquents, and others for illegal purposes. As with any technological inventions, they can be used for good or for illegal purposes. It all depends on the human being that is using the technology.

Birth of the Internet

The global collection of networks that have evolved in the late 20th century to become the Internet represent what could be described as a "global nervous system" transmitting from "anywhere to anywhere" (now more fiction than fact, but will one day be fact) facts, opinions, and opportunity. However, when most managers, security, and law enforcement professionals think of the Internet, it seems to be something either vaguely sinister or of such complexity that it makes it difficult to understand. Popular culture, as manifested by Hollywood and network television programs, does little to dispel this impression of danger and out-of-control complexity. One should remember that the Internet is simply a high-tech communications tool. It is not, at least not yet, the be all and end all of high-technology efficiency. A simple power outage can wreak havoc on those dependent upon the Internet.

The Internet arose out of projects sponsored by the Advanced Research Project Agency (ARPA) in the United States in the 1960s. It is perhaps one of the most exciting legacy developments of that era. Originally an effort to facilitate sharing of expensive computer resources and enhance military communications, the Internet has

---

[1]This chapter is adapted from *I-Way Robbery: Crime on the Internet*, written by Boni and Kovacich for Butterworth–Heinemann, 1999, and provides the readers an overview of the Internet.

over the 12 years, from about 1988 through today, rapidly evolved from it's scientific and military roots into one of the premier e-commerce and commercial communications media. The Internet, which is described as a global meta-network, or network of networks,[2] provides the foundation upon which the global business marketplace will be built (global business—another word for e-commerce and e-business).

However, it was not until the early 1990s that Internet communication technologies became easily accessible to the average person. Prior to that time, Internet accesses required mastery of many arcane and difficult to remember programming language codes. However, the combination of declining microcomputer prices, enhanced microcomputer performance, and the advent of easy to use "browser"[3] software were key enabling technologies that created the foundation for mass Internet activity. When these variables aligned with the developing global telecommunications infrastructure they allowed a rare convergence of capability.

It has now become a simple matter for average people, even those who had trouble programming their VCRs, to obtain access to the global Internet and the huge volume of information it contains. In the United States alone, tens of millions of people are accessing the Internet on a regular basis. Millions of others around the world are logging in, creating a vast environment often referred to as "cyberspace" (see Figures 3–1 and 3–2) and the Global Information Infrastructure (GII), which has been described as the virtual, online, computer-enabled environment, and distinct from the physical reality of "real life." As businesses have looked at China's population as one billion customers, the Internet has the potential for providing businesses literally billions of new customers. With the falling cost of communications and prices, increased access will undoubtedly continue exponentially.

The most commonly accessed application on the Internet is the "World Wide Web" (Web). The "Web" was envisioned by its inventor as a way to help share information. The ability to find information concerning virtually any topic via search engines, such as Google, Alta Vista, HotBot, Lycos, InfoSeek, Yahoo, and others, from among the rapidly growing array of Web servers is an amazing example of how the Internet increases the information available to nearly everyone. One gains some sense of how fast and pervasive the Internet has become as more TV, radio, and print advertisements direct prospective customers to visit their business or government agency Web sites. This trend may exponentially increase as free Internet access is proliferating through a variety of sites.

---

[2]Information Superhighway: An Overview of Technology Challenges GAO-AIMD 95–23, p. 11.

[3]Software that simplifies the search and display of World Wide Web supplied information.

In the first part of the 21st century, worldwide revenues via Internet commerce are expected to reach perhaps hundreds of billions of dollars, an unparalleled growth rate for a technology that was effected only since the early 1990s. The "electronic commerce" of the early 21st century is expected to include everything from online information concerning products, purchases, services, and also the development of entirely new business activities.

The Global Marketplace

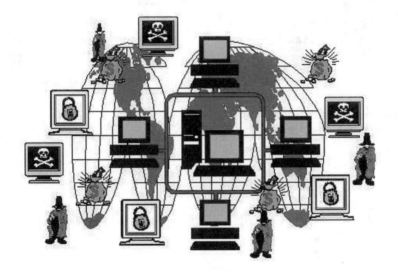

Figure 3–1 The "new world."

An important fact to understand, and that is of supreme importance for managers, security, and law enforcement professionals, is that the Web is truly global in scope. Physical borders as well as geographical distance are almost meaningless in "cyberspace"; the distant target is as easily attacked as a local one. This is an important concept for corporate and government managers, security, and law enforcement professionals to understand, as it will impact their capability to successfully protect corporate assets against Netspionage agents.

The annihilation of time and space makes the Internet an almost perfect environment for Netspionage agents. When finding a desired server located on the other side of the planet is as easy and convenient as calling directory assistance to find a local telephone number, technospies have the potential to act in ways that we can only begin to imagine. Undeterred by distance, borders, time, or season, the potential bonanza awaiting the techno-spies is a chilling prospect for those who are responsible for safeguarding the assets of a business or government agency.

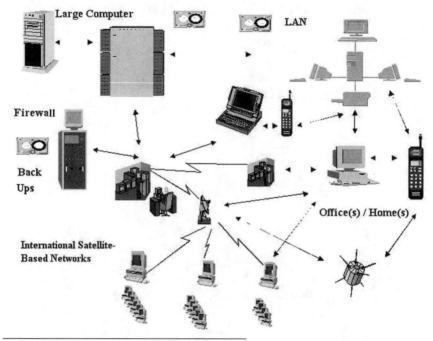

Figure 3–2 The "new world of communication."

Future Shock

With appreciation for Toffler's book, *Future Shock*, the reaction of people and organizations to the dizzying pace of Internet "progress" has been mixed. Although some technologically sophisticated individuals and organizations have been very quick to exploit the potential of this new technology, many have been slower, adopting more of a wait and see posture. The rapid pace of evolution of the Internet does raise some questions as to how much a society can absorb, how much can actually be used to benefit organizations in a such a compressed time frame. Sometimes lost in the technological hype concerning the physical speed of Internet enabled communications or the new technologies that are making it easier to display commercial content, is the fact that the Internet's greatest impact ultimately is that it is providing unprecedented access to information. The access is unprecedented in the breadth of the total volume of information that is moving online and may be tapped for decision making and other uses against competitors.

It also is unprecedented when we consider the increasing percentage of the world's population that enjoys the access. As more and more information moves online and becomes available to more and more people, it is causing some fundamental changes in how we communicate, do business, and think of the world we live in. Consequently, it is also causing fundamental changes in how Netspionage agents and techno-spies commit crimes.

Roadmap for the Internet

The Internet can be compared in some ways to a roadmap for a superhighway. Some basic examples will help explain the Internet in common terms.

When multiple computers (whether microcomputers or larger) are linked together by various communications protocols to allow digital information to be transmitted and shared among the connected systems, they become a network. The combination of tens of thousand of organizational networks interconnected with high capacity "backbone" data communications and the public telephone networks now constitutes the global Internet. However, there is a major difference in this environment that is important to consider.

When the isolated "by-ways" of individual business or government agency networks become connected to the global Internet, they become an "off-ramp" accessible to other Internet travelers. The number and diversity of locations that provide Internet "on-ramps" is vast and growing. Today, one can access the Internet from public libraries, "cyber" cafes in many cities around the world, even kiosks in some airports. These and other locations provide Internet on-ramps to anyone who has a legitimate account or a Netspionage agent who can "hijack" one from an authorized user.

Typically a business or government agency will use centrally controlled computers, called servers, to store the information and the sophisticated software applications used to manage and control their information flow. These systems could be equated to a superhighway interchange.

Commonly business and government agency networks are considered private property and the information they contain as proprietary for the exclusive use of the organization. These business and government agency "networks" are connected to large networks operated by Internet service providers (ISPs) (such as, UUNET, GTE, AOL, and ATT) who provide the equivalent of toll roads and turnpikes that provide the highways for the flow of information.

The Internet: No Traffic Controls

The Internet challenges the security and law enforcement professional with an array of new and old responsibilities in a new environment. From the perspective of managing risks, this new access to information creates new kinds of dangers to businesses and government agencies. It also allows well understood security issues to recur in new or unique ways. No longer can organizations assume they will obtain any security through obscurity, no matter where they are physically located. In other words, because there is an Internet off-ramp organizations will be visible to Netspionage agents. Everything from a nation's most critical defense secrets to business information is vulnerable to easy destruction, modification, and compromise.

Too often managers who are careless (overworked or just plain ignorant of the real-world threats) fail to take adequate measures to safeguard sensitive information, which result in premature disclosure with attendant adverse impact. The major part of the controllable risk arises from inadvertent disclosure to the ever-vigilant eyes of the Netspionage agent and others such as competitive intelligence analysts with Internet access.

No Central Management or "Internet Police"

When the Internet was limited to scientists, academic researchers, and government employees such a collaborative framework was probably a very cost-effective means of controlling the virtual world. However, in the early 1990s, for the first time there were more commercial sites than educational and governmental sites using the Internet. Since that time, matters have become increasingly complex. The informal array of social sanctions and technical forums for cooperation is no longer capable of ensuring a modicum of civilized behaviors. There is no Internet police force that corporations can call to track down techno-spies.

What Has Been the Impact of the Internet?

In business, it has become in some ways a David versus Goliath world, where the advantages don't always accrue to the corporation that can field the bigger battalions. Advanced information technology was once the province exclusively of governments, the military, universities, and large corporate entities. This is no longer true. Now anyone with a modest investment in hardware and software can acquire a powerful processor and attach it to the Internet. It should be obvious that Netspionage agents, techno-spies, and others with criminal intentions also have access to powerful information technology. The question remains "how will they use it?"

As we consider the potential for Netspionage actions directed against organizations, it is critically important to consider these factors. The same information technology we use to manage our organizations can and will be used by savvy Netspionage agents and techno-spies to the detriment of governments, businesses, and others.

Whereas the innocent e-mail user sees only increased speed and volume of communication, managers, security, and law enforcement professionals must understand how damaging even one message could be to a business or government agency. A single e-mail message could contain the whole strategic business plan of the organization or the source code to a breakthrough product, and be transmitted anywhere on earth in a nanosecond or for now maybe at 56kbs.

New Challenges for Security and Law Enforcement Professionals

The Internet has brought with it many new challenges to the security professional. Just learning the vocabulary and technical terms arising from the Internet is a significant issue. Some also look at the challenges from the Internet robbers, fraudsters, techno-spies, and terrorists, as something completely new. However, looking closer we find that there is little that is truly new for the Internet Netspionage agent. Few of the basic techniques or objectives of these criminals have changed. What is actually new is the environment in which they operate. It is now the Information Age and all business and government agencies that operate in the Information Age today inhabit a technology-driven environment. It is the microprocessor-based, network intensive environment alone that is new. Make no mistake, the "bad guys" still have the same motives, opportunities, and rationalizations for spying.

Netspionage agents, techno-spies, and other criminals are attempting to do what they have always done: to steal, defraud, and subvert others for personal, corporate, national, and/or political gain. The methods they use, for the most part are the same and only change when the Internet environment requires them to change to achieve their objectives.

If we really think about it, do we have any reason to believe spies are much different today than they were throughout history—even before the days of Sun-tzu? Even in a world featuring computers, coupled with the digital, virtual Internet, and the increased use of Internet commerce, Netspionage agents and techno-spies still have the same objectives: take someone's information and convert it for their personal, corporate, or nation-state benefit. However, the Internet now allows them to have global mobility and escape in nanoseconds! They are no longer bounded by physical locations, physical procedures, personnel controls, or very much by time.

Internet, Techno-Crimes, and Law Enforcement

When placed in perspective, one can see the Internet robbers of the information age have much in common with the highway robbers of the Industrial Age. Based on the above, managers and security and law enforcement professionals should therefore understand that little has really changed over the years. Therefore the problems, issues, and approaches to dealing with them will be very similar. What must be emphasized, what did not work before, will not work now and what worked before may or may not work in the present or future.

One overwhelming distinction is obvious. Whereas in the earlier, pre-information age era, the United States Government could respond to citizens' concerns about rampant lawlessness by empowering the FBI to enforce federal laws, times are now different. The Internet is global in scope and growing fastest in nations and continents that are not likely to take direction from the United States, and where the United States has no jurisdiction. How will managers and security and law enforcement professionals of a nation, influence the global response necessary to confront the more serious risks that the Internet will create? In the absence of a global "Internet Patrol," each individual nation's response is likely to fall short of effectively addressing the complete spectrum of criminal threats.

At a news conference after an all-day meeting at FBI headquarters of the Justice Ministers of the G-8 countries (the largest industrialized countries in the world) in December 1997, United States Attorney General Janet Reno said, "Criminals no longer are restricted by national boundaries. . . . If we are to keep up with cybercrime, we must work together as never before."[4] The news release from this important meeting went on to list the following areas where these major nations have agreed to collaborate:

- Assign adequate number of properly trained and equipped law enforcement personnel to investigate high-tech crimes.
- Improve ways to track attacks on computer networks.
- When extradition is not possible, prosecute criminals in the country where they are found.
- Preserve key evidence on computer networks.
- Review the legal codes in each nation to ensure that appropriate crimes for computer wrongdoing are proscribed and to ensure that the language makes it easier to investigate the crimes.
- Close cooperation with the private sector to develop new ways to detect and prevent computer crimes.
- Increased efforts to use new communications technologies, such as

---

[4]"Nations Band Together Against Cybercrime" Reuters 10, December 1997.

video teleconferencing to obtain testimony from witnesses in other nations.

These are essential steps, even if they are general in nature. However, the track record of nations cooperating in such efforts has seen little success. For example, "law of the sea" has taken more than 40 years to ratify and it is still not signed by all countries. Therefore, one should not be overly optimistic about the future based only on these actions. The global reach of the Internet and the difficulties of obtaining jurisdiction over perpetrators is one of the greatest challenges in dealing with Internet miscreants. To the extent that the collaboration of the G-8 nations ultimately extends to the other nations of the globe, perhaps under the broader auspices of the United Nations or other agencies, organizations may eventually be able to have increased confidence that even the most sophisticated Internet miscreants may ultimately face prosecution.

As law enforcement has adapted its methods and incorporated new technology to combat criminals, private organizations also have adopted various strategies to combat risks to their interests. It is likely that many organizations, confronted with increasing risks from the Internet will choose to respond as the railroad industry did in the 1880s in the United States. In that time the railroads, frustrated at the largely ineffective nature of geographically limited law enforcement, engaged the Pinkerton Detective Agency to help protect corporate interests against the James gang and similar highly mobile criminal gangs. It is possible, indeed likely, that many large organizations will choose to engage the resources of private sector specialists (cyber-sleuths or digital detectives) to help them resolve Internet enabled crimes directed against them. This may happen because the limited resources in the public sector are directed to larger or more serious crimes, or simply because public agencies will generally take longer to complete an investigation due to the many competing priorities.

National and International Juvenile Delinquents, Wannabe's, Fraudsters, and Other Miscreants

As the vulnerabilities of such technologies' hardware, software, and firmware became known throughout the world, there were those who were there to take advantage of it. The Internet is the latest in a series of technological advances that is being used not only by honest people to further their communication, but also by miscreants, juvenile delinquents, and others for illegal purposes.

As previously mentioned, with any of the technological inventions, they can be used for good or for illegal purposes. Technological inventions are really no different than other inventions such as the handgun.

The handgun can be used to defend and protect lives or to destroy them. It all depends on the human being that is using the technology.

Because of the advances, increases in power, and decreases in costs of computers, cell phones, PBX's, etc., technological inventions have proliferated over the years. Technology has not only been purchased by people who wanted to use the tools to support their goals, but also by the miscreants as tools to support their goals.

The scum of humanity who are always willing to take advantage of an honest person for their own selfish reasons, either to satisfy their little egos, for monetary gain, power, or sexual gratification, etc., have found fast, cheap, and often anonymous ways to ply their trade. Such things as viruses, logic bombs, Web site attacks, computer fraud, piracy, and copyright violations have grown in numbers with damage inflicted and intensity throughout this century in one form or another.

These high-technology scams have been going on throughout the 20th century, and will obviously continue as long as there are human beings that want to gain at the expense of others. As technology has increased and been made available to more and more people, it also has made that same technology available to more and more miscreants.

Now, knowing the amount of chaos, damage, and destruction some 14-year-old hacker can do to your systems and Web sites, imagine what a highly-trained Netspionage agent backed by an international corporation or government agency can do.

Roadblocks to the Techno-Spies: Are They Working?

Many information technology managers are quite concerned about the potential for techno-spies to harm their organization. Some managers may believe that if the United States government can't prevent intrusions, such as the high profile defacing of the CIA and FBI Web sites, how are businesses and other government agencies, with significantly lower security budgets, going to stop these Internet miscreants and Netspionage agents?

Stopping these *miscreants* is more than just a theoretical issue. A recently published study conducted by WarRoom Research,[5] showed that most Fortune 1000 companies have experienced one or more incidents where an outsider successfully penetrated system defenses. More than 50 percent of the responding companies experienced more than 30 system penetrations in the past 12 months and nearly 60 percent reported losing $200,000 or more from each intrusion.

In a separate study published jointly in 1998 by the Computer Security Institute and the FBI, 520 United States companies reported total losses of $136 million from computer crime and systems security

---

[5]War Room Research Report summarized in *ComputerWorld*, August 1998.

breaches in 1997. This represented a 36 percent increase from 1996. Nearly 54 percent of respondents cited the Internet as a frequent point of attack, about the same percentage of those who identified internal systems breaches as a frequent point of attack.[6]

With the vast increase in the numbers of people accessing and using the Internet, it seems likely that more attacks will be attempted by outsiders. Prior to the Internet, most security staff considered the threat to be 80 percent internal and 20 percent external. However, the 1999 Information Week Security Survey fielded by PricewaterhouseCoopers found that 52 percent of incidents involved insiders, but 48 percent now involve outsiders. It is not known how many intrusions are simply never detected. What is known is that many of those that are detected are not reported to law enforcement for investigation.

According to the same FBI–CSI 1999 study[7] of the companies that knew they experienced a computer crime or detected system break-ins, now nearly 40 percent are not reporting known crime to law enforcement. The most common reason cited in the survey for not reporting known computer crimes to law enforcement is the fear that the corporation will suffer adverse reactions from customers and prospective business partners due to negative publicity.

Capabilities and Limitations of Law Enforcement

If tidal waves of criminal enterprise are about to overwhelm the Internet and impact this new commercial medium, what can we expect from the "Internet patrol?" Unless things change drastically, it would seem not much. We must remember that, at present, there is not any single, central organization with responsibility and capability to patrol and protect the global Internet. The reasons are readily apparent considering the current state of planetary political affairs.

Rather than creating a global Internet patrol, it's more reasonable to expect updated extradition treaties as probably the best short-term answer to the problems of obtaining jurisdiction over these Internet "robbers." The inconsistencies in legal language, statutes, and codes from country to country are just one of the major problems associated with policing the global Internet. In the absence of well-developed international agreements and treaties, and lacking any sort of Internet patrol or even common policing standards, it is likely that corporations will be subject to criminal activities originating in another country. If this situation arises, there may be no local authority capable or willing to pursue a criminal investigation against the Internet robbers. One should remember there is a great deal of time lag between creating

---

[6]See CSI-FBI 1999 report.
[7]Ibid.

national laws, let alone international laws. In some instances, we may be waiting decades—or longer.

Global Connectivity via the Internet = Global Exposure

As recently as the late 1980s, the most common form of non-employee computer crime probably involved a teenager in the local telephone dialing area using a "war dialer" to try to emulate the movie "War Games." In that era, a company could protect itself against a wide range of risks with relatively inexpensive security technology. However, in today's era of global connectivity and access, one should not assume that what was sufficient for simpler times will suffice for the present. Those corporations that choose to ignore their increasing vulnerability and trust haphazard security measures may well suffer serious losses. Potential Internet robbers are not likely to ignore forever poorly protected on ramps that have valuable assets.

An Internet robber is no more likely to ignore an easy network-firewall penetration any more than his distant relative in the 1930s would have passed an unlocked bank vault. This means that just as banks and businesses in the past had to harden their facilities, hire trustworthy guards, install video surveillance camera's and alarms to safeguard their cash vaults, today's "digital data vaults" require enhanced protection. When organizations fail to invest adequately in protection they run the risk of damage or loss of their key assets.

Summary

Careful study of information in this chapter and other publicly available data concerning Internet crimes reveals several common themes. First, it appears that Internet and computer/network enabled crimes are a rapidly growing component of global crime statistics. Second, no one in business, government, or academe really knows the full extent or the complete nature of Internet crimes that have already been committed or are happening at this moment. Lastly, we can conclude that although the Internet and information access enabling technologies like the Web browser-server combinations are creating more complex environment's, we should not expect that complexity alone will protect valuable resources against losses. Spies over the ages have proven themselves highly adaptable, and they already appear to be capable and willing to exploit the new Internet environment for greed and benefit.

4

The Global Business and Government Revolutions

From Physical Assets to Information Assets

Today, very few individuals in our information-based societies, businesses, and government agencies would argue that one of the greatest assets of those entities is the information that is processed, stored, and transmitted by information systems. For without their information systems, modern societies, businesses, and government agencies would not be able to continue to provide the support to social, business, and government services and processes.

We would no longer even be able to make some of the products that are being made with ever-decreasing costs, such as electronics. From computerized controlled traffic signals, microwave ovens, weapons systems, aircraft, air traffic control, modern automobiles, to watches and kids' toys, they all rely at least in part on microprocessors.

Hopefully information and the information systems are still considered no greater than second place in businesses and government agencies as far as valuable assets, with people still being in the number one spot. However, one could argue that as more and more automation takes place, the need for humans to accomplish more and more tasks is no longer needed. The computer-driven machines can do a better job, faster and cheaper. In fact, there are some jobs that only computerized machines can do. If you doubt that, try making one of today's microprocessors by hand.

So, we continue to believe that people are the number one assets, and human relations people will also say that, as well as management. To say otherwise, even if it may be true, would not sit well with employees—or probably with any human being. That aside, even to entertain such thoughts smacks of science fiction and robots taking over the world. It seems wrong somehow. However, looking at it objectively, have we already come that far? Are we so dependent on our technology "toys" and information that it is now a matter of survival? Yes. We literally would not be able to maintain our current business processes without them, nor our government services, nor our current lifestyle. In fact, more and more humans around the globe owe their jobs and, in fact, their lives to information and information systems. High-technology has truly become a global, indispensable asset to the Information Age societies.

As was stated earlier: In the near 21st century, the money is in the information coursing through cyberspace and the global Internet. By some estimates intangible assets of the enterprise: the knowledge, trade secrets, and sensitive proprietary information utilized by an organization already constitute 50 percent or more of the value of a modern business corporation. Such assets are now most commonly found in digital form somewhere in the corporation and often on the corporate Web site.

Yes, we have come that far. For these reasons alone, it is imperative that managers and security professionals protect the sensitive, proprietary, and trade secret information, the "crown jewels," of their corporations, government agencies, and the like. Also for these reasons, Netspionage is growing and will continue to grow.

The Changing Business and Government Environments

In today's global marketplace, businesses must rapidly adapt to changes. However, in government agencies these changes come more slowly and sometimes threaten the very existence of some government agencies. For example, the need for a Department of Education and a Department of Commerce seems to be debated with the advent of each congressional session.

One clear example of these changes is the U.S. Post Office (USPO). The USPO must compete with such businesses as Federal Express, DHL, and United Parcel Service (UPS) for the delivery of letters, documents, and packages. However, as more and more people around the world get "online" and send electronic mail, legally-binding contracts, and other documents through national and international networks, the need for an Industrial Age government agency such as the USPO may become less and less important as information systems provide immediate, international communications.

To combat this trend, it appears that the USPO may try to position itself to be the authenticator of e-mail messages. In others words, stay in business by being the intermediary between the e-mail of senders and receivers to verify and validate that the senders are in fact who they are supposed to be.

Another example is the U.S. Internal Revenue Service's increasing use of the Internet to receive and process tax returns. Because of the vulnerabilities of systems as alluded to earlier, the opportunity for Netspionage agents to gain valuable, personal information cannot be overlooked.

One does not have to look far to also see the vital need for managers and security professionals in corporations and government agencies to be concerned about such things as privacy and liability issues. There are techno-spies that are trying to steal that information and use it for the benefit of themselves and others.

Corporations are storing more and more personal information on networked systems and in massive databases. This is a common and basic business tool that corporations and government agencies rely on in order to conduct their business more effectively and efficiently. However, this is not without some serious concerns. For example, several software companies have been identified as collecting statistics concerning consumer uses of their products without advising their customers that this was happening. The companies expressed surprise that consumers were upset about the collection of their personal information without their knowledge. This is a good example of the disconnection between business interests and the customers brought on by today's technology. In the past, it was never possible to easily obtain this type of information, and businesses had to rely on personal surveys. Now they can easily create software to monitor consumer behavior on a massive scale. As they continue to expand and grow, the violation of privacy rules and laws will increase liability issues for corporations.

This type of collection method is also a great tool for the Netspionage agents and techno-spies as they target both individuals and the corporations' massive databases. These databases if compromised provide competitors a great deal of information to help them gain market shares.

The Three Revolutions

There are three primary revolutions that are taking place (see Figure 4–1). These revolutions will continue for the foreseeable future and will have a major impact on corporations and the global marketplace. Of primary importance to corporations is the economic revolution (see Figure 4–2), as this revolution will determine how corporations do business in the global marketplace.

Many nations are making foreign trade a national objective because they realize that economic power is the most important contribution to global power. By doing so, they can become a dominant force in the world. One only has to look at Japan and Taiwan to see how economic power can be translated into world power, even if the nations are "small islands" in physical size, they can be very large in the economic world. The balance of trade and increased exports is a key element that is being used (see Figure 4–3). Now, imagine the shift in world economic power as China continues to become a global economic giant—with the rest of the free world's continued help. These nations are only able to accomplish such objectives due to today's technology and the Internet that has brought on these new phenomena called the global marketplace. Many of the global businesses of the world are merging to form global, mega-corporations wielding global economic power sometimes larger than the gross national product of many of the world's nations. For example, it has been suggested that Microsoft alone would be the world's 18th highest-ranking country in terms of GNP.

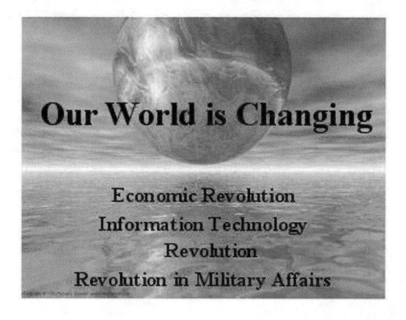

Figure 4–1 Three revolutions taking place.

New World Order

Some say we are in the midst of a "New World Order." We do know that the world is rapidly changing and that change is being fueled by high-technology. The end of the Cold War has brought with it a new era with new foes and new threats. This New World Order is to bring with it peace dividends. However, we see more wars and more chaos than we have seen for some time.

As alluded to earlier, this new, chaotic world order coupled with global networking brings with it more need and opportunities for

Netspionage. Such things as information warfare, economic espionage, industrial espionage, new threats to national security, business warfare, and economic warfare all offer great opportunities for the Netspionage agents and techno-spies to sell their services during the chaos and rapid changes of business and government.

Economic Revolution

- Lester Thurow, noted economist and former Dean of MIT's Sloan School of Management says in *Winning in the 21st Century: New Rules & New Strategies for the New World Economy*

  – Five fundamental revolutions are changing the nature of the economic game we play:
    1. The end of communism
    2. A shift to man-made brain-power industries
    3. Demography (the population moving and aging)
    4. The development of a global economy
    5. The dawn of an era without a dominant world power

Source: 1997 Price Waterhouse World Energy Conference. Nov. 10, 1997

Figure 4–2 Elements of the economic revolution.

This New World Order and technology-driven new frontiers cause us to rethink old methods of everything. These rapid changes have left a void with the demise of the super powers, also brought on by technology. One may believe that the United States and possibly China and Russia are super powers, at least in a military sense. However, a closer look shows that this is not the case. The United Stated is often defeated in the world political arena when it wants to take some action, for example the actions taken against Iraq throughout 1998. Neither the Chinese nor the Russian military has a global sphere of influence.

There is also the growing trend of not only Internet firms plying their trade on the Internet, but also the more conservative and older "bricks and mortar" firms beginning to see the advantage of doing electronic business; thus, making more businesses vulnerable to the Netspionage agents and techno-spies.

Globalization

- Increase Trade Exports
  - Why?
    - **Broaden Economic Base**
    - **Expand the Number of High Paying Jobs**
    - **Improve the Standard of Living**

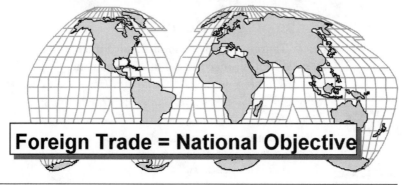

Foreign Trade = National Objective

Figure 4-3 Reasons why trade exports are a prime concern of nation-states and corporations.

Electronic Commerce

Electronic commerce is the new "buzz word" of the information age. Electronic commerce is basically the use of computers, telecommunications, and related high-technology devices used to conduct business transactions and to communicate between entities for the purpose of conducting business. It is also called "electronic business."

A broad definition of electronic commerce is provided by Electronic Commerce Australia (ECA, formerly EDICA) in one of its reports as:

> *The process of electronically conducting all forms of business between entities in order to achieve the organization's objectives. The term "electronic commerce" embraces electronic trading, electronic messaging, EDI, EFT, electronic mail (e-mail), facsimile, computer-to-fax (C-fax), electronic catalogs and bulletin board services (BBS), shared databases and directories, continuous acquisition and lifecycle support (CALS), electronic news and information services, electronic payroll, electronic forms (E-forms), online access to services such as the Internet, and any other form of electronic data transmission.*

Electronic Business on the Internet

Why is the Internet the "electronic vehicle of choice" for electronic business? It is because the Internet is global and has the potential of making businesses more efficient and the potential for reaching literally billions of potential customers in the future at less cost. For example,

> *Texas Instruments Corporation reengineered their procurement processes lowering average purchase order processing costs from $49.00 to $4.70.*
>
> *A U.S. Medical Center reduced its supplies inventory by 25 percent in a two-year period, while orders processed increased by more than 50 percent.*
>
> *U.S. Department of Defense identified a potential savings of $1.2 billion through automation of the 16 most-used forms (over a-ten-year period).*
> *(http://www.usc.edu/dept/ATRIUM/EC_on_the_Inet.html)*

Besides, the Internet is too large to ignore. Like any nonelectronic business, doing electronic business only needs three items: (1) Sellers, (2) Customers, and (3) and an Infrastructure to transfer goods and services. The Internet provides the infrastructure, and sellers and potential customers are already on the Internet. In order to conduct business on the Internet, it is now easier than ever before. All one has to do to create a presence worldwide is to develop a Web site. With today's many software suppliers for Web development, even children are creating their own sites.

Businesses on the Internet can: (1) distribute catalogs; (2) provide product support information; (3) generate sales leads and respond to requests for information; (4) interact with customers, suppliers, and employees; and (5) conduct any other transactions which can be accomplished other than physically delivering a product—unless that product is software, audio, text, graphics, and video. Also, many business people do not realize that their competition can also see what they are doing because for some reason, many businesses place information on their Web sites that they never would have previously made available in the nonelectronic business environment. In addition, more information can be found on the Internet that can help give a business a competitive advantage.

Internet Business Problems

Although businesses are rapidly pushing forward to conduct more and more business through the Internet, most of the potential customers are concerned about using it as a consumer, primarily because of security concerns. This is quite understandable and their concerns are valid. Their concerns can be summarized as concerns about confidentiality—keep information private; integrity—trust the information is accurate; and availability—it is accessible when needed or wanted. The potential customers are concerned about threats from such things as malicious codes (for example, logic bombs and viruses), natural disasters, and power fluctuations. They also read about and are concerned about systems' vulnerabilities relative to poor security, e.g., UNIX, Windows NT, etc. And quite frankly, they have a right to be concerned because there are risks. Are the risks high? Medium? Low? The answer is that it varies based on how the Internet is used for business, the security used, the cost of a loss, etc. It is perceived differently depending on the people, circumstances, and environments.

Business people try to lure potential customers into electronic business because they see the billions of potential customers out there in cyberspace. However, until the security issues are addressed, the potential will remain mostly that—potential.

What are some of the problems that have been publicized that may cause such concerns? They include the following:

1. Businesses bordering closely on infringing on domain names, e.g., "NASA.gov" will allow you to access the U.S. Mars mission information; while "NASA.com" may show you an advertisement with naked women. Does a closely associated domain name infringe on a business or agency?
2. Credit card information is stolen in transit or from Web sites and corporation databases.
3. Personal information is sent in clear, unencrypted texts allowing others to gain access for criminal use.
4. ISP's and businesses' sites are hacked, changed, orders re-routed, and customers' personal information is compromised.
5. Internet's hardware and software are vulnerable to numerous types of attacks by anyone in the world from anywhere in the world.
6. Accidental changes and damages, as well as attacks, deny use of sites for stock trades, business communications, online ordering, etc.

Internet's Security Problems Affecting E-Commerce

The Internet security problems have increased for several reasons to include:

1. A more distributed computing environment

2. More networking nationally and internationally
3. Blurring of computers and telecommunications systems
4. Capability for more remote systems maintenance
5. Cheaper hardware and software
6. Poor information systems security because it is a low priority
7. More individuals growing up with computers have turned into computer vandals. Why break a business' store windows when you can break their Microsoft Windows?
8. Less morality and social pressure to conform to societies' standards
9. Opportunity for criminal gain with little international recourse by law enforcement agencies
10. General standardization on specific hardware and software, e.g., UNIX and Windows NT environments—UNIX and NT have known vulnerabilities
11. Systems are easier to use
12. More hackers, although on average, less technically competent than in the past
13. Smart, very sophisticated hackers with a great deal of technical competency

The Dark Side of Electronic Commerce

It's become obvious that many executives are placing their businesses on the Internet with little or no appreciation of the massive increase in risks they are creating. As they rush to embrace the many advantages of e-commerce they assume that this new business model will only create increased revenue for their business. Total e-commerce (essentially retail) sales are already exceeding $101 billion according to a research study of the Internet economy sponsored by Cisco. As businesses begin using the global Internet to solicit and provide prices, products, and services to business partners and creating extended electronic supply chains, total e-commerce sales are likely to explode, and could exceed $1.2 trillion globally in the early years of the 21st century according to some estimates.

Although advantages are undeniable, there is an issue that is rarely discussed in the media, the fact that such a tidal wave of money will bring with it those who make money the old fashioned way . . . by stealing it! Consider for just a moment the huge amount of "conventional" frauds, abuse, and business disputes arising from the traditional "bricks and mortar" economy. The Association of Certified Fraud Examiners estimates that well run U.S. companies lose, on average, $9 per day per person to fraud, which means the losses in the United States alone may exceed $400 billion annually. There is no reason to suppose that electronic systems will be immune to similar levels of abuse. Assuming the same percentages hold for the electronic economy, we could reasonably expect that losses from cyber-fraud and abuse alone could well exceed $60 to $100 billion by 2001.

We expect that fraud abuse and disputes over the operation of e-commerce systems will follow the Internet straight into the heartland of cyber commerce. This will happen for many reasons. Some of the major issues to be considered include the following:

- People must use systems for commerce, and humans represent the inevitable weak line in every system of technical controls. Most computer users don't really understand computers. Thus, to aid them, "help desks" have been established. By their very nature they are there to assist employees. This may run counter to security philosophies. People have been subject to weakness of character, manipulation and sloth since time immemorial. Criminals and con artists will continue to ply their trade on the Internet, and any system that does not consider human factors is doomed to failure. Most design and technology staffs have no understanding of fraud elements, so we expect little will be done to mitigate these vulnerabilities in current and future systems.

- Design failures arising from complex systems will encourage and abet cyber and computer crimes. Many organizations are stringing Intranets, Extranets, and the global Internet together in a Byzantine maze of hardware and software communications pathways that are often so convoluted that few technical employees or consultants ever understand precisely how they work. Sloppy software development processes, as exemplified by the Y2K issues, did not end with COBOL. Human nature has not changed. Shortcuts and expedient solutions to meet implementation deadlines will create much otherwise avoidable vulnerability.

- No one really knows how much cyber crime has already occurred or is happening right now. The reason is simple, there is no one that is trusted enough by business management to collect and analyze Internet crime statistics on a global basis. This is a serious problem because it limit's every corporation's ability to prevent schemes. Inability to analyze known and suspected incidents and abuses, and share that information will reduce every corporation's ability to respond effectively, since each corporation's knowledge base will be limited to only what they have actually experienced. As a consequence, there is no global or national system of advance warnings. Thus, there is nothing to prevent schemes from rippling through linked business partners. The persistent resurgence of the "Explorer.zip" and "Melissa" viruses demonstrated how successful methods of attack would be adapted and reused by Netspionage agents and techno-spies.

The longevity of the famous "Nigerian" advance deposit fraud, which is estimated to have netted hundreds of millions of dollars over the past 10 years, shows that even conventional frauds flourish in the global marketplace. As security and audit professionals, it is not difficult for us to imagine how electronically networked commerce systems—where the parties to a transaction may have never met and operate at the speed of light—will facilitate similar schemes in cyberspace. Those that exploit technical glitches or problems in systems environments to obtain money or valuable information will experience even greater success since fewer people will actually understand how the act has occurred.

Global Mergers and Acquisitions

If it comes to choice, the signals from the financial markets take precedence over those from the product markets. Managers will readily divest divisions or sell the entire company if this will enhance shareholder value; they maximize profits rather than market share. Managers must either acquire or be acquired in an increasingly integrated global market; either way they need a high price for their stock (Soros, 1998).

Mergers and acquisitions were in vogue at the end of the 20th century, and this "feeding frenzy" will undoubtedly continue well into the 21st century. Sure, mergers and acquisitions have been taking place as long as there have been businesses. However, not on such a global scale as we have witnessed over the last decade or so. As an example: In Canada, "Canadian merger and acquisition activity has surged to a six-year high, and the pace is expected to continue well through the year 2000."[1]

What is interesting to note is that many mergers and acquisitions were global, and a sizeable number of companies are now part of one corporation. What does this do to competition to maintain lower prices through that competition? Will it help in the global marketplace competition? Interesting questions that will not be addressed here, but something to think about as we continue to see many more of these types of actions by global corporations. One thing for certain, the competitive intelligence professionals are undoubtedly working overtime, and the Netspionage agents might be also.

So, why are these mergers taking place? There are many individual reasons that are probably unique to each one. However, the main driving force for all of them is the need for increased marketshares and developing a competitive edge in their respective national and global marketplaces.

---

[1]http://www.emp.on.ca/046_2.html

How would one go about determining who to merge with or who to acquire? What mix would offer the best benefit for the shareholders? How much should the merger or acquisition cost? Many of these answers may come from the competitive intelligence professionals. Maybe some of that information may not be readily available unless formal talks were initiated from one to another. However, maybe a Netspionage agent could provide some of the more sensitive information up front.[2]

Not everyone is happy with mergers and acquisitions taking place, at least in the United States. Korey C. C. Kemp wrote:[3]

> *What does this all mean? Well, I believe it means that we are repeating history. Corporate America is returning to the 1800s with the likes of Carnegie steel and other monster conglomerates. We are returning to a time when big business ran our country and the so called "little-guy" was left working long hours for little pay. If these corporations are allowed to continue to merge into these huge conglomerations, the voice of the common man will become obsolete.*

Yet others such as the Social Democrats (SD), U.S.A., take a more nationalistic view going back as far as 1995:[4]

> *In 1975, there was $12 billion worth of mergers and acquisitions. Last year, there was over $300 billion. No corporation, no matter how large or how strong, is now immune from the threat of an unwanted takeover. Until this decade, mergers and acquisitions were business tools used to increase profits by diversifying into new markets. In contrast, many of today's players have neither financial strength nor managerial experience. They are slick market operators who bid on companies, and then blackmail or gut them to profit from the deal.*

As political activism grows on the Internet, one can expect more aggressive acts against those businesses that the political activists consider acting not in the best interest of society. This has and will continue to happen on a global basis. The defacing of the Web site of Indonesia over East Timor and of a furrier over the killing of animals for their fur are just two of many examples. These attacks may spill over into the merger and acquisition arena as well as other arenas. The

---

[2]We certainly are not saying that any illegal information gathering took place on any mergers or acquisitions identified. We are only pointing out, as an example, that such information could save a corporation millions of dollars if they had the right information before merger talks began. Thus, there may be the incentive for someone in some firm to take it upon themselves to acquire much needed information in any possible way.

[3]http://www.drgerlich.com/merge.html, 05/12/98

[4]http://www.idsonline.com/sdusa/mergers.html

activist attacks may often include Netspionage to gain evidence against those businesses that do not meet the desired profiles of the activists.

It appears that the trend of global mega-mergers will continue with no end in sight. As noted above, not everyone is happy about mergers. Certainly the employees of such firms know that they have a much better chance of being laid-off when such mergers and acquisitions occur. So, should these employees remain loyal to a firm about ready to lay them off, in their middle age, with no pension, after 20+ years of service? Obviously, few would remain loyal. Therefore, these employees provide an opportunity for the Netspionage agent, and the employees themselves may become Netspionage agents in order to further their careers or harm the firm that is about to merge and lay them off. The incentive, for some, is there. It has been said that 75 percent of all corporate monetary losses from computer crime activities are attributed to disgruntled corporate employees. It is obvious that these employees would be easy targets for recruitment by Netspionage agents. Are merging corporations doing enough to safeguard their sensitive information from these potential spies? The answer: probably not.

A Snapshot of Global Marketplace—Ripe for Netspionage[5]

The following is a list of events that took place in a narrow part of the global marketplace during a one-month period:

> *Racal rockets on bid hopes; DLJ in Japan ECN deal; Vodaphone surrenders Airtel; Metro to sell $2.8B assets; a banner in '99 mergers; KCP&L pulls out of deal; Humana to sell subsidiary; Statoil sell U.S. gas unit; Argentine telecon deal; Lycos invests in iCOMS; Rolls eyes Pratt merger; Britons to reign in Spain; $3B British defense deal; HSBC warps Safra deal; WMI sues over Eastern deal; CMGI buys stake in Adtech; Gateway sells Amiga line; Intel sells flash card line; U.S. West cuts cable stake; May acquires ZCMI; Stellmaker blocks takeover; Colt eyes Euro gunmaker; CBS, Viacom inch closer; ABB to sell nuclear biz; Sprint sells D.C.-area GSM; U.K. insurer up on bid talk; Fairchild Aerospace sold; Private group buys Jostens; BestBuy takes e-town stake; Internet Gold, Microsoft in deal.*

Look at the above and envision the possibilities for Netspionage—having advanced information about mergers, sales, acquisitions, etc. What could you do with that information? What if you were interested in merging with another corporation? Wouldn't it be nice to know exactly what their bottom line agreement deal would be in advance of negotiations? Illegal? Probably. Useful? Undoubtedly. Profitable? Indubitably. Provide you with a competitive edge and the ability to

---

[5]http://www.cnnfn.com/news/deals/continued.html

make or save literally millions if not billions of dollars in many instances? Most assuredly. Remember, just because they didn't teach Netspionage in the Harvard Business School does not mean that it is not happening daily on a global scale.

The Global Stock Markets

The stock markets of various nations are now intricately linked. What happens in one nation and in one's stockmarket has a major impact on other stockmarkets around the world. With the time differences, 24-hour trading and the like, how these markets react to bad and good news travels like a tidal wave around the world impacting everyone. From a Netpionage standpoint, time may be a factor. Also, because of the linking and interactions between markets, one may attack a target in Asia for the sole purpose of effecting a market half way around the world. As more and more stock traders with expertise in one sector begin to expand to trading in like sectors in other parts of the world, this linking will undoubtedly grow stronger.

Another factor worth considering is that corporate management may not want to hurt their corporation's stock prices—possibly for personal gain—and only report good news. If your competitor continued to report only good news in a down market where everyone in that sector was losing, that would be suspicious. Therefore, a competitor may want to verify that everything was really that good at the competitor's business. One would want to know that so they could find out why and maybe copy some of their techniques.

Also, if it were not true, wouldn't that be worth passing on (anonymously of course—maybe through chat rooms and disguised Internet mail) to the media? We are not, of course, talking about what is legal and what is not, nor are we advocating such techniques. We are talking about business warfare and Netspionage being an integral part of that warfare. The techno-spy and Netspionage agent could be hired to find out the real story.

Another example of the changing business world and our links to each other is the financial community and the stock market of the many world nations. If the Asian economic crisis didn't make that fact perfectly clear, it should be obvious by watching how one nation's stock market impacts others:

With few exceptions, stock investors around the world headed for the exits again on Wednesday, gripped by anxiety over potential interest rate increases and determined to preserve the profits of last year. From Singapore to Santiago, selling was heavy and analysts were saying that market corrections were underway. In Hong Kong, the Hang Seng

Index dropped more than 7 percent. But, a rally on New York's Dow Jones industrial average injected some confidence into the markets late in the global trading day.[6]

Digital Intellectual Property and Business Secrets: Understanding Global Risks

Recently there has been substantial media attention in the United States on the vulnerability of the U.S. national infrastructure to information warfare, hackers, cyber-terrorists, and computer criminals. These increasing reports of technical lapses that result in penetration of governmental and civilian networks, and computer systems must also be paired with the information documenting increased losses of U.S. companies' trade secrets and competitive information. The losses are ascribed to a wide range of threats. However, it is believed that the two are already closely linked and will become even more apparent in the near future.

The advent of Netspionage agents and techno-spies capable of trolling the global networks and scavenging unsecured digital assets will drive the alignment of these trends. This is an issue that will become increasingly challenging the more businesses operate electronically in the global marketplace. There have been many media reports that have highlighted the increased incidents of cyber crimes and thefts of economically valuable information. Incidents demonstrating the value of stealing poorly protected information have surfaced in the United States, United Kingdom, Japan, Germany, Australia, and many other nations where advanced computer and network technology have been used to enhance businesses. This array of incidents from around the world demonstrates that this is a global problem. As more people, government agencies, and businesses gain access to the Internet; as global marketplace competition increases; and as more people become aware of how poorly most corporations are protecting their assets a tidal wave of Netspionage activities is quite likely.

In the United States, another trend has erupted that shows there is another aspect that must be considered for safeguarding digital information assets. There has been a dramatic upsurge in intellectual property litigation in the United States between companies. Many of these suits allege theft or misappropriation of a corporation's digital products or business secrets by competitors and/or former employers. In some cases, the competitors have actually penetrated the networks or systems of their opponents in order to steal valuable information. At the same time, world wide losses to U.S. companies in the software and

---

[6]http://www.cnnfn.com, 01/05/00

entertainment industries, where digital products are already the basis for commerce, have continued to swell as digital piracy becomes sophisticated and joins the underground economy supporting organized crime.

In recognition of their vital contribution to the U.S. economy, the U.S. government has become more active in helping U.S. software and entertainment companies to combat piracy by using diplomatic and economic pressures. Countries and regions that have been hostile to intellectual property rights are being coaxed and coerced into making at least token efforts to protect them. The fact is that protecting a corporation's business secrets and key intellectual property assets is a difficult but increasingly important responsibility of executives in the global marketplace, a responsibility that cannot be ignored as these assets make growing contribution to the bottom line profits of major companies.

Decreasing product development lifecycles have wreaked havoc on intellectual property and proprietary information protection mechanisms. In the past, developing and producing new products occurred at a much slower pace. This longer time frame allowed the corporation to carefully plan and execute a well thought out patent development program. Violation of patents could then be dealt with through litigation for patent infringement, which itself would often result in a long-term process with often uncertain results. However, with products now being developed and deployed in short time intervals, sometimes less than a year, emphasizing patent protection may be problematic at best and ineffectual at worst.

Many companies spend heavily on legal fees associated with patents, trademark, and copyright protection, but fail to invest sufficiently in measures to prevent or detect efforts to steal trade secrets and proprietary information. The old protection strategy that emphasized patent filing and litigation or prosecution helped deter losses, but in the global marketplace and a world of increasingly compressed product lifecycles it no longer suffices. Such a reactive strategy risks loss of critical assets as well as the company reputation and may ultimately put the continued survival or success of the corporation at risk.

A similar misallocation of protection resources has occurred in corporate security programs. It is common for large corporations to spend tens of millions of dollars on physical security measures such as gates, guards, alarms, and CCTV surveillance cameras. Careful examination of the incident reports from such corporations will typically reveal that theft of physical assets such as parts, products, etc., result in a few hundred thousand dollars in annual losses. Unfortunately a single successful Netspionage incident may be expected to result in average losses of $50 million for a manufacturing corporation and $15 million for a high technology company.[7] These results far surpass the typical incidents of physical theft of products and components that are the principal focus of most corporate security programs.

Summary

As they become more information- and technology-dependent, the global businesses are moving from an emphasis on physical assets to an emphasis on information assets. The world is changing, and revolutionary changes are taking place in societies, governments, and businesses. These changes are often chaotic with mergers and acquisitions taking place at a rapid rate as the global competition for market share and enhanced shareholders' value dominates the New World Order.

The thirst for information, no matter how it is acquired, may be quenched by Netspionage agents and techno-spies. Covertly and with no fanfare, they are accomplishing their missions, and some believe the end justifies the means.

As Richard A. McGinn, chairman and CEO of Lucent Technologies, summed it up in the company's 1999 Annual Report:

> The industry in which we operate has never been more dynamic. At a growth rate of more than 14 percent a year, the market will approach $815 billion by 2003. That growth is being propelled by customer demand for next-generation networks: converged networks that deliver new services in any form—voice, data, or video. This is creating a wealth of opportunity . . . Enterprise customers around the world are responding to new competitive challenges as commerce on the Internet continues its explosive growth. E-business has become the Internet's latest growth phenomenon, and enterprises are looking for network solutions to give them new operating efficiencies while helping them improve their relationships with customers . . .

References

Greider, William. *One World, Ready or Not, The Manic Logic of Global Capitalism.* New York: Touchstone, 1997.

Schwartz, Evan I. *Digital Darwinism, 7 Breakthrough Business Strategies for Surviving in the Cutthroat Web Economy.* New York: Broadway Books, 1999.

Soros, George. *The Crisis of Global Capitalism (Open Society Endangered).* New York: Public Affairs, 1998.

---

[7]Loss estimates based on the averages reported in the 1999 ASIS=PwC Loss of Property Information Survey. Full report available at http://www.pwcglobal/Information Loss.

C　　h　　a　　p　　t　　e　　r

5

A Short History of Espionage:
Industrial, Economic, and Military

High-Technology Spying, Economic, and Industrial Espionage on the Internet

When we look at rapid, technology-oriented growth, we find nations of haves-and-have-nots. We also see corporations who conduct business internationally and those that want to do so. The international economic competition and trade-wars are increasing. Corporations are finding increased competition and looking for that competitive edge, competitive advantage.

One way to gain the advantage, the edge, is through industrial and economic espionage. It is true that both forms of espionage have been around since there has been competition. However, in this Information Age, competitiveness is more time-dependent, more crucial to success, and has increased dramatically, largely due to technology. Thus, we see the increased use of technology to steal that competitive advantage and ironically, these same technology tools are also what is being stolen. In addition, we now have more sensitive information consolidated in large databases on Internet networked systems whose security is often questionable.

John F. Quinn, Managing Director of Quinn International and international business intelligence expert says there is a difference between competitive intelligence and espionage. He explained that Business Intelligence (BI) and Competitive Intelligence (CI) is generally under private sponsorship using an "open" methodology. Whereas, espionage may be either government or privately sponsored and clandestine.

Espionage—What Is It?

According to Webster's *Ninth New Collegiate Dictionary*, espionage is *the practice of spying or the use of spies to obtain information about plans and activities especially of a foreign government or a competing company.* The Encarta[1] defines it as *the use of spying or spies to gather secret information. (Late 18thC. From French espionnage, from espionner "to spy," from espion "spy." Ultimately of prehistoric German origin.)*

Industrial and Economic Espionage Defined

To clarify what we are talking about here, definitions of industrial espionage and economic espionage are in order. According to FBI agents, industrial espionage is generally defined as an individual or private business entity sponsorship or coordination of intelligence activity conducted for the purpose of enhancing their advantage in the marketplace.

Also according to the FBI, economic espionage is generally defined as *government-directed, sponsored, or coordinated intelligence activity, which may or may not constitute violations of law, conducted for the purpose of enhancing that country's or another country's economic competitiveness by the use of the information by foreign government or by providing it to foreign private business entity, thereby giving that entity a competitive advantage in the marketplace . . .*

Proprietary, Intellectual Property, Trade Secrets, and Other Sensitive Information

According to the FBI, proprietary, sensitive, intellectual property, trade secrets, and the like generally means *all forms and types of financial, scientific, technical, economic, or engineering information including, but not limited, to data, plans, tools, mechanisms, compounds, formulas, designs, prototypes, processes, procedures, programs, codes, or commercial strategies, whether tangible or intangible . . . and whether stored, compiled or memorialized physically, electronically, graphically, photographically, or in writing . . . provided that the owner takes reasonable measures to protect it, and it is not available to the general public.*

Military Espionage Defined

A general definition of military espionage is the practice of spying or the use of spies to obtain information about plans and activities of the military, especially of a foreign government.

The goal of this book is to address the Netspionage issues related primarily to the threats to businesses through industrial and economic

---

[1]Encarta World English Dictionary, St. Martin's Press Microsoft Encarta.

espionage in today's network, e.g., Internet environment. The problem of military espionage will not be addressed in any level of detail except as it relates to the use of military spies to gain businesses' sensitive, proprietary, trade secret, and intellectual property information.

The Purpose of Industrial and Economic Espionage, and Netspionage

The purpose of Netspionage, industrial and economic espionage, is to obtain unlawfully or clandestinely sensitive financial, trade, or economic policy information, proprietary/sensitive economic information; or critical technologies; or to influence unlawfully or clandestinely sensitive economic policy decisions of a government or business.

The Rising Profile of Economic Espionage

In today's environment, proprietary intellectual property and economic information in the global and domestic marketplace have become the most valuable and sought after commodity by all advanced nations.

The theft, misappropriation, and wrongful receipt of intellectual property and technology, particularly by competitors and foreign governments and their agents, directly threatens the development and making of the products that flow from that information. Furthermore, it can also result in:

- Loss of market share
- Loss of profits
- Loss of business
- Weakened balance of trade
- Weakened economic power of the country
- Weaken the country's ability to provide for its citizens and national defense, e.g., Asian nations cut back on defense modernization programs due to their economic crisis

Threat History

The United States is still the dominant economic power in the world today and thus a major target of espionage and in particular Netspionage due to the massive information infrastructure.

- At one time, the FBI stated that they were investigating approximately 800 economic espionage matters, and that 23 "foreign powers" were directly implicated.

- Another United States Government agency was alleged to have stated that 126 countries have computer espionage programs, and 12 countries are assessed to be actively targeting the United States—including so-called allies.
- On another occasion, the FBI indicated that of 173 nations, 57 were actively running operations targeting U.S. companies; 100 countries spent some portion of their funds targeting U.S. technologies.
- One unidentified survey disclosed 21 percent of attempted or actual thefts of proprietary/sensitive information occurred in overseas locations.
- A CIA survey found that 80 percent of one country's intelligence assets are directed towards gathering information on the United States and to a lesser degree, Europe.
- Current and former employees, suppliers, and customers are said to be responsible for 70 percent of proprietary/sensitive information losses (not deleting a former employee's User ID and password from a corporate system makes it so much easier).

Because of the sensitivity of such matters, many corporations do not report such incidents to law enforcement. If they do, law enforcement usually agrees to not release the information to the news media or others. However, somehow the information often seems to be leaked to the news media.

Espionage and Netspionage Vulnerabilities

To be targeted is one thing; management has no control over that. However, to be vulnerable is inexcusable. Some reasons for the vulnerability of corporations are:

- Proprietary/sensitive information not identified
- Proprietary/sensitive information not adequately protected
- Computer and telecommunication systems not adequately protected
- No or inadequate policies and procedures
- Employees not aware of their responsibilities
- Management attitude of "We don't have proprietary or sensitive information" or "It can't happen to us"

  Therefore, the combination of:

- A nation's or corporations' information which is valuable to other nations and businesses
- The amount of money which some are willing to pay for that information

- The increase in miscreants willing to try to steal that information
- The increase in Internet connections to businesses and government agencies
- The vulnerabilities of systems on the Internet, e.g., Web sites
- The lack of security as a high priority for businesses and government agencies
- The ability to steal that information on a global scale

All add up to some very dangerous times for those with information worth protecting and major challenges to the managers, security personnel, high-technology crime investigators, and law enforcement professionals with the responsibility for that protection and investigating incidents.

When corporations fail to adequately protect their information, they are taking risks that will, in all probability, cause them to lose market share, profits, business, and also help in weakening the economic power of their country.

Tofflers' Three Waves of Evolution Applied to Espionage and Netspionage

The use of the Tofflers' model of technological evolution provides a useful framework for discussing information as it relates to espionage and Netspionage.

The First Wave is the time of the hunter-gatherer and the agricultural revolution, which has taken thousands of years to develop, mature, and in some countries, has begun to fade. According to the Tofflers, this period—at least in the United States—started with the beginning of the human race up to about 1745. Obviously, agriculture is necessary for us humans to survive; however, in modern societies, it does not have the force that it once had. During this period, people lived in small and sometimes migratory groups, feeding themselves through fishing, foraging, hunting, and herding. Subsequently, migrating into clusters then towns, and then cities.

During this First Wave period, information was passed by word of mouth or in written correspondence, usually sent by a courier. People were more dispersed, and transportation more primitive. This meant that there was less communication amongst people. During this period, the number of people who could read or write was relatively little in comparison to the total world population.

The threats, e.g., theft of information in the written form, were minimal since most of the people of the world could not read, or their reading was very limited—although they could destroy the written message. Perhaps, this type of destruction was the first instance of "denial of service." Information verbally relayed could be misinterpreted, or changed. A method that still poses a threat to successful Netspionage today.

Espionage during this period was a manual and human intensive profession. The First Wave espionage relied almost entirely on personal observations and one-to-one contact. Cryptography and stenography were in their infancy in this period.

The Second Wave-what Tofflers' call the "rise of industrialized civilization" (Toffler, 1994) took less than 300 years. This was the age of steel mills, oil refineries, textile plants, mass assembly lines, etc. The people migrated to centralized locations to work in these industries. This period lasted until just a few years after World War II. In the United States, its decline, according to the Tofflers, is believed to have started about 1955, when for the first time, white-collar workers outnumbered blue-collar workers.

The Second Wave period saw the building of the great cities of the world, the period of great inventions like the telegraph, telephone, air transportation, and computers. This period saw increases in education, mass transportation, and exponential growth in communications—the sharing of information.

The sharing of information became easier due to the invention of communications systems and the increased consolidation of people into large cities. This made it easier to also educate the people, a needed skill in order to work in the more modern factories and offices of the period.

The sharing of information through various communication channels brought new challenges. For communication protection, cryptography came into its own during this period. Cryptography primarily was a government-used high-technology anti-espionage tool. This was due for the most part because the federal government owned most of the computers. Although businesses were beginning to look at the use of computers, most were cost-prohibitive; these systems were primarily operated in stand-alone mode. In other words, the computers did not talk to other computers.

Although espionage—intelligence collection—has been around for centuries, it really started to come into its own in Europe and the United States in the late 19th century and 20th century. For example, in 1882 the Royal Navy was producing valuable economic intelligence collections by observing the movements of the commercial, foreign merchant ships. With the new 20th century came "His Majesty's Secret Service," the Kaiser's spies, the Czar's spies, the Codebreakers, and aerial reconnaissance.

There were also the train watchers, the French spies, the Russian spy networks. Spying really began developing with the advent of World War I where *for the first time in war, technology was a major factor in gathering intelligence* [Richelson 1995]. Later came Lenin's spies, the development of spy agencies by all the major world countries. To supplement the human element, as technology developed, technology-based spying equipment was developed, e.g., the SR-71 and U2 aircraft, the spy satellites, and other technologies too numerous to mention here.

What were the main techniques? Of course, human intelligence collection was still the primary technique. One just has to look at what technology was available at that time for communication—telegraph, telephones, and radio communications. So, what did the spies tap into? Of course, those communication links used by the adversaries. So, is it any wonder that as communications—the flow of information—moved onto computers, networks, and now the Internet, that the espionage agents would not also follow suit as techno-spies and Netspionage agents?

During this period pagers, cellular phones, private branch exchanges, and even computerized telephone switches did not exist, or if they did, it was on a small scale.

For much of this period, anti-espionage measures for businesses and government agencies consisted of some form of physical security, e.g., combination of locks, guards, alarms, and fences, and was thought of as primarily a government and military problem. After all, weren't spies after military secrets? This is a misconception that still exists today, at least in the United States.

As the computer became more sophisticated, the main protection mechanism used for computers changed very little. The reliance was still on physical security, and the espionage detection and investigation concentrated more on the physical aspects such as busted locks, cut wire fences, with theft being the reason for the crime. The thief was after physical documents and physical equipment.

After all, why worry about such things as access control other than physical security? Besides physical security, the primary emphasis was on personnel security—hiring honest and ethical employees. One must remember that in those days not many people knew how to use the computers in the first place. In the beginning of this period, very few people worked in the computer field, and those that did, had to know how to "program with punch cards." Therefore, at first the threats to these information systems and their information were small.

The Third Wave, the age of technology and information, is sweeping across the earth and will have done so in decades not centuries.

This Third Wave period that we are now in has seen more advances than the First and Second Wave periods combined. This period has seen the rapid growth of high-technology that is playing a major role in our rapidly changing world.

Remember the old business saying, "Time is money?" Well, in our world of international, global competition, that saying is truer now than ever before. Managers and security professionals must also understand this better than ever before. Espionage and Netspionage concerns cannot be a roadblock to business. However, the concerns must be addressed.

The San Jose Mercury News *ran a series of articles, Silicon Valley Secrets for Sale, May 2–9, 1982, which indicate that not much has changed over the years. A glance at the headlines disclosed:*

- Greed, more than high-tech spies, threatens . . .
- Bumbling efforts at control; agents baffled by technology
- Capitalists in the United States sell their soul to show a nice balance sheet to stockholders
- Chip thieves play for high stakes
- In the quest for U.S. high-technology, money talks; electronic devices flow
- Europe's high-technology smugglers deal amid elegance and sophistication
- They (high-tech companies) discourage problems. They don't want stockholders to know they've lost millions of dollars. They don't want their competitors to know
- We've had crooks tell us they take the damn thing when the guy's out to lunch—and nobody misses it—Pat Moore, a sheriff's deputy
- Crackdown on high-tech espionage urged
- Access to U.S. technology can be easy when foreigners own the company
- High-tech theft: some solutions—employee incentives, better security, tougher probes, and appeals to allies

One of the challenges of management and security professionals is to assist in deterring and preventing espionage, and Netspionage. Such crimes can be mitigated, in part by controls, security measures, and considering espionage and Netspionage when looking into violations of business policy and procedures. It is also important to as well as aggressively investigating and identifying those that commit violations of corporate policy, procedures, and/or laws. In addition, the management supported by security professionals is undoubtedly responsible for providing a cost-effective anti-espionage and anti-Netspionage program within their corporations.

Netspionage agents who attack through high-technology systems, especially those that are networked, e.g., to the Global Information Infrastructure, Internet, generally use a common attack philosophy and methodology. Their sequence of attacks usually follows the scenario as shown in Figure 5–1.

Basic Use of Physical and Human Intelligence Collection Methods: Theft and Social Engineering

Based on the general, systematic approach, the Netspionage agent or the attacker must gather information about the target from some source or sources.

Let us use the example of a Netspionage agent or techno-spies whose goal is to obtain information about a company. Let's begin with the Internet, Global Information Infrastructure (GII), and National Information Infrastructure (NII), because these massive networks are excellent examples of the new high-technology environment where the miscreant will ply their trade, now and into the future.

The Internet itself provides an excellent vehicle for the attackers to share and collect information on a global scale. They can use the Internet to search out their targets, and to share information about that target and attack technique with others around the world. Remember that these massive networks are global communications systems. Thus, the Netspionage agents use them as they would a telephone, telegraph, or letter a few years back.

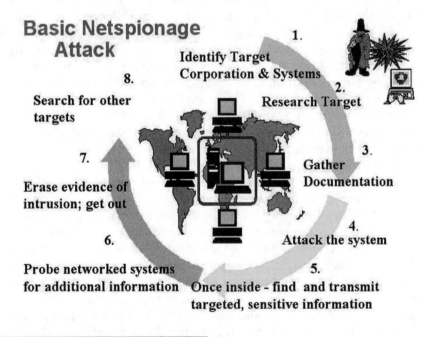

Figure 5–1 A general attack methodology.

Sometimes it may be necessary to gather information directly from the target, whether it is a business or government agency. The basic methods for doing so are by personally collecting the information on the target's site, through theft, social engineering, or a combination of both.

You may recall watching a typical television drama where the police, trying to catch a criminal involved in fraud, drug dealing, etc., covertly take the person's garbage and sift through it for information that can be used to help their investigation. The Netspionage agents often use the same technique. They frequently rummage through the trash bins of their target looking for clues to assist them in successfully attacking that target.

So, what are these "dumpster divers" looking for? They are seeking information that will tell them more details about the computing environment of the target. For example, there may be boxes in the trash that had been used to transport new computer hardware and software. One of the boxes may have been used to ship the target's new Internet firewall product, its new network server, routers, switches, as well as the new version of their operating system.

In addition, they will look for memos, telephone books, anything with names, positions, and telephone numbers that may give a hint as to the User ID's and passwords people may be using; possibly passwords themselves. Even expired passwords provide good information because they may indicate a pattern that would allow easy guessing of the new password. For example, if I am required to change my password every month, I may choose a word with a sequential set of numbers. So when I have to change my password, I use "password2" in February. Then in March, when I am again required to change my password, I use "password3." This meets the security requirements to change passwords on a monthly basis as well as the security requirement to use alpha-numeric characters for my passwords, but it also means anyone who finds my old password could easily predict my current and future password.

The information also may be gathered by posing as an employee, vendor, prospective employee, or even as a janitor on a night shift (when there are probably less people around). All it takes to obtain almost unrestricted access to a target site is either getting hired by the janitorial service or finding out what work clothes the janitors use, stealing a set or buying a similar set. Photo ID Badges used by the organization pose little deterrent to a determined Netspionage agent. With just a little bluffing, a Netspionage agent may tell the security guard that he is a new employee and has an appointment to get an ID badge in the morning. In the interim, the janitorial company has told them to sign in as a visitor. More likely than not, the guard will allow the access for the single evening, which may be all that is required.

This is only one way of social engineering your way into the targeted facility. The objective is to convince someone to allow you access to the target facility. Once inside, you have many hours to find information that will assist you in breaking in. If you are lucky, maybe someone even left their computer operating and connected to the organization network at the end of the workday. Such a lucky break will allow the fortunate intruder to act as an "authorized" user with access to the system.

Social engineering is used quite often for gathering information necessary to successfully attack a system on the Internet. Social engineering is nothing more that the ability to "con" information out of people and/or make them do what you want them to do.

For example, taking an organization's phone book out of a garbage dumpster may give the Netspionage agent the names of people who may have the information required to break into a major network or application containing the most critical information of the organization.

Another approach that has been used is to call during nonbusiness hours, the later at night the better because all the higher level managers, if not all managers, will most likely have gone home. You call the systems operations group, who typically will be working 24 hours a day, and tell them you need access to their maintenance port to do some online maintenance. You give them as the name of your company, their primary computer vendor, e.g., Sun, IBM—whatever works!

You know what systems they have from documentation you obtained in your previous searches or by calling up someone in the target and asking them what computers they are using. Again, social engineering techniques apply. You can say you were a high school student and looking for a company, which has a certain type of computer, for your high school science class to tour. Normally, you will be referred to the public relations or marketing people. In either case, these individuals have been known to give out a great deal of information.

You can also pose as a computer salesman, or anyone else who can get information because of who they claim to be. The most essential skill for social engineering is the ability to make other people believe what that person is telling them.

If the operations person is hesitant in providing that information, some nice talking may work: "Look, I understand your concern and I appreciate your position, but we both have our jobs to do. Mine is to do some system maintenance for you. Your company called in the first place so it's not like I want to be here this late at night either. Look, is Bob Johnson there? (You found Bob Johnson's name in some targeted documentation and found that he was the Director of Operations.) His name is listed on the work order with telephone number 234–2345."

Normally, it's the specific and detailed nature of the information provided to the contact that causes them to believe the request is legitimate. After all how could anyone know that much information unless they were legitimate?

If that approach does not work, then some intimidation may work: "Look, if you don't give me the information I need to perform the maintenance, I really don't care. I can go home early, no problemo! Let me have your name and position please so that when my boss asks or this Johnson guy asks why the work was not done, I can tell them to talk to you. I don't care!" That technique works quite often, and once you are in, you are in!

Social engineering works because people basically think other people are honest and unless they had some guidance and awareness briefing on what to say and *what not to say*, they are normally very helpful and provide the requested information.

Other Computer-Related Techniques Used by Netspionage Agents and Techno-Spies: Both Insiders and Outsiders[2]

The following are some methods that may be used by these Netspionage agents and techno-spies:

- Data Diddling: Changing data before or during entry into the computer system. For example, forging or counterfeiting documents used for data entry; exchanging valid disks and tapes with modified replacements
- Scavenging: Obtaining information left around a computer system, in the computer room trash cans, etc.
- Data Leakage: Removing information by smuggling it out as part of a printed document; encoding the information to look like something different and removing it from the facility
- Piggybacking/Impersonation: Physical access is one method used. For example, following someone in through a door with a badge reader. Electronically using another's User ID and password to gain computer access; tapping into the terminal link of a user to cause the computer to believe that both terminals are the same people
- Simulation and Modeling: Using the computer as a tool or instrument to plan or control a criminal act
- Wire Tapping: Tapping into a computer's communications links to be able to read the information being transmitted between systems and networks

---

[2]These definitions are the generally accepted definitions used by the FBI and others. The FBI provided these definitions in 1979. Obviously, not much has changed.

System Manipulation

Software applications have been written and techniques used by the Netspionage agents, hackers, and techno-spies. The term for these types of application programs have become standardized over the years. Many Netspionage agents can use a variation of hacker tools. They generally are often classified as follows:

- Trojan Horse: Covert placement of instructions in a program that causes the computer to perform unauthorized functions but usually still allow the program to perform its intended purpose. This is the most common method used in computer-based frauds and sabotage.
- Trap Doors: When developing large programs, programmers tend to insert debugging aids that provide breaks in the instructions for insertion of additional code and intermediate output capabilities. The design of computer operating systems attempts to prevent this from happening. Therefore, programmers insert instructions that allow them to circumvent these controls. High-technology criminals take advantage of these trap doors, or create their own.
- Logic Bombs: A computer program executed at a specific time period or when a specific event occurs. For example, a programmer would write a program to instruct the computer to delete all personnel and payroll files if his/her name were ever removed from the file.
- Computer Virus: Malicious code that causes damage to system information or denies access to the information through self-replication.

Using the GII, Internet, and NII to Search for Tools

When a Netspionage agent or techno-spy needs tools to attack their targets, especially those on the massive, global networks, they usually come from four sources:

- Fellow spies
- Government agencies
- Developed themselves
- The Internet

The first three speak for themselves, so only the Internet will be addressed. Very little equipment or skills are needed these days to attack systems on the Internet. It must be remembered that these are just some examples and are far from all-inconclusive. Some "network patches" have been developed by manufacturers and others that defend against such attacks. Furthermore, new vulnerabilities, patches and attacks seem to be identified on what seems to be a daily basis.

- The attacker obviously must have access to the Internet, which is usually through some Internet Service Provider (ISP), and for our purposes that is assumed.
- Once on the Internet, the attacker points the mouse to the "SEARCH" icon and then types in "hacker," "hacker software," or specific tools that the Netspionage agent had heard about.
- Then, the Netspionage agent must be able to download the tool. This is also generally an easy task, as often the attacker only has to click on the Download icon.
- Netspionage agent then identifies the target or randomly attacks various targets by executing the attack tools programs.

Try Catching These Miscreants

The ex-KGB,[3] ex-CSR, and ex-GRU (as well as active) agents are professionals, but the most dangerous are the Ph.D. computer scientists that were trained by the KGB, GRU, and others. They have many decades of experience, have reversed engineered IBM mainframes in the "good ol' days," and these are the ones to most fear. These are the ones who, without sheer luck and/or a lot of money spent on security, will not be caught.

If they are caught, it will be a challenge to investigate the matter and be able to build a case that would stand up in court.

Summary

In many countries, the "Three Waves" are simultaneously impacting societies, although with various degrees of speed and force. With it comes various degrees of social unrest, conflicts, and tensions as the "old wave" supporters try to hold on to the past. This all leads to the potential for increased Netspionage. Governments, businesses, and people are all being impacted, as the Tofflers have pointed out.

Economic espionage, that espionage supported by a government to further a business, is becoming more prevalent, more sophisticated, and easier to conduct due to technology.

The increase in all forms of economic espionage is also largely due to the corporate vulnerabilities to such threats. Corporations do not

---

[3]Central Intelligence Service–*Centralnaya Sluzhbza Razvedkyin* (CSR); remaining elements of the Committee for State Security, the *Komitet Gosudarstvennoy Bezopasnosti*, or the KGB; and the Chief, Intelligence Directorate, the *Glavnoye Razvedyvatelnoye Upravleniye*, or the GRU.

adequately identify and protect their information, nor do they adequately protect their computer and telecommunications systems.

They do not have adequate security policies and procedures; employees are not aware of their responsibilities to protect their corporation's proprietary information. Many of the employees and also the management of these corporations do not believe they have any information worth stealing or believe "it can't happen here."

When a corporation fails to adequately protect their information, they are taking risks that will, in all probability, cause them to lose market share, profits, business, and also help in weakening the economic power of their country.

The ever increasing value of trade secret information in the global and domestic marketplaces, and the corresponding spread of technology have combined to significantly increase both the opportunities and the motives for conducting Netspionage. Remember: what your country's businesses do impacts the economic power of your nation-state. Ask yourself what are your responsibilities to defend against this threat.

References

Bequai, August. *Techno-Crimes, The Computerization of Crime and Terrorism.* Lexington: Lexington Books, 1987.

Deriabin, Peter S., and Jerrold L. Schecter. *The Spy Who Saved the World.* New York: Charles Scribner's Sons, 1992.

Dulles, Allen. *The Craft of Intelligence.* New York: Harper & Row Publishers, 1963.

Estimiades, Nicholas. *Chinese Intelligence Operations.* Arlington: Newcomb Publishes, Inc., 1998.

Fialka, John J. *War by Other Means.* New York: W.W. Norton and Company, 1997.

Kahaner, Larry. *Competitive Intelligence, How to Gather, Analyze, and Use Information to Move Your Business to the Top.* New York: Touchstone, 1996.

Kuzichkin, Vladimir. *Inside the KGB, My Life in Soviet Espionage.* New York: Pantheon Books, 1990.

Lunev, Stanislav. *Through the Eye of the Enemy.* Washington D.C.: Regnery Publishing, Inc. 1998.

Richelson, Jeffrey T. *A Century of Spies, Intelligence in the Twentieth Century.* Oxford: Oxford University Press, 1995.

Schweizer, Peter. Friendly Spies. New York: *The Atlantic Monthly Press,* 1993.

Sheng, Wang. Political Warfare. Taipei: Minister of Defense, 1963.

Winkler, Ira. *Corporate Espionage.* Rocklin, CA: Prima Publishing, 1997.

Section II: Who Does What to Whom, Why and How

This section will provide the reader with a description of how effective use of a wide range of technologies has made the efficient collection and dissemination of timely intelligence information an effective tool for savvy managers in both business and government. We will define and describe technology enabled ethical competitive intelligence, and distinguish this vital element of corporate success from the criminal acts involved in actual spying.

Chapter 6: Competitive Intelligence and the Networked World

This chapter will discuss the migration of information to the web as businesses use it to automate their value chain and build tight linkages with customers, suppliers, vendors, employees, and government agencies. It will detail e-business as fundamentally changing the web and Internet; increased importance of competitive intelligence collection and analysis; as well as the increased temptation to cross the line and commit Netspionage to supplement the publicly available information.

Chapter 7: Information Collection in the Gray Zone

This chapter discusses what can be accomplished by operating in the ethical and legal "white zone," the unethical and legal "gray zone," and the unethical and illegal "black zone." It will explain that because of today's global networks connected to the Internet, information brokers, hackers, and private investigators are among the groups of people selling information to those with the money to buy.

Chapter 8: The Black Zone, Who Uses Netspionage, How and Why

This chapter discusses operating in the black zone where principles such as ethics and legal issues no longer apply. Discussions will include techniques and software products that can be used by the Netspionage agents against multiple and vulnerable corporate targets.

Chapter 9: Case Studies of Netspionage

This chapter identifies and analyzes Netspionage-related cases; as well as discusses their meaning and impact.

6

Competitive Intelligence and the Networked World

What Is Competitive Intelligence?

It is essential to define Competitive Intelligence (CI) before we discuss how it is a key enabler of business success in the Information Age. It is also important to distinguish CI from other forms of information collection that may be misrepresented as CI.

The need to gather information for decision makers has been playfully described as the second oldest profession, and one with a romanticized history played out in endless movies, novels, and plays over the centuries. The domain of the spy and spying has fired the imagination of countless people over the years. However glorious espionage may have been, it has mainly been associated with defense and military efforts. The advent of vast global organizations competing for survival at the speed of online connections, has brought the term competitive intelligence to the forefront of business operations.

Competitive intelligence has been well defined as " . . . *a systematic program for gathering and analyzing information about your competitors' activities and general business trends to further your own company's goals.*"[1] Note that the definition does not imply or address legal or ethical factors, it is neutral, merely describing the objective: to gather useful information to support the company's goals.

There are schools in various nations these days that have courses in business intelligence and competitive intelligence. According to one source, there is at least one school in Paris, France, and others in Idaho and Florida in the United States, just to name a few.

One cannot begin any serious discussion of competitive intelligence without recognizing the influence of The Society of

---

[1]*Competitive Intelligence* by Larry Kahaner, p. 16.

Competitive Intelligence Professionals (SCIP). SCIP is a large professional society dedicated to the advancement of the field of competitive intelligence. With over 7,000 members from dozens of countries around the world SCIP[2] is a recognized leader in the effort to promote "ethical business intelligence."

One of the major contributions of SCIP has been to provide a code of ethics for member practitioners (see Figure 6–1):

SCIP Code of Ethics for CI Professionals

• *To continually strive to increase respect and recognition for the profession.*
• *To pursue one's duties with zeal and diligence while maintaining the highest degree of professionalism and avoiding all unethical practices.*
• *To faithfully adhere to and abide by one's company's policies, objectives and guidelines.*
• *To comply with all applicable laws.*
• *To accurately disclose all relevant information, including one's identity and organization, prior to all interviews.*
• *To fully respect all requests for confidentiality of information.*
• *To promote and encourage full compliance with these ethical standards within one's company, with third party contractors, and within the entire profession.*

Figure 6–1 SCIP Code of Ethics.

Note that this code *does* state that members will comply with *applicable laws*. However the admonition to accurately disclose one's identity and to avoid unethical practices falls a little short of language explicitly stating that members must not deceive, lie, or steal information, even though that is obviously the intention of the code. The other area for consideration is that the SCIP code, although promulgated by the leading professional association for competitive intelligence professionals, has little force on nonmembers. It may even fall short of deterring unethical activities by members for whom the local "applicable law" may include tolerance or even encouragement of collection activities that are proscribed in other countries. This issue becomes very significant later when we discuss how the Internet access facilitates exactly this type of transnational access and may allow CI staff to exploit "ethical confusion."

---

[2]Additional information may be found at the SCIP web site http://www.scip.org.

The various state and Federal laws in the United States that deal with theft of such sensitive information as proprietary and trade secret information are much more effective in efforts to discourage theft of sensitive information. These laws create significant adverse consequences for anyone who is considering crossing the line from CI into the gray and black zones[3] where the practices of industrial and economic espionage flourish. There may also be more significant issues. In some nations (the United States in particular), the taking of another corporation's proprietary information, trade secrets, and other intellectual property is a serious, criminal offense. However, in many other countries, especially newly developing nations such as in Asia, there tends to be little interest in safeguarding the intangible assets of non-indigenous businesses. Violations for piracy are often considered a relatively minor offense and receive little attention from the local authorities, especially if the thefts are directed against "rich" companies from a distant and alien land. Regardless of any differences as to what is ethical, legal or not, there are factors that are increasing the demand from corporate executives for more information

Competitive Intelligence, Industrial, and Economic Espionage

"Intelligence" differs from mere information. Information is purely fact based, one can point to specific sources and documents, e.g., an annual report states that a plant is being closed, that a small start up company has been acquired in Silicon Valley, that a senior executive has retired to academia.

Competitive intelligence is much more than merely the acquisition of heaps of facts. The key distinction is that *Intelligence . . . is a collection of information pieces that have been filtered, distilled, and analyzed. It has been turned into something that can be acted upon. Intelligence, not information, is what managers need to make decisions. Another term for intelligence is knowledge.*[4]

Whereas the facts cited in the previous example are in themselves interesting, the analyst may infer much more based on long experience and other information. For example, the closed plant described may represent an unsuccessful product line now discontinued; the start-up may represent new technology that is required to transform the core business of the larger corporation; and the departing executive may have been the advocate of a now disgraced strategic initiative built around the discontinued product. These assumptions may be proven or

---

[3]The gray zone refers to information collection activities that clearly are unethical but may be legal; the black zone refers to the activities that are both illegal and unethical.

[4]*Competitive Intelligence*, by Larry Kahaner, p. 21.

disproved by additional facts acquired in a systematic process that is typically referred to as a "collection plan." At the end of a series of iterative collection and analysis steps, the raw facts will have been filtered, distilled, and interpreted through the skilled efforts of the analyst, placed into perspective and given meaning. No computer yet invented can replace the human, the "carbon based units" in performing analysis. The insight that comes when unexplained fact meets intuition and insight to infer meaning and determine the operational implications of facts in a context meaningful to the corporation.

When one thinks of industrial espionage (IE), one often views it as the use of illegal means, which may include all means of clandestine information collection characteristic of the national intelligence services to acquire a business' sensitive information. Typically, IE is performed by one business against another. The purpose may include such tasks as obtaining a superior manufacturing process, advance release of key details of a marketing campaign, or the parameters of a breakthrough product. The objective is to gain the competitive advantage

The means that may be employed to accomplish IE include physical acquisition by paying or bribing rogue employees, trash collectors, or others for copies of key documents. Another popular technique is the assignment of penetration agent(s) (in the intelligence community commonly referred to as "moles") to operate inside a target organization. The reader should not believe such matters are pure fiction nor are they confined to only advanced information-based nations. A recent article in a leading trade publication from India discussed the rampant use of "dummies" (employees of a detective agency) placed on the opponents payroll to ferret out the key information of the business rival.[5] Further evidence of such behavior can be found in legal journals and court documents, for example, in Silicon Valley.

Covert photography, especially in industry where the appearance, design factors, and such are often the source of an advantage, may be very effective. The widespread availability of concealed surveillance video devices camouflaged to appear as fountain pens, pagers, and even eyeglasses has added the potential for full video to the ever present threat of a high powered telephoto lens and a 35mm camera. Wiretaps are relatively simple to install and offer the potential to monitor every telephone conversation. They are basically radio frequency transmitters known in the intelligence community as "bugs." Wiretaps are cheap and when installed by professionals offer the capability to monitor the conversations and presentations in key areas. The targets for bugs include corporate boardrooms, executive offices, and especially off-site meeting rooms at luxury hotels and resorts where security is notoriously poor against these types of threats. The rule that may apply to some CI specialists is to do whatever it takes to obtain the targeted

---

[5]http://www.the-week.com/98apr12/biz1.htm Spies on Board the Week 4/12/98.

information, use any means that offers the corporation access to the targeted information.

In the United States one of the most famous (or infamous depending on your point of view) cases of industrial espionage was Hitachi against IBM in the early 1980s. In this incident, the Japanese company was accused of trying to convince an employee of IBM to sell the engineering drawings and designs of the company's next generation computer system. The materials contained trade secret and proprietary information of the IBM Company and under the laws of the United States selling these materials to another company, any other company, would have been a crime. IBM with the help of the FBI thwarted the plot.

Another incident involved a former career engineer from Kodak, who after retirement offered to sell to Kodak's competitors confidential information concerning new products under development and to which he had access during his long tenure as a trusted employee. As FBI Director Freeh described this case: *Harold C. Worden was a 30-year employee of the Eastman Kodak Corporation who established his own consulting firm upon retiring from Kodak. Worden subsequently hired many former Kodak employees and stole a considerable amount of Kodak trade secret and proprietary information for use at his firm. The market share at risk could have been in the billions of dollars. As a result of investigation, Worden signed a plea agreement with the U.S. Attorney's Office for the Western District of New York in which he pled guilty to one felony count of violating Title 18, U.S.C., Section 2314 (the Interstate Transportation of Stolen Property). Worden was sentenced to one-year imprisonment, three months of home confinement with monitoring bracelet, three years of supervised probation, and a fine of $30,000.*[6]

It is instructive to note that Worden's penalty, although significant, is hardly draconian. The fact that the downside consequences of such crimes are limited and the potential upside so great is one reason why there seems to be an increasing supply of people willing to risk the sanctions in exchange for a chance at successful Netspionage.

Economic Espionage

Some major governments have authorized their national services to use any and all methods, including illegal means by the official agents of the nation-state to acquire businesses' sensitive information. It may also include actions by the agents of a nation-state or transnational entity against the national economic information of another country.

In recognition of the increasing damage done to U.S. interests by industrial and economic espionage efforts the Congress enacted the

---

[6]Director of the FBI Louis Freeh, Testimony to Senate Select Committee on Intelligence 1/28/98.

Economic Espionage Act of 1996, which made both forms of espionage against U.S. companies a federal felony with very serious sanctions (see Appendix 1).

The major difference between competitive intelligence and both forms of espionage is clear. CI is the use of legal and ethical means to acquire information that will be used to create actionable intelligence for business decision makers. Espionage, by definition involves violations of laws and ethics. Competitive intelligence is a legitimate tool that should be embraced by managers to address the need for better information for decision making.

Demand for Competitive Intelligence Support

A wide range of factors has driven the increasing demand for competitive intelligence, most significantly the very competitive global marketplace. The speed of business has become so fast that past practices of informal information collection and analysis are simply too slow and too inefficient to meet the need for actionable information for decision makers, who want the information yesterday.

Some of the factors which are driving the explosive growth in competitive intelligence include but are not limited to the following:

- There is simply too much information (sometimes referred to as "info glut") impacting every corporation and manager. The challenge is to have methods and techniques that cull out the nuggets of key information. For example, a typical manager in business receives dozens to hundreds of electronic mail messages daily. In addition, their in-basket groans under the weight of stacks of management reports. The manager seldom has time to monitor the trade press for key developments and the general business press is a critical source of external business-related data. A well-developed CI program provides a structure for weeding out irrelevant information and focuses on producing refined products that support the company's decision makers by telling them what they need to know to help them make better decisions.

- The economy in the modern information-based nations is rapidly becoming global. The popular media provides a fine example that highlights this fact. A recent television advertisement for e-business shows a foreign manufacturing company that cannot find sufficient parts in country for their need. However, the crisis is averted as a young manager used the Internet to locate a supplier in the United States. As laudable as the tale may seem for highlighting the global economy, there are many unanswered questions. How does the foreign company know anything about the U.S. company, who owns it, how big they are, what is their production quality? The key challenge in global e-business is how to know with whom you are dealing with on the other side of the planet. The chance that one may make a bad decision is very high unless there is some method of knowing about prospective suppliers and business partners as well as the competitors in other regions of the global marketplace. A comprehensive CI program that addresses business operations issues can provide the much-needed information.

- Other challenges derived from globalization brought on in large part by the Internet include differences in ethics and standards for business practices. In some nations there are different standards for "sharp dealing" compared to material misrepresentations or misstatements of facts inspiring detrimental reliance by another organization. Without a business intelligence program to identify and manage these differences, the company could suffer serious problems. Therefore, there is need for accurate, complete, and timely information before selecting business partners, and deciding which initiatives merit resources or run unusual risks. Providing this information is a task for CI.

- Technological innovations, primarily the Internet and the deployment of e-business systems are key drivers for increased interest in CI. The need for nonstop operations impacts the information needs of corporate management. From the perspective of the CI analyst, the Internet provides both new means and methods to accomplish traditional means of collecting information as well as entirely new means of acquiring information and generating intelligence. There are now many new and different avenues for reaching the most productive sources of intelligence. From the CI perspective the Internet is a vast electronic "candy store," just waiting to be exploited. However, meeting the needs of the e-business management for fast, timely, accurate market information requires a structure process, which is what CI provides.

Competitive Intelligence in Practice

The practice of ethical competitive intelligence collections is derived from the classic intelligence cycle (see Figure 6–2) taught at every national intelligence service around the planet. Note that this is a circular, iterative process that progressively should move closer to the limits of questions that can be answered without intrusive (read unethical or illegal) methods and techniques.

How Has the Internet Impacted the Intelligence Cycle?

Let's examine how the Internet and the web have impacted the steps in the classic intelligence cycle.

• Planning and Direction: First, the web allows the savvy manager to create and sustain a "virtual intelligence organization" (VIO) using the full range of communication technology to leverage both internal and external resources. The VIO will include regular employees, full time intelligence staff, specialist consultants, information brokers, online databases, trade and business publications, and other specialized or industry unique reference materials. A competitive intelligence department in an advanced corporation undoubtedly uses a web-based Intranet server, either custom crafted or off-the shelf. This system serves as the primary information repository and operations base. The intelligence organization may solicit or request input and collection assignments from the entire corporation or only selected organizations, e.g., the marketing department, via web forms or electronic mail. This is how the CI unit is determining what needs to be known. The CI manager will develop an overall plan and strategy, prioritize requests and assign tasks to both internal and external sources of information.

The Competitive Intelligence Collection Cycle

1. *Planning and Direction* - Determine what the business needs to know

2. *Collections* - Obtain the information needed

3. *Analyses* - Understanding what the information means

4. *Dissemination* - Getting the right information to the right people at the right time; obtain feedback; get re-tasked

Figure 6–2 The Competitive Intelligence Collection Cycle.

Commercial Databases

Commercial databases can provide a wealth of additional sources for a fee. Although not strictly limited to competitive intelligence, these resources can and do provide those with access to them a wealth of useful information. For example, CI staff at a company where one of the authors worked in the early 1990s carried subscriptions to over 900 different commercial databases. The available information included everything from current names, addresses, vehicle registrations, bankruptcy, liens, judgements, to aircraft, maritime vessels, and more.

Typical public record databases are often classified according to the following categories:

Identifier Databases (Autotrak, CDB Infotek, Lexis-Nexis)

Business Databases (Lexis-Nexis, Dun & Bradstreet, Dialog, InfoAmerica)

Media Databases (Lexis-Nexis, Dow Jones)

Legal Databases (Lexis-Nexis, CDB Infotek, Pacer, InfoAmerica)

Asset Databases (Lexis-Nexis, CDB Infotek, Autotrak)

Licensing Databases (CDB Infotek, Lexis-Nexis)

Specialty Databases (Dialog)

The CI staff probably employs a relational database system to capture and retain information on competitors and other relevant topics. These systems allow managers and authorized users to craft custom queries at any time it is convenient to the user. Thus reports, analysis, and information may be accessible at all times. This last aspect is increasingly important for global businesses upon which the "sun never sets," and who operate with different holidays, working shifts, etc. It's just not sufficient in today's global marketplace to promise to get the information to an internal customer the next (local) working day. It is sometimes difficult for managers and staff to really think globally, but it is essential in the intelligence business.

The server(s) may be fed automatically from various information sources. Many services exist that comb through the vast array of online publications, chat rooms, forums, and other sources. For a nominal fee these services will provide regular updates and a tailored report that will identify the most recent information concerning target companies or other relevant topics (e.g., new technologies). These inputs may be pre-filtered and fed directly into folders in the core database so that all public reporting on the key topics are retained and available to assist company managers in tracking positive or negative trends. Ironically, these databases which are one of the crown jewels of many organizations are themselves often the targets of competitors engaged in Netspionage. After all, by knowing the questions asked by management as well as the answers provided by the CI unit, the competitor will likely be able to forecast with great accuracy the direction and plans of the company, their competitor.

In addition, the information collection system probably allows the collective knowledge assets (both institutional as well as human) of the global enterprise itself to provide answers to important collection tasks. For example, the manager of the London or Tokyo offices of the company may themselves know the name of, price, or status of a particular product that the research centers in San Francisco or Sydney need to know for strategic planning. By some estimates, as much as 80 percent or more of what mangers and executives need to know in order to make better decisions is already available to them *inside their own company*. Often the elusive element is within the knowledge of their own staff or contained in documents or materials the business has created. However, categorizing these resources and managing them in a way that keeps them productive and accessible to queries has been very difficult in the past. The web and advanced software technologies now facilitates the efficient use of these resources.

The collection phase will also include a general web search using common search engines, specialized commercial databases and online research as noted above. Most often the inquiries received from line and executive managers will fall into one or more of the following broad categories:

- Research all public information about a specific company, organization, or agency
- Provide all current news relevant to a specific topic
- Search out primary sources who can advise concerning the above or special topics or issues

The obvious starting place for nearly every collection project is the target companies own Web site and sites affiliated with the target. If a Web site itself is of interest, the contents may perhaps be captured in part or in full using various search utilities and saved for off-line examination in detail and for inclusion in the report. If there is a search utility on the site itself, it may be used to identify the most relevant or promising materials for capture. It is interesting to note that sensitive information is often posted to a company's Web site without anyone ever considering its value to competitors. These Web sites have become a gold mine for CI specialists and Netspionage agents. Ironically, if you were to telephone the company and ask for such information, you would probably (hopefully) be told that the information could not be provided to non-company personnel, and yet, there it is on the company's Web site for the world to read.

Additional business information on major companies may be found via such sites as the Securities and Exchange Commission's EDGAR site (http://www.sec.gov/cgi-bin/srch-edgar). The various online news archives and major newspapers (Web sites) may provide essential background on a target. Zeroing in on a local newspaper or regional magazine can sometimes provide additional details that are critical for analysis. Consulting the Newslink site (http://www.newslink.org) that provides access to over 3,300 U.S. and over 2,000 non-U.S. newspapers and magazines is another good source that may have coverage of the target.

If the target is a major competitor, it's likely that the CI staff will also use one or more of the electronic clipping services to sift through the vast array of information, widely casting an electronic net in order to find potentially relevant materials. Some free services allows the user to receive an alert via e-mail whenever there is an article, headline, or posting to specific Web sites concerning the target organization. Although some are free, others require a subscription fee. One of the best of these appears to be eWatch (http://www.eWatch.com) that will, for an annual subscription fee, provide information updates on selected businesses whenever information appears in many of the different online locations.

The service of greatest relevance to CI purposes is a comprehensive system for monitoring the activities of competitors. This is done in a process that tracks keywords or topics in a variety of venues which the company claims includes *more than 1,000 editorial-based sites on the web . . . more than 63,000 Usenet groups and Electronic Mailing Lists . . . hundreds of public discussion areas on AOL, Prodigy, CompuServe, and MSN and finance/investor bulletin boards on Yahoo!, Motley Fool, and Silicon Investor.* An interesting feature is the ability to track and report on a line-by-line basis any changes (both additions and deletions) that are made on designated Web sites. This type of comprehensive tracking of competitors' activities is very useful. The mere fact that such services exist demonstrates that the web provides valuable insight about competitors' activities.

The general Internet search engines are also useful for basic research. For example both the Fast Search and Transfer (FAST) search engine and the Northern Light system claim over 200 million indexed web pages, while AltaVista's database includes 250 million web pages.[7] Although these are impressive numbers, by some estimates there may be 800 million or more web pages, which would mean that even the best of the search engines only have somewhere between 25 and 30 percent of the web indexed. Also, given the various indexing strategies and techniques, identical searches on each engine will return different results. Given this fact there are many utilities that will be used by an

[7]Reconnaissance Over the Web Special to washingtonpost.com 1/3/2000.

advanced CI group to minimize the time spent searching the web for relevant content. Enhanced search utilities like WebFerret[8] and similar products engage multiple search engines simultaneously and will quickly find hundreds of sites containing key words.

- Collecting–Primary Sources: All search engines are merely searching the Internet and Web sites for information that has been made publicly available. However, every public site in the world and every news report ever published together probably does not contain all the information needed by the CI staff. To get to the really significant information the CI staff will also use other methods such as human sources that are in a position to augment the public information. The identification and use of human "primary sources"[9] is a major part of an effective CI program. Finding knowledgeable people was always the most difficult part of the intelligence process in the past; however, this is an area where the Internet has made the task of the CI practitioner much simpler.

  There are several tools that may help anyone find the primary sources that should be consulted. Directory services like 411, public search tools like DejaNews, and other resources may locate people, organizations, or companies with the expertise or access needed to meet the tasking.

  Another means to do this is to watch for prospective sources that can be identified though their activity on the Internet or other public activity. Sometimes they can be located by a provocative posting to a key forum, chat room or Web content site, which may generate a flurry of responses that help identify additional individuals. Once they have been identified, they may be contacted directly through private e-mail communications. Such direct communications may result in a primary source disclosing sensitive information they would not post where it could be seen by other participants, including managers or coworkers who may disapprove of a discussion on a particular topic.

  Occasionally during their activities on the Internet, the CI staff may encounter or develop a "virtual walk-in," which is an intelligence community term for someone who volunteers to provide information. Such information could potentially expose the individual source to adverse consequences if they were discovered to be responsible for divulging the information (e.g., they may lose their job, or worse if they are in some countries). Using such sources should be carefully weighed against the potential consequences. The CI staff must also remember that the information provided by the "walk-in source" may itself be a provocation or an attempt to mislead or misdirect the CI analyst and corporate management.

---

[8]http://www.ferretsoft.com

[9]Primary source means a person who is knowledgeable of the relevant topic.

One advantage of primary sources is most companies operate an Intranet that contains information the contents of which could be very useful to a CI analyst. These systems should be protected by strong security measures such as enhanced authentication (like biometrics or token based security systems), cryptography and intrusion detection tools to monitor the access and activity. However, network security measures may be neutralized with relatively little risk if the CI analyst can identify and convince one or more people who work with the desired information to just share some of the contents. The key to successfully executing this technique is to find such people and then recruit them as sources. As an additional advantage the Internet is also a nearly ideal mechanism for transferring information, between a source and the CI staff. Once a source has obtained the desired information, the information may be attached to an e-mail or uploaded to a "free drive" on the web (a digital dead drop) or perhaps compressed and concealed using some form of cryptography, and the password communicated to the CI analyst.

The ability to overcome technological security barriers by recruiting or developing sources internal to the target demonstrates the power of a Netspionage approach in the age of the global Internet. Finding someone with access will be possible because someone must use the information and have access to it as part of his or her job. Once that someone is located, they may be persuaded or influenced by an appeal to political, economic, ideological, ethnic affinity, or old fashioned greed (by offering money). One technique that may prove successful is when the CI staff finds that one of their competitors is downsizing its staff. A prime candidate for recruitment may be someone from the competitor who will be downsized or can be convinced to "see the writing on the wall" that they may be the next to go. Thus the company loyalty conflicts can be avoided. After all, would that employee still be loyal to a company about to lay them off? In short, what CI staff are doing is trying to find people, perhaps inside the target corporation, who they can talk with in order to obtain information. During the interaction with primary sources, the CI staff runs the greatest risk of crossing over the line from clearly legal and ethical collection, which is the focus of CI into the gray and black zones.

How can a primary source be contacted using the Internet? The following example is provided from one of the author's personal experiences: A security manager at a high-technology company received a copy of an e-mail message that had been sent to a scientist at the company. Since this scientist was working on a new product technology, it was not too surprising that the message contained a survey questionnaire concerning the same field. The sender encouraged the addressee to answer all the questions and to provide incentive; the addressees were promised either their choice of $300 or a Palm Pilot device as an "honorarium" for their time spent answering all the questions. In reviewing the questions, several were innocent and generic, but several also pertained to the new product. Although the scientist did not respond, the company had no way of knowing at that time, how many people received the same message and did respond! Is the sender at any risk of prosecution for such activities? Probably not, after all tracking down the real identity of the sender via the Internet could be difficult. Even if they did obtain sensitive information from the respondents they would likely claim that they had no way of knowing the materials they received were sensitive and that the corporation was to blame for failing to train its employees about proper release of such materials. The story could be believable to a judge or jury and prosecutors are not likely to push too hard to take on such a case.

- Analysis: Analysis may benefit from the knowledge base of the enterprise if they have a formal knowledge capture and retention program or process. At a minimum, the CI analyst will probably use link analysis tools, and graphic and data mining, and other net enabled tools for filtering, displaying, and presenting the results of the analysis.

- Dissemination: Dissemination brings us back to the Intranet and perhaps extra-net services as well as e-mail list managers to distribute to the internal audience a summary report with hot links to the internal and selected external Web sites for the additional detail that may not be needed by every recipient. The CI staff probably uses web tracking and reporting software (similar to that any commercial Web sites might use). The purpose is to determine which elements of the e-listed reports generate the most web traffic, which groups, individuals or units access which information, how often; which pages or segments generate the greatest repeat traffic, etc. Careful attention to these indicators supplemented with periodic satisfaction surveys (perhaps again done via web-based survey engines) will keep the CI unit focused on the areas where it has the greatest demand from its constituency.

Some Downsides of the Internet

It is important to understand that anyone can post almost anything to the Internet. Their reasons may run from fraud to revenge to deliberate attempts at misinformation and manipulation. When reviewing the contents of web forums, chat rooms, and other postings, it is difficult to assign credibility to the source of a particular piece of information. Many of the people posting to these sites will be using measures to conceal their true identities for various reasons. There are both tools and techniques one can use to ferret out the true identity of a particular poster, but without a subpoena or search warrant, legally penetrating the secret identities of anonymous posters is almost impossible—except by maybe government intelligence and investigative agencies. And, for those who use the current generation of privacy tools (see the Annonymizer and the Freedom tool) the chance of finding the real person behind the online persona becomes increasingly more difficult.

Another downside to the information found on the Internet is to assume that everything worth having can be found on the public network. So much information is already available on the web and so much is added every day that it creates the impression that everything that could be needed is available online. One author coined the term "net disease," which he characterizes as *a condition that allows otherwise rational business people to think that CI begins and ends with the World Wide Web that if the data is not on the Net or in databases, then it probably can not be found at all.*[10]

As we have already seen in most cases, the Internet will provide substantial information, but it will need to be supplemented by the contribution of primary source experts and analyzed for accuracy before it could become actionable intelligence.

Summary

More information is migrating to the web as businesses use it to automate their value chain and build tight linkages with customers, suppliers, vendors, employees, and government agencies. Electronic business is fundamentally changing the web and Internet, and will increase the importance of competitive intelligence collection and analysis. The pressures will also increase the temptation to cross the line and commit Netspionage to supplement the publicly available information with the guarded contents of systems and servers. However, not everything that will be desired will be accessible. As a consequence there will be demand to fill in the gaps by obtaining sensitive information from primary sources.

References

Kahaner, Larry. *Competitive Intelligence: How to Gather, and Use Information to Move Your Business to the Top.* New York: Touchstone Book, 1996.

---

[10]July–September 1999 (vol. 2, no. 3) Overcoming "Net Disease."

7

Information Collection in the Gray Zone

The Murky World of the One Type of Netspionage Agent: The Information Broker

From the mid-1990s onward, new phenomena arose. With the advent of the global Internet and the increasing availability of on-line databases to provide useful information, a new class of freelance information providers came into being. A cross between the classic shady gumshoe of mythic detective tales and the online reference librarians, these people offered to get desired information, for a fee. In some cases, they used entirely ethical means derived from their understanding of online research techniques and knowing which databases to go to for the kinds of data desired by their customers. In other cases, they also have offered to provide other types of information, some of which are prohibited by federal or state laws.

Suddenly the web was full of sites that offered anyone access to all manner of highly confidential information about specific persons or organizations. Such information would be of great benefit to private investigators working on behalf of legitimate clients such as abandoned spouses seeking child support payments, merchants defrauded by debtors who skipped out on debts and others. However, potential stalkers and other unstable persons could also abuse the information by tracking down those with whom they had a real or imaginary grudge. In many cases, all a prospective customer needed to do was to provide a credit card or money order. The information brokers claimed to be able to provide information such as the home telephone call records of a specific individual, bank account information, financial information, and the like.

Some of these information brokers are most comfortable in the gray zone between ethical and legal conduct, and unethical behavior and conduct. They are willing to sell information to whoever wants it, as long as they get paid for it.

For the Netspionage agents, information brokers can also be used to provide a convenient buffer between themselves and their targets. The agent could contact the information broker through e-mail using anonymous user techniques, provide a credit card number account to pay for the information, have the information sent via e-mail, and never have personal contact with anyone. The credit card could be a valid one or it may be one that was stolen from a database. Why use a valid credit card if one wanted to remain anonymous? If the Netspionage agent resided in another country and/or was using a bogus company name as a front, what difference would it make? Even if the agent was identified, the odds that they would be prosecuted are small, especially considering the extradition procedures that would all but make extradition impossible.

Finding the Facts and Selling Secrets

It is an ironic by-product of the information age that information brokers can obtain personal data on almost anyone. The same technology that has made it easier to bring business competitor's information to the eyes of business intelligence analysts has also made it increasingly a simple matter to pull together the previously disparate pieces of information about an individual. It is now possible to create almost a complete dossier of a person; how much money they earn, how much they have in their checking and savings accounts, how much stock they own, what sort of medical care (including psychological treatments) they may have received and other elements. This information would be invaluable to a Netspionage agent targeting an individual for recruitment or to obtain information about the executive management of a competitor's corporation.

According to a recent news program, the typical prices for such details are relatively small: the list of medications and doctors will cost about $150; a non-published telephone number, $75; details and a copy of a credit card charges about $195.[1] All this and more are available for a price from the ubiquitous eyes of the online snoops and digital detectives. One source told us that he used a "$39.00 special" offer to verify an address, property ownership, telephone listing, etc. He also used an online source for a "minimal $100 a year for member access" to "track down eight years of past financials on a target firm."

Although some people doubt that much can be found, there have been numerous examples where various people have volunteered to be test subjects for such online profiling. In one recent example, a test was conducted with the person's permission. Without any special training and at a cost of less than $100, they discovered that a great deal of personal information were easily accessible. They were able to obtain a

---

[1] ABC News 20/20 television program: "Information Brokers—Secrets for Sale" transcript available at: http://www.abcnews.go.com/onair/2020/transcripts/2020 _990628info_trans.html 6/28/99.

copy of the person's signature (that could have been scanned and used for other information request purposes); copies of recent telephone bills; the current value of the individual's house; and other useful financial information. They learned the exact day and place where the individual had been born by Caesarian section and even details about the individual's cat's diet by "dumpster diving" into his abandoned trash.[2]

The most troubling of these may be the signature sample that could be digitized by scanning software. Since so many organizations will accept a fax as proof of a request, it would be a trivial matter to fax copies of completely bogus requests using the signature sample and get even more information. Worse abuse is also possible for someone willing to go farther. With a little creativity, copies of the digitized signature could be pasted into almost anything. With a personal computer and common fax software someone could close another person's bank account, turn off the electricity or telephone services at their home or find other interesting means of discomfiting a target.

The combination of the exact birth date coupled with the exact name and social security number would allow a "researcher" to impersonate the target or even to commit full-fledged identity theft. It's also worth recalling that in many web-based applications, the last four digits of a person's social security number are used as the default password or personal identification number. So by having the actual number, one may be able to get into company applications as well as personal systems, request information under the assumed name, and the like. By use of e-mail systems, further anonymity could be maintained as the personal identification of the victim could be provided via the e-mail system.

Operations in the Gray Zone

How do information brokers get all this information? Some of it is available through public databases if the researchers know how to search for it. Personal and confidential information can sometimes be obtained by bribing an employee who works at a bank, credit agency, or even some law enforcement agencies. It's interesting to note how many former and retired law enforcement officers' (LEOs) work as private investigators and information brokers. Contact with their former colleagues and friends can often provide them with a rich source of information about prospective targets, and more than one former LEO has been prosecuted for using information obtained from criminal justice resources for the benefit of private clients. Note: As with corporations' lax security practices, some government agencies fail to delete ex or retired officers from computer systems. Thus, they continue to access the information, but now for private clients.

---

[2]*New York Times* Expert in Computer Security Finds His Life Is a Wide-Open Book, 12/13/99.

Some of these information brokers turned Netspionage agents may work in the "gray zone" defined as using unethical but legal techniques to obtain information (see Figure 7–1).

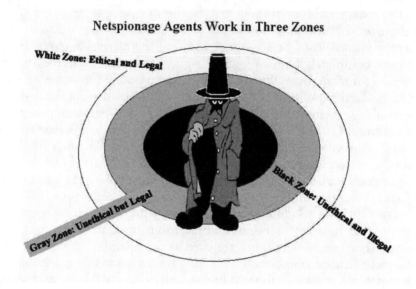

Figure 7–1 The world of the Netspionage agent who operates in all three zones.

Many times all that is required is a variant on the techniques used by hackers—social engineering. In a surprising number of cases, all it takes is a skilled person to con people into disclosing private information by manipulating them emotionally and deceiving them during a telephone call or even through e-mail. People feel most comfortable trusting people like themselves. Too often all that is necessary is to convince the person on the other end of the telephone conversation that you are just like them, that you have a problem, and that they can help you by providing some information. Another way that often works is to convince others that you are working on an important but sensitive investigation and that they are the key to solving the case. Many people in large bureaucratic corporations seem to respond surprisingly well to an opportunity to help a private investigator. Playing on the dreams of corporate "Walter Mittys" is more dangerous than the alternatives, but may be just the right option in some cases.

Target Identification

The basic technique employed by the most successful brokers and many private investigative agencies to obtain sensitive information about a corporation or corporate employee is very straightforward. First, they identify the specific piece of information that must be obtained to meet their client's need or to advance their overall investigative strategy. Next they figure out where that information can be found. Third, they learn the policies, practices, and procedures that control when and to whom the organization will disclose the information. Once they know who can obtain the information and what it takes to get it released, it's simply a matter of assuming the identity of that person.

For example let's say that a client has approached a Netspionage agent to determine if two corporations were discussing a merger or acquisition. Part of the assignment is to determine whether a specific person, let's call him Joe Smith, Corporate CEO, has traveled to a given location to meet with certain people of another corporation. In developing a strategy, the Netspionage agent may decide one element of the inquiry will be to get copies of the credit card records for the period in question. If the Netspionage agent has a source in the credit card company or bank that issued the credit cards, they may be able to get a copy of the monthly billing by paying that person a small amount of money. Although that industrial age method still works, it carries with it more risks. However, in today's information age, the Netspionage agent covertly enters the credit card or bank's database through Internet or other networks interfaces, obtains the information and logs out. No other individuals need be involved, thus lowering the odds of being identified and/or caught. This method can work from half way around the world. Remember that there are no physical boundaries in cyberspace.

For most people the basic identification information is widely available. The Netspionage agents typically starts with the target's name (in the case of the individual), and then attacking online databases, they can obtain a current or past address; the social security information from mortgage applications, real estate records, or rental applications. With these pieces of information, they can often get telephone, electrical, or gas billing records. Each piece of additional information makes it easier to get other pieces and any subsequent deceptions are better supported. It is interesting to note that a person's date of birth, social security number, and mother's maiden name are the three common methods of identification. They are all easily attainable in today's databases.

The Netspionage Agent—Information Broker Industry

All this has become a multi-billion dollar industry. Hundreds of brokers have gone online and are actively marketing their services using the Internet. Experts on privacy have called for more and detailed laws to control information brokers, and to better protect the companies and individuals they target. Most companies, especially banks, telephone, and credit card companies do make some effort to keep customer information and records private. However, many believe that these companies do not appreciate the full scope of the problem. "There is really a shocking lack of awareness on the part of the banks and the telephone companies. Their personnel need to be trained and made aware of the threat that this poses."[3]

The really expert Netspionage agents are able to get almost any information they need concerning anyone. However, they claim that the information they obtain through the use of pretext and other techniques is never intended to be used for improper purposes, that they have no intent to commit illegal acts. Since they do not intend to hijack the bank accounts or impersonate an individual to steal their credit cards, they may not have committed any criminal offense. In some investigative businesses, they claim they limit their operations to cases where it's appropriate, like fighting fraudulent insurance claims or tracking down deadbeat spouses for failure to pay alimony or child support. But others familiar with the industry say that personal ethics are of little importance, that the client's ability to pay is more significant than any concern about how the information could be misused.

In a recent case that received considerable publicity, the owners of a California liquor exporter called Saybrex claimed that an information broker tricked employees of their telephone company into providing copies of their telephone bills. These documents showed the telephone numbers called by Saybrex employees and included all Saybrex customers. Saybrex alleged that a competitor then used these telephone numbers to steal millions of dollars of business. The competitor, of course, denied the allegations but the case was settled out of court so the real truth in this matter will remain a mystery.

Following a month-long undercover operation begun in 1998, the Federal Trade Commission filed suit in the U.S. district court in April 1999 claiming that Touch Tone's deceptive practices caused substantial injury to the consumers. Rallying to defend a member of the community, the information brokers and private investigators claim that the use of "pretexting"[4] is a critical and legitimate tool for investigators.

---

[3]ABC News *20/20* television program: "Information Brokers–Secrets for Sale," 6/28/99.

[4]Misrepresenting whom you are to obtain information that would otherwise not be available. It is sometimes called a specialized form of social engineering.

Another tool that may prove useful for Netspionage agents is "NetEraser." The U.S. CIA has invested $3 million in the program thus far. A CIA official is quoted as saying, "The key application is that our analysts have to monitor foreign sites. We would prefer not to do it in a manner that discloses it is the CIA." This program allegedly constantly changes a computer's Internet protocol address which would allow a user to covertly access foreign systems or Web sites without leaving the user's address.

Hiring Hackers as Netspionage Agents: Business as Usual?

It seems that many corporations are surprised to find they have on their payroll, some of the very people that the information security staff is trying to keep out of their networks—hackers and perhaps even crackers. This situation came to public attention last year when the FBI interviewed and arrested a number of people who they claimed were involved in the attacks against various U.S. government web pages as part of the "Global Hell" cyber gang. In one high profile example, a young 22-year-old whose underground handle was VallaH, lost a job as a contractor with Microsoft Corporation. The hacker lost his job even though he claimed he had no knowledge or involvement in any hacker attacks or other illegal acts for the year he was employed at Microsoft working on the Windows2000 product.[5] Following the incident, a Microsoft spokesperson claimed "We don't recruit people who are involved in illegal activities."[6]

Although there is no reason to doubt Microsoft's assertion concerning their policy about hiring people involved in illegal activities, it is interesting to note that technically, VallaH was a contract employee, one who was actually employed by a temporary services company, not Microsoft per se. He claimed in press reports that "his Microsoft employers knew he came from the scene," and even knew he still communicated with hackers. Only the embarrassment of the raid cost him his job.[7] So perhaps in truth the company does not hire them, but only uses them in an advisory role, such as when they are designing a new operating system, like Windows2000?

That leads one to speculate on the use of hackers as Netspionage agents. If the hacker is hired to keep the company posted about activities in the cyber underground, there is a risk that they may have actually engaged a double agent on the payroll, who may trade useful bits of internal company information and product code to outsiders in

---

[5]Perils of moonlighting as a hacker, MSNBC, 6/2/99.

[6]Ibid.

[7]Ibid.

exchange for useful pieces of intelligence to benefit the company. . . . thus effectively playing off both sides against each other for personal gain. This Netspionage agent may also be in a position to plant a Trojan horse, trap door, or other malicious codes in the product for later use. The agent could also be sending, through e-mail, copies of the software code being developed to a competitor or a software company that will build new programs based on the new code. By having that code in advance, it would give the software company a competitive edge in getting new software products to the customers sooner than their competition.

In today's competitive marketplace, it is indeed possible that other companies do knowingly and deliberately hire hackers, and expect to use their skills for many purposes, some legal, some in the gray zone, and some in the black zone. For example, it is instructive to recall that just before Kevin Mitnick went on his last episode of hacking that resulted in a set of criminal charges, his last employer was a private investigations (PI) firm in Southern California. The firm claimed that they only used Kevin's knowledge of computers for internal support. If a PI firm or other company has a hacker on its payroll, it's a fair bet they could be tempted to use the hacker's unique skills to hack into targets on behalf of the employer. Such intrusions could perhaps find information or evidence for the PI firm that would be helpful, maybe even decisive for the matter under investigation. Such matters, of course, could range from marital infidelity to competitive intelligence.

If you find that one of your competitors has hired a notorious hacker group as security consultants to teach them how to defend themselves against other hackers, should you be concerned? It may be the true reason for the contract, but then again, maybe they are using the hackers to prepare a full scale Netspionage attack against the most important computer systems and networks your organization uses. After all, if the competing firm first understands how to break into systems and then protects itself against such attacks, it will understand the mechanics of conducting network break-ins and how to cover their tracks to minimize the chances of being detected.

Official Government Personnel Working for Businesses

According to a recent press report, Britains GCHQ, a top secret government agency that allegedly taps communications and collects data from spy satellites (the equivalent of the National Security Agency in the United States) has allowed its Communications-Electronics Security Group (CESG), to market its services to industry and the public sector.[8] The available services include "access to the expertise of CESG's pro-

---

[8]*London Sunday Telegraph*, 07/11/99.

fessional computer hackers, who can carry out "hits" on clients' systems to identify any weaknesses that might be exploited by infiltrators."[9]

Although it appears that the majority of the work of this group has been for the United Kingdom's Ministry of Defense (the equivalent of the U.S. Department of Defense) it has also helped other British government agencies combat computer crimes and computer espionage. Members of this team are all carefully screened, but contrary to the practice prevailing in the United States, the British government allegedly does not employ ex-hackers.

The official position is that making these experts available, at a cost, to private sector organizations will both help cover the agency's costs, and also allow them to help protect critical national infrastructure (such as electrical and telephone utilities, etc.) in the national interest. It is an interesting turn of events that some of the most secretive intelligence agencies are moving into public visibility. One can admire the British efforts here to marry market incentives with national interest to the benefit of improved protection of their critical national infrastructures from Netspionage and other threats.

The offer to help out British companies does raise possible concerns for non-British companies. Such foreign companies may believe the real purpose of these specialists is not merely to help British companies defend themselves, but to teach them how to more effectively use the Internet and associated technologies to steal information from their foreign rivals. One may perhaps forgive businesses from perennial rivals like the French and Germans, with whom the British have had a stormy history for the past 300 years, for being a little suspicious. After all, it may be reasonable to infer that by teaching British companies how to optimize their defense against intruders, and especially by conducting simulated attacks against the companies' defenses, they are really teaching them "best in class" penetration techniques.

Such suspicions and concerns will manifest themselves any time official government agencies make their expertise available to corporations. Is it possible that these specialists are also breaking into the corporations of British corporations' competitors in order to provide sensitive information to the British corporations?

Hijacking E-mail

An interesting development that is clearly in the gray zone are the increasing efforts made to exploit errors, negligence, or mistakes to obtain access to sensitive information. The clever opponents of various corporations have established what may be described as clone sites that

---

[9]Ibid.

closely mimic the web and e-mail addresses of their target. These clone sites rely on the fact that most corporations use the same address for both their web and e-mail addresses. For example, a canny opponent could establish a site where the target is the organization with the address of http://www.association.org, but the clone site is set up as http://www.association.com or vice versa. In this way, anyone trying to send a message to the executives at the actual target who key in the common but wholly incorrect address suffix (.COM) will actually be sending it straight into the hands of their opponents, who may then examine it for a variety of reasons. Taking advantage of this type of human error does not require advanced programming knowledge or skills. Many web-hosting services require only a modest increase in the monthly fees and they are pleased to enable the e-mail receipt functions. The technique is so simple that one should assume that some companies are already using hijacked e-mail to spy on their competition.[10] Corporations should check to see who owns web sites with similar names or same name ending in a different suffix, e.g., .com, .org, .net.

In fact these efforts may well be illegal, but there are competing precedents offered by the parties involved. Some see nothing wrong with the practice, claim that picking up e-mail is "similar to picking up the phone when someone has dialed a wrong number."[11] This seems very disingenuous, and perhaps the actions are closer to trying to set up a toll free number that mimics another so as to steal users from the competing service.

It seems that every new technical innovation brings with it potential abuse by those looking for an easy way to power and influence over others. The ease of Internet e-mail communications carries a high degree of risk for any unsecured contents. The possibility that someone would set up a clone site is relatively benign. Such efforts provide a degree of plausible deniability because the original site has not been penetrated, and the victim can claim that the victim bears at least partial responsibility for anything received. After all, this technique relies on human error and mistakes to capture information from negligent senders. However, it is only a relatively small step, albeit a crucial one, that takes the perpetrator across the gray border into the black zone. If the intruder makes modifications to a poorly protected Web site or e-mail server, and diverts the e-mail traffic or other information from the opposing site to one controlled by the techno-spy, they have crossed the line. They have left behind the comfortable haziness of the gray zone and are well into the "black ops" mentality of true Netspionage.

---

[10]WSJ Interactive Edition, Hijackers lay traps for errant e-mails, 11/9/99.

[11]Ibid.

Summary

Netspionage can be accomplished by operating in the ethical and legal "white zone," the unethical and legal "gray zone," and the unethical and illegal "black zone." Because of today's global networks connected to the Internet, information brokers, hackers, and private investigators are among the groups of people selling information to those with the money to buy.

8

The Black Zone, Who Uses Netspionage, How and Why

Setting the Stage

Netspionage as we have defined it, is using networks, computers, and associated capabilities to steal corporations' secrets. It is a totally new concept that is becoming increasingly important. Although it has not yet penetrated deeply into the awareness of most business leaders, it is already well understood at the national governmental levels in the United States and other major global powers. Press reports[1] highlight the claim that the United States, in cooperation with its closest allies, the United Kingdom, Australia, and Canada, are suspected of creating a global monitoring and surveillance system. This system, reportedly code named ECHELON, is supposed to track all "telephone conversations, electronic mail messages, and faxes."[2] One can assume that this wholesale collection effort will undoubtedly include sensitive information being transmitted between corporations.

In similar fashion, major European nations like France and Germany, as well as former Cold War enemies like Russia,[3] the Peoples Republic of China, and even Sweden have all been accused of implementing technical means of surveillance to deal with all forms of electronic communications. If any of these allegations are true, there is already a great deal of Netspionage being conducted by legions of governmental analysts.

Although a major concern, passive monitoring, no matter how pervasive, depends on the negligence of the sender for success. Since

---

[1]*Secret Power—New Zealand's Role in the International Spy Network*, Nicky Hager, Craig Potton Publishing, ISBN: 0-908802-35-8.

[2]ECHELON Examined, article by Barbara Starr, ABCNEWS.com, 11/22/99.

[3]Russia establishes Internet surveillance network
http://www.zdnet.co.uk/news/1999/48/ns-12023.html, 08/12/99.

sensitive information is often transmitted in an unprotected medium, such as an unencrypted e-mail message or an unencrypted cellular telephone call, it is vulnerable for collection by government agencies and competitors. The evolution of a "surveillance society" where every communication may be reviewed by faceless agents, competitive intelligence specialists, and others is very troubling.

We are even more concerned about active measures taken by both "Big Brother" government agents as well as "Little Brother" agents working for companies or private corporations to search out and obtain, covertly, the most critical and valuable information of a corporation or an individual. Such measures include the systematic application of tools and techniques to achieve the classic objectives of espionage, acquisition of secret information by covert means. Such mechanisms have been used for centuries with varying degrees of success by nation-states and more recently by various governmental agencies. CIA Director Tenet said in testimony to the Senate Governmental Affairs Committee that "Potential attackers range from national intelligence and military corporations, terrorists, criminals, industrial competitors, hackers, and disgruntled or disloyal insiders."[4] Tenet went on to say that the fundamental shift in the hacking challenge from that posed by individuals and terrorist groups to governments is already underway and that "Down the line we are going to encounter more [hacking] and it will be more organized."[5] By one estimate "23 countries are believed to have the capacity to engage in state-sponsored, surreptitious electronic raids. Among the most sophisticated: India, Syria, and Iran . . . "[6]

Monitoring, especially on a global basis may now be the exclusive purview of large sophisticated governmental entities with vast budgets, huge numbers of people, and a large number of very fast and powerful computers. However, government-based corporations or global, mega-corporations also have the resources for such activities. In contrast, other techniques of Netspionage may be engaged in by an individual or may involve the coordinated efforts of dozens to hundreds of collaborators distributed around the planet in a carefully orchestrated, yet "virtual" campaign to ferret out the digital treasures of a targeted corporation.

Netspionage is made possible and indeed is inevitable due to the convergence of several major trends. The first, and most obvious of these is the increasing connectivity of all corporations via the global Internet and the attendant evolution of electronic business and operations. This vast increase in the nature, extent and duration of connectivity provide the potential access pathways for positive purposes, but also for abuse.

---

[4]*The Boston Globe*, CIA chief warns of computer warfare, 06/25/98.

[5]Ibid.

[6]"Cyber raiders," Scripps Howard News Service, 11/5/99.

The second major trend has been the increasing digitalization of the most valuable assets of corporations. Corporations are rapidly transitioning from the world where the greatest value has been created primarily by the physical contribution of people, manufacturing plants, and raw materials to a time where the acquisition, preservation, and exploitation of knowledge provides the primary competitive advantages. The products or services provided by most corporations already reflect the increasingly important contribution of intangibles, such as the proprietary information and other intellectual properties created by the knowledge workers of the corporation.

Whereas the first two trends are largely benign or at least neutral the third trend is essentially negative. We have entered a time when there is widespread availability of both the software tools as well as the knowledge of how and why to exploit vulnerabilities in networks and computer systems. This is compounded by an increasing number of knowledgeable people who can operate these tools at the same time there is a general and rapid increase in the pool of people who have access to networks and computer systems as part of their work environment. The advent of what may be characterized as "electronic burglary" tool kits now allows nearly anyone with malice in their hearts to attempt to access, or control the systems and networks that contain the valuable assets described above. As an ever-increasing number of the planet's population gain access to the global Internet, they have the potential of using these tools against their employers, governments, and other corporations in an attempt to gain personal benefit. The era of "security through obscurity," which assumed that no one knew where to go or what to do to hijack systems is now a fading memory. The barbarians are literally at the virtual gates, or maybe, on the payroll.

Given these trends, one might expect that companies would create strong protection programs to safeguard their sensitive information. Sadly, the protection of most corporations' information assets is generally weak. Thus, they are vulnerable to those that operate in the "black zone." There are many reasons that protection is generally inadequate, including the fact that corporation's organization with protection responsibilities typically do not coordinate their functions and tend to operate in segregated stove pipes:

- Lawyers do the lawyer tasks: They get nondisclosure agreements signed and patents, copyrights, and trademarks established and defended.
- Information Technology (IT) management makes sure everyone has a password and ensures network connectivity. The principal focus of IT is to facilitate easy access to information. IT management sets up the Internet connection, and extends the Extranet to key vendors, suppliers, and others. If anyone is responsible for

information systems security, they typically lack the training, experience, and wherewithal to adequately address the threats.

- Security (often called physical or corporate security in most corporations) most likely has an exclusive focus on physical asset protection: gates, guards, and alarms. Their emphasis on physical protection has little impact on the "cyber enterprise," which is the ultimate extension and combination of inter, intra, and extranets. The "cyber enterprise" encompasses an extended corporation perimeter that includes business partners, key vendor/suppliers, and others.

Sounding the Alarm

The U.S. National Counterintelligence Center was one of the first agencies to alert businesses and other government agencies to the threat of Netspionage as a tool for compromise of both classified (national security) information as well as proprietary and sensitive business or economic data. In an article in the July 1998 issue of the official publication "Counterintelligence News and Developments" titled "Internet: The Fastest Growing Modus Operandi for Unsolicited Collection,"[7] the agency noted that: . . . *The Internet offers a variety of advantages to a foreign collector. It is simple, low-cost, non-threatening, and relatively "risk free" for the foreign entity attempting to collect classified, proprietary, or sensitive information.*

The article went on to describe how foreign intelligence collection was already exploiting the new access provided by the global Internet to obtain not just classified military information, but also economic and competitive information from corporations. This demonstrates that several years ago professional intelligence specialists had recognized that the Internet was revolutionizing their field. In the recent past, clandestine intelligence operatives would have likely been forced to engage in the risky business of recruiting foreigners to work on behalf of the spy agency in their plots to obtain information. Now, thanks to the ubiquitous Internet, the collector may sit safely at a keyboard in their most secure homeland site and execute a Netspionage attack. Exploiting a variety of means (some of which we will discuss in this chapter), they have the potential to engage in wholesale looting and plundering of the official economic and business secrets of their enemies.

The 1992 presidential campaign slogan, "it's the economy, stupid" captured a fundamental truth of life at the beginning of the new millennium. Economic power, the ability to transform knowledge and information into goods and services—is now and will be for the fore-

---

[7] Complete report available at NACIC Web site: www.NACIC.gov.

seeable future—the basis of national power. Most other countries understand very well that the United States is a not only a military superpower, but also a technology and economic superpower. Otherwise friendly nations and their indigenous businesses have already directed efforts to penetrate the systems and networks that are the core strength of the economic and information infrastructures of the United States.

As global power is increasingly the result of the application of technology to the national economy, one inevitable result of this will be that business corporations will become caught in the crossfire between those competing for global advantage. As incidents of network enabled information theft proliferate, directed in some cases by competing national intelligence services, it is likely that business leaders have already concluded that the rules of the global business game have fundamentally changed. They will soon begin to use more aggressive tactics to survive and flourish and will use Netspionage as a weapon in the global economic and business warfare arena.

There is some historical precedent for this transition, which demonstrates how quickly attitudes may change. In the early 20th century, before WWI, a senior government official dismissed the idea of using spies to intercept official communiqués between foreign nations with the comment that "gentlemen don't read other gentlemen's mail." Such an idea now appears quaint and hopelessly idealistic in the late 20th century and early 21st century as we review the crucial role that precisely such interception played in WWII and other conflicts in the past century. It is inevitable that legal and ethical constraint against aggressive techniques of Netspionage by businesses and quasi-governmental entities will totally vanish over the next 5–10 years as businesses struggle to exert control and gain dominant position in the global competition for survival and success. It is quite probable that early in the new century, such tools will be considered as fundamental to business success as marketing plans and business strategies are today.

Netspionage is also gaining significance as a threat against other countries key industrial areas. According to Josef Karkowsky of the German Association for Economic Security, *the data net is not only used to make business contacts—it often also opens the way for modern spies. German companies in particular ignore security measures, making "self-service stores" out of themselves for computer spies.*[8]

Digital Tradecraft

The Internet and specifically the web, has now made available to increasing numbers of people, with widely varying legal, ethical and

---

[8]http://www.berliner-morgenpost.de/bm/international/inhalt/2897/tunnel_2.html In the Sights of the Spies.

personal motivations, and constraints, the tools and technologies that are nearly ideal for the theft of the increasingly valuable digital assets of the typical corporation. The global reach now afforded to prospective techno-spies by the expanding connectivity provided by the Internet, has created a situation of unparalleled opportunity for anyone who is willing to go after a corporation's assets.

The pages that follow describe software programs and utilities that allow even unsophisticated attackers to steal the prime assets of their own or other corporations, then safely transfer these assets to others.

Our focus in this section differs somewhat from a description of traditional hacker tools and how they have been used. Whereas a hacker may chose to engage in Netspionage, it is also possible for a Netspionage agent to commit Netspionage without being an accomplished hacker. In fact, successful techno-spies may never need to engage some of the sophisticated technical tools, such as port scanners and attack simulators. Such powerful software requires technical knowledge and tends to be the hacker's weapons of choice for neutralizing traditional information security technologies. Instead we will discuss a new application of software and technical tools, which we describe as "digital tradecraft."

Tradecraft is defined as "the technical skills used in espionage"[9] and traditionally would include knowledge of lock picking, clandestine photography, secret writing, surveillance, and dead drops.[10] As one can deduce from such examples, a great deal of the traditional spy's life revolved around the means of acquiring information and then communicating it to the sponsoring agency for processing and analysis. Of course, it is obvious that such means are intended to allow the spy to operate in stealth and with anonymity, largely in hopes that the spy might continue to survive and perhaps even someday return safely to his or her homeland.

In many ways the objectives of Netspionage are exactly the same as they have been for traditional espionage. The new tools are intended to allow the virtual agents operating against online business corporations to penetrate the internal systems of the target. Once successfully inside, the agents may obtain information without detection, then communicate it so the sponsoring corporation may operate with the advantage of superior information while the attacked corporation remains blissfully unaware of the nature and extent of its losses.

Let's take a closer look at some of the tools that comprise what may be characterized as "Netspionage tradecraft":

---

[9]*The Ultimate Spy Book*, H. Keith Melton, p. 159, DK Publishing 1996.

[10]Ibid, p. 161.

Trojan Horse Software

There has been a literal plague of what have been described as "Trojan horse" programs. These software tools, are named in honor of the famous beast of history that allowed the mighty walls of the city of Troy to be breached by cunning Greek warriors. Today's Trojan software is more likely to appear in the guise of a cute little e-mail attachment sent by what appears to be a friendly e-mail account. These programs represent a fundamental change in the threat matrix; they are particularly dangerous in the small and medium sized businesses where there may not be any formal information security program.

All the various Trojan software provide a common core of functions that typically include the following:

1. Operate concealed, in "stealth mode" without any indication to the user of their presence. Nothing will be visible in the WINDOWS system tray or will appear if the user activates the Close Program dialog box.
2. Open and close the CD-ROM drive.
3. Run programs already resident on the target system remotely without the user's intervention.
4. Capture (log) user keystrokes without alerting the user.
5. Capture screen shots.
6. Reboot the computer.
7. Upload (and execute) programs to the "target" computer without the user's knowledge.
8. Operate microphones, web camera's, modems, and other peripherals to gain information, to include remotely turning on computers, downloading their contents and turning them back off.

BackOrifice2000

The program that probably best exemplifies the large number of new software tools that are magnifying the risks of network enabled espionage is called BackOrifice (BO), which in it's most current form is known as BackOrifice2000 (BO2K). Named in a mocking double entendre to deride Microsoft's BackOffice, the software itself is no laughing matter. The original software was developed by a hacker who goes by the name Sir Dystic in what he has claimed is an effort to get Microsoft to improve the security features of the widely used Windows operating systems. The original version was released by the hacker group the Cult of the Dead Cow at the annual DefCon hacker conference in Las Vegas July 1998 and only operated under Windows95. The BO2K version operates under Win95, 98, and NT 4.0 (sometimes).

The software is shareware, and is available for free to anyone, anywhere in the world with an Internet connection. By some estimates, several hundred thousand copies of this tool were downloaded in 1998 alone, and it continues to be very popular among hobbyists and hackers and others with interest in computer and network security.

The program has a number of features that set the standard for other tools to follow and also has several unique features that distinguish it from the many copy cat utilities. Some of the features included in the software itself and described in the documentation that are of greatest interest for the application of the product to Netspionage include the following:

- Session and keystroke logging
- HTTP file system browsing and transfer
- Direct file browsing, transfer, and management
- Multimedia support for audio/video capture, and audio playback
- NT registry passwords and Win9x screensaver password dumping

A computer user must be running either Windows 95 or 98 to allow BO2K to automatically infect a target machine. The software will not install itself automatically on an NT system. The software comes in two parts—the client and the server. The server is installed on a target computer system. The client is used from another computer to gain access to the server and control it. The client connects to the server via a network.[11]

Once connectivity is established, it is possible to exercise almost complete control over the server/ target system. For example, the server (target) can be made to send an e-mail message to a designated address with key information about the system included in the message. It is also possible to connect to an Internet Relay Chat (IRC) server to inform all the users of a particular IRC channel that a specific computer is now available for remote operation and control.

What Does This Mean?

If someone successfully installs BO or one of the many imitators on a target system, he has at least as much control as the assigned owner/user. Anything the user could do while sitting at the keyboard can probably be done by the techno-spy sitting at his own computer, which may be located in the same building as the target or could possibly be located on the other side of the world. The techno-spy, running the client software is able to search through the file listings of the target system, find any that are of interest and copy, modify, or delete them as desired, or transmit them to another computer for future use.

---

[11]This information is derived from the BO documentation.

Cached passwords (passwords stored on the computer) for example to login to a remote system or Internet service provider, can likewise be copied and transmitted. The keystroke logging allows the client to capture any passwords entered by the user (for instance, those that have not been cached) and use them for later, perhaps to impersonate the authorized user and gain access to an important database system.

The fact that the BackOrifice product accommodates plug-ins provides more reasons to be aware of this tool. As if the basic functionality was not dangerous enough, there are extensions that allow even unsophisticated users to package BO into another program. What this does is allow BO to "infect" a target when the doctored program is executed. The plug-in, called SilkRope, also modifies BO so it can't be found with a common file scan. These tools are one reason why the various holiday executables can be a source of real danger. Although the "dancing Santas" or "happy Halloween ghosts" executable may be cute, it's a very simple matter to load BO into the file and send it out via e-mail to the desired target. When the target executes them, they enjoy the display, unaware of the infection and subsequent control over their system enjoyed by the operator of the client code.

These are features that are nearly ideal for the purposes of theft of sensitive information from computer and network systems. These tools are optimized for theft of passwords, documents, and other materials right out from under the noses of the often unsophisticated users (such as senior executives, managers, and other less technical staff), which means they are ideal tools for Netspionage.

Defenses

Although BO and it's variants and imitators are potentially very dangerous, the makers of security and anti-virus software have largely neutralized the threat from unsophisticated use of these tools. Common anti-virus tools often detect them in their normal state and can even "disinfect" systems that have been attacked. However, in the hands of experts, one should not assume that off the shelf anti-virus tools alone are sufficient. It is possible for BO to be compiled in a manner that will change it's file signature and thus defeat file comparison anti-virus software. The network operations group of the corporation should monitor network traffic for unusual transmissions using the UDP protocol that BackOrifice uses to communicate between the client and server.

Regardless of the current effectiveness of specific protective measures, there is a running arms race between the developers of attack tools such as BO and those who develop protective tools. The mere fact that the capability now exists insures that some Netspionage agents and techno-spies will exploit the vulnerability.

Potentially, any one of the many Trojan software programs could be used by a techno-spy to steal sensitive files, or modify or delete data, from any computer running Windows 95 or Windows 98, and many systems running Windows NT. However, there are a few factors limiting their effectiveness at present.

First, every one of these programs requires some sort of server application to first be installed on the target machine that the techno-spy is seeking to plunder. Achieving this installation requires either physical access to the computer system or some way of convincing the authorized user to install it. Where physical access is not feasible, it is often possible to trick an unsuspecting user into installing the code by inserting it into some pretty executable, then sending it to the target via e-mail. Alternatively, the operator of a targeted system may be invited to a Web site/URL to download a copy of the modified executable onto the target system. Once the unsuspecting user double clicks on the downloaded file, the user will unknowingly install a copy of the Trojan onto the system.

Once a copy is installed, the techno-spy must then find the Internet Protocol (IP) address of the target machine before the software can be activated and controlled remotely. The Netspionage agent can often use his client application to search through a range of possible IP addresses. However, this is a serious challenge if the agent does not have enough information about the network to limit the range of addresses to be searched, because there are "four billion" possible IP addresses.

The installation of a properly configured firewall between the target machine and the Netspionage agent will probably make it from difficult to impossible for the Netspionage agent to communicate with the target machine (depending on the skills of the agent and strength of the firewall). Since many corporations install firewalls between their internal networks and computers and the Internet this means that, if the firewall operates correctly, there should not be any Trojan remotes controlling internal systems via the Internet. More likely, the use of a Trojan utility will occur inside the corporation since internal compartmentalization of networks using internal firewalls is not common.

Although a leading anti-virus vendor advises that corporations can defend themselves from Trojan software problems by "following safe computing practices, for example, not downloading or running applications from unknown sources . . . ,"[12] this advice is too simplistic. Users are increasingly likely to do just that, download software from new and unknown sources, and therefore, remain vulnerable to these tools. And, of course, if the operator of the Trojan is a trained Netspionage agent who has infiltrated the corporation in the guise of a "lowly temporary employee," the agent won't be downloading anything, except possibly the crown jewels of the company via a Trojan utility.

---

[12]http://www.sarc.com/avcenter/venc/data/backorifice.html.

Other Trojan Software

For those Netspionage agents operating in the black zone, BO is not the only sophisticated tool available. There are many others. An excellent listing of many additional "network Trojan" software programs can be found at http://xforce.iss.net/alerts/. The X-Force service, sponsored by ISS has documented more than 120 tools for the various versions of Windows. This site also provides a full technical description of how the software operates as well as techniques for detecting and removing Trojans from computers.

The following is a short list of some of the most common additional tools and the special features associated with each software program. Please note that the feature described is not the only function the software performs, most of them have the full complement of basic features similar to BO but also other unique features:

- NetBus Pro presents itself as a remote administration and spy tool
- NetSphere will operate the "ICQ" real time messaging utility
- SubSeven uses Internet Relay Chat or ICQ to inform the attacker when a target is infected

Digital Dead Drop

Imagine you are a techno-spy, and you need to set up a secure place where you can stash copies of the critical information you have obtained from the penetrated corporation. As good as you are, there is always the chance, no matter how small, that the authorities may raid your computer someday. If they find the copies of the stolen crown jewels on your company computer system, you are going to be in big trouble. One way to avoid such professional embarrassment is to load a "digital dead drop" with the copies of the stolen valuables and get them out of your system as quickly as possible.

There is no need to purchase a server and set up an Internet connection as there are already many services offering 10, 20, 30, or more megabytes of online storage for free. The most generous provide 300MB of personal "Free Disk Space" on secure servers.[13] All they require is some personal information about the subscriber, which, of course, could be completely fabricated, even if the service made some effort to verify the subscriber's information. The advantages to the techno-spy are obvious. The agent gets a free online storage place that is accessible from anywhere on the Internet at any time of the day or night. Of course, if the techno-spies are especially careful, they will protect the valuable stolen contents by using one or more methods of cryptography, perhaps even steganography (see below) to ensure that even

---

[13]http://www.freediskspace.com.

an examination of the files deposited in the dead drop will be fruitless for investigators. Those that use such services should also be aware that the sites might be excellent targets for Netspionage agents.

Even if the process is detected and investigated by the security group they face an uphill battle. If the techno-spy uses digital dead drops properly, the control agent from the Netspionage team or customer contact will be unloading the contents soon after the agent loads them. This downloading operation will be done using another expendable account; probably a new web mail or front company address for every transmission. This will be done from a safe location, probably outside the country. The contents will then be transferred to a safe location inside the sponsor's home corporation, probably outside the target's homeland. Using a number of foreign locations for the transfer and processing of the stolen contents will make recovery more complicated. It will reduce the ability of the security officials to gain search warrants and execute them on a timely basis against multiple foreign locations and operations.

Steganography

Hiding information by embedding a file inside another, seemingly innocent file is a technique known as steganography. It is most often used with graphics, sound, text, HTML, and PDF files. Steganography with digital files works by replacing the unused bytes of data in a computer file with bytes that contain concealed information.

Steganography (translated from the Greek for "covered writing") has been in use since ancient times. One technique was to carve secret messages into wooden objects and then cover the etched words with colored wax to make them undetectable to an uninitiated observer. Another method was to tattoo a message onto the shaved messenger's head. Once the hair grew back they were sent on their mission. Upon arrival, the head was shaved revealing the message. The microdot, which reduced a page of text to the size of a typewriter's period so that it could be glued onto a post card or letter and sent through the mail, is another example.[14]

Usually, two types of files are used when embedding data into an image. The innocent image that holds the hidden information is a "container." A "message" is the information to be hidden. A message may be plain-text, ciphertext, other images, or any thing that can be embedded in the least significant bits (LSB) of an image.[15]

Steganographic software has some unique advantages as a tool for Netspionage agents. First, if an agent uses regular cryptographic software on their computer systems, the files may not be accessible to

---

[14]http://webopedia.internet.com/TERM/s/steganography.html.

[15]http://www.jjtc.com/stegdoc/.

investigators, but they may be visible. It may be obvious that the agent is hiding something. Steganographic software allows the agent to hide "in plain sight" any valuable digital assets the agent may have obtained until the Netspionage agent can transmit or transfer the files to a safe location or to the customer. As a second advantage, steganography may be used to conceal and transfer an encrypted document containing the acquired information to a digital dead drop. The agent could then provide the handler or customer the password to unload the dead drop but not divulge the steganographic extraction phrase until payment is received or the agent is safely outside the target corporation. As a final note, even when a file is known or suspected to contain information protected with steganographic software, it has been almost impossible to extract the information unless the pass phrase has been obtained.

Computer Elicitation

Information requests via the Internet are likely to become a regular part of the techno-spies arsenal. After all, e-mail communication using a sanitized account or free-mail (see below) can be direct, quick, and inexpensive, and if it is successful, the requested information may be transmitted via return messages within minutes. Many people are now accustomed to receiving e-mail requests from persons that they do no know and few employees will take the time to verify the sender's identity and physical or Internet address when an unusual request is received. Even if a request was received from an unknown person, many people will likely just do their best to respond to the request without considering who is asking for what. The art of obtaining meaningful information from an unsuspecting source is known as "elicitation" in the intelligence community. It is really a skill to manipulate a conversation in such a way as to encourage a person to disclose sensitive information they know without raising their suspicions. Since e-mail in many corporations now takes the place of conversations, it offers the potential access to knowledgeable persons from whom information may be elicited.

The U.S. National Counterintelligence Center has advised that the following could be indicators of attempted collection efforts via computer elicitation:[16]

- The return e-mail address is from a foreign country.
- The recipient has never met the sender.
- The sender may claim to be a student or consultant working on a special project.

---

[16]http://www.nacic.gov, Counterintelligence News and Developments, 11/96.

- The sender identifies his/her employer as a foreign government or claims the work is being done for a foreign government or program.
- The sender may advise the recipient to disregard the request if it causes any security problems or if it is for information the recipient cannot provide due to security classification, export controls, and so forth.

Van Eck Interception

There are two important research papers that together provide some of the first unclassified descriptions of the formerly highly sensitive area known as TEMPEST. The first paper published in 1985 by Wim van Eck, a Dutch scientist was titled, "Electromagnetic Radiation from Video Display Units: An Eavesdropping Risk?"

The second was published in 1990 by Professor Moller of Acchen University and was titled; "Protective Measures Against Compromising Electromagnetic Radiation Emitted by Video Display Terminals."[17] Together these papers describe how it is possible to obtain meaningful information by intercepting the electromagnetic signals given off by various parts of the computer, especially the monitor.

Although there are many competing theories as to the meaning of the word, most believe TEMPEST to have been a word assigned by the U.S. National Security Agency to describe the interception and analysis of electromagnetic radiation for intelligence information.[18] The issues around TEMPEST have been highly classified for years and much of it remains so at the present. However, it appears that TEMPEST and Van Eck interception are largely directed at the same issue.

It is possible to intercept sensitive information from computers by capturing radio-frequency emissions. Furthermore, the equipment is available for $60,000 or less. But it is possible that a software radio, specially designed to let computers tune into radio signals in any waveband, could make eavesdropping on computer signals easy and inexpensive. Some believe such a system could cost as little as $2,000–$3,000. It could be available in the very near future (if it is not already on the market).[19]

When a commercial system is developed, it will allow a Netspionage agent to capture the contents of PC monitors inside corporations. If such a system is created, they could monitor everything from passwords and User IDs for approving wire transfers in banks to

---

[17]http://www.thecodex.com/c_tempest.html.

[18]http://www.eskimo.com/~joelm/tempest.html, The Complete Unofficial Tempest Information Page.

[19]http://www.newscientist.com/ns/19991106/newsstory6.html, New-wave spies.

the keyboard input for anything of value. This will all be done remotely without any need for physical access to the computer or perhaps the building itself depending on the range and size of the interception unit. The ability to intercept all types of sensitive information from the monitors and microcomputer peripherals will make this type of device a very powerful and dangerous new tool in the hands of the Netspionage agents and techno-spies.

Network Mapping and Attack Tools

Software has become available that allows the techno-spy to probe even the largest networks for vulnerabilities. This probing is done in a way that creates the appearance of participating in a multi-nation attack force. This freeware allows the attacker to simulate any number of TCP/IP addresses as the originating points for these reconnaissance efforts. According to information security specialists, it is possible that by embedding attack scripts in the software, an attacker could exercise "one button takeover of commercial or military computers."[20] It is now possible to execute very sophisticated scans for vulnerabilities and then to add the exploitation script for the specific vulnerabilities that have been detected. Once root/superuser access is obtained, the attacker will then have complete control of the system.

Military and commercial espionage has never been so easy. Competitors inside or outside the country have little stopping them from closing down an enemy's electronic commerce and other network based services.[21]

The tool is called NMAP,[22] and it is easy to use, which has made it accessible to a wide range of potential users. For the Netspionage agent seeking an easy method of finding and exploiting vulnerabilities, NMAP has a lot to recommend it. Not only is it freeware, it can be configured so as to mislead the opponents into thinking people from an ostensibly hostile country are scanning them. Such misleading information can add a whole new level of protection to a collection effort. Imagine the excitement of a Republic of China (Free China on Taiwan) competitor with a good network security officer who detects a series of scans that appear to be originating from mainland China, or vice versa. As he leaps to the conclusion that hostile forces are mounting an attack, the techno-spy could quietly complete his assignment. Once he provides the stolen information to his European sponsor, he can have confidence that even if his efforts were detected, the company will be searching in the wrong direction.

---

[20]The CIO Update published by the SANS Institutue, Vol 2 Number 3, 3/8/99.

[21]Ibid.

[22]"Cracking Tools Get Smarter" Wired News 3/19/99.

Free Mail

One of the most important tools of choice for the successful Netspionage agent is a web-based e-mail service. There are many available and none that seem to have any particular advantages over the others. Two of the most commonly used are Hotmail and Yahoo Mail; however, so many sites offer web-hosted e-mail as a service that it's a matter of personal preference as to which one to use. These services are useful in part because, like so many other products and services on the Internet, they allow anyone to register, and they don't appear to make an effort to verify any of the information provided by the registrant. They are accessible from any Internet access point.

When the techno-spy is operating inside a target corporation, there are several ways the spy could be tripped up. One of the most dangerous is to be caught in possession of documents or files techno-spies are not authorized to possess. They obviously need get the rid of the "crown jewels" quickly, and they need to get them to the customer. The longer they have the crown jewels in their possession, the more chance that a search could discover the incriminating possession of critical information. If the knowledge worker has a web-browser on his desktop computer, then he can use web-mail to send the materials out of the corporation. A couple of key caveats apply. First the contents to be transmitted should not exceed the total bandwidth capacity to be sent. For most documents and files this should not be a problem. Larger files may need to be compressed using "zip" or "tar" utilities, or perhaps subdivided into smaller components to avoid detection or to avoid crashing the mail gateway.

The reason web mail is better for Netspionage operations is because many companies have now begun monitoring outbound e-mail message traffic at the e-mail gateway. The SMTP gateway commonly has some sort of filter, perhaps one created by the information technology group or maybe a commercial product. If the neophyte techno-spy is foolish enough to send a critical document containing key words that trigger the filter, their career will likely be over. Of course, this includes key assumptions. First, that the keywords correspond to the current target. Since filters will tend to change over time, it's possible that even a very good filter may not contain current priorities. The second is that someone notices and actually responds in a timely manner. Given the workload of most network and information systems and security personnel, it is very possible that even if filtering software is installed the transmission will not be detected. Reviewing the reports and logs is rarely a high priority, and it's possible the techno-spy could perhaps complete the assignment and be long gone before anyone had the opportunity to respond.

On the other hand if a web-based e-mail package is used, the techno-spy can transmit the stolen files to a safe holding position, perhaps one of the digital dead drops mentioned earlier. Since there is no practical limit to the number of free mail accounts or free drive server space to which they have access, the Netspionage agent can operate without worrying much about running out of space, and with no chance that filtering software will detect their activity.

The only way to prevent a Netspionage agent operating within the corporation from using web-mail would be to deny all personnel at the location the option of using HTTP, which is the protocol used to surf the web and engage in basic Internet research and searching. This means it is not likely that corporations could take the steps to prevent Netspionage agents from bypassing the company provided (and monitored electronic mail system) in favor of the "free mail" access path that avoids detection.

Erasing Digital Fingerprints

Once stolen digital assets are transmitted to a safe location such as a digital dead drop, the Netspionage agent must then use a product that will help cover his trail and eliminate any digital evidence that could link him to the activity. There are a number of tools such as East Tec Eraser[23] that destroy much of the electronic evidence of the crime. These tools were developed specifically to defeat computer forensic techniques used by law enforcement and security organizations. Their capabilities go far beyond the delete or erase functions provided by Windows and other operating systems. As almost everyone knows, files that are deleted or erased by earlier editions of the Windows operating system are not physically eliminated from the disk, but merely renamed and their assigned disk space is opened to receive new data. Often such files can be completely recovered by simple "Undelete" utility software. Forensic eliminators not only wipe (overwrite the clusters assigned to a specific file) the files that were sent, but also clean out the disk cache, file slack, all temporary files, and free space. Once these procedures are completed; they dramatically reduce the possibility that even a full computer forensic investigation of a computer system will uncover useful evidence.

The Honey Pot and Sexpionage

In the old days of espionage before Internet and mass global communications, one of the well-known ways of getting information from someone was to compromise them through sex-related blackmail. The adversaries provided members of the opposite sex or the same sex, depending on the individual target's profile and sexual preferences.

---

[23]http://www.east-tec.com.

With the advent of mass global communications such as the Internet and World Wide Web, one can now find many romance sites. Most of these sites are probably legitimate. For a price, they introduce two people to each other. However, these sites could also be ideal fronts for identifying new targets for exploitation. Also, the sites may be legitimate, however, one or more of the people listing on the site, could be an agent for an adversary or competitor.

For example, on one site alone, 31 countries were listed with a total of more than 3,528 women. Of those 807 were Chinese from the People's Republic of China and overseas Chinese, 127 were from Russia and 415 from the former Union of Soviet Socialist Republics (USSR), excluding Russia itself.

Included on the Web sites were colored photographs and the description of the women to include their personal profile, their hobbies, as well as telephone numbers and e-mail addresses where they were available. Most of the women identified were professional, spoke at least some English, and many were college educated. One listed her occupation as Chinese army officer! Although it's obviously not possible to know just by reading the sites' web pages whether any of the listings are in fact agents, it is likely that some foreign services are already exploiting this approach.

The use of men and women willing to exchange sexual favors for information is not new, of course. However, in the pre-Internet days such encounters were done person-to-person. Therefore, there was the risk of being caught by the intelligence agents of the targeted country. With the advent of the Internet "romance Web sites" this is no longer the case.

Let's look at an example of how such a system could be used. A country or foreign business that is seeking to obtain sensitive information from an American business relating to the development of its new microprocessors directs their Netspionage agents to list himself or herself on one or more romance Web sites. The agent can be male or female, and his background or description is not important. The Netspionage agent creates profiles to attract the type of individuals they are seeking. The Netspionage agent would, of course, get or invent photos of an attractive female or a handsome man (depending on the target) and ensure the individual is fluent in the language of the targeted country where the target business is located, in this case English. That person could also be a college student or a college graduate majoring in computer systems or electrical engineering. Thus, the person would naturally attract potential Netspionage targets of like interests.

Now along comes Fred, an American at work surfing the Net out of boredom or looking for the one person to light up his life. So, this American computer engineer from Silicon Valley who is an extreme introverted nerd, makes contact with Natasha. She appears to be the girl of his dreams and another computer nerd. They share so many common interests. Fred, of course, had never been briefed on the dangers of such contacts and what to watch for, or totally ignores the warnings that have been provided. So, Fred sends off an e-mail to request a password to register for the site, or he logs into a URL to begin the registration.

Immediately the site collection begins. From either Fred's e-mail header information or from the details provided by his web browser, the adversary can determine the primary domain server associated with Fred's employer. Consulting Internic or equivalent commercial registry services they can learn the corporation name and street address associated with the IP address. They will also learn the telephone numbers and fax numbers associated with the corporation, as well as a system administrator and technician's telephone, fax, and e-mail information.

Once Fred completes the registration form, the adversary will have some additional information. Since this is a romance Web site, they may ask questions that are very personal and could open the person to blackmail. The answers on the registration form can also be used to create a psychological profile of Fred so that he can be more effectively manipulated. Although Fred is under no obligation to answer truthfully or completely, the odds are good that he will give up some very useful information that helps the psychologists broaden their profile of Fred.

Since Fred works for a targeted company and is in one of the right groups with access to targeted information, a prompt response will be received from his new friend. Over time many conversations via e-mail would take place and this new digital pen-pal would gradually gain the trust of the targeted engineer who would, of course, open up and begin to share information as to what he was working on. It may be that the Netspionage agent would be able to gain valuable information without ever actually meeting the targeted engineer. And if discovered, what is the result? There are no laws that can be enforced to prosecute that agent, especially not while they remain safely in Russia, China, or another country.

A variant on the above scenario would be to identify a specific business and identify individuals within that business to whom e-mails can be sent to develop a relationship over time. The Netspionage agent interested in biotechnology for example would target biotechnology firms. Once the individual was identified, the Netspionage agent would send an unsolicited e-mail, "Hello, you don't know me, but I heard your lecture at the conference last week (or read your paper in the proceedings or . . .). I am also working on research in the field for a similar corporation in Peking. As a fellow scientist, I would like to share information on topics of mutual interest for the benefit of humanity. We are currently working on developing a prototype of XXX. What are you working on?"

There are, of course, so many variations that one can think of to begin the contact that may ultimately lead to compromise of sensitive business information. Remember, especially in nations like China and Russia, Internet e-mails, telephone calls, and other communications activity are subject to being monitored. This means that if an innocent relationship did develop through the Internet, the Netspionage agents of that nation could use the opportunity to require their citizen to gather information—and in countries like China, you do not say no to the government!

Potential Targets for Netspionage

The most important step in determining what assets to protect in a corporation is to first determine what may be valuable and important, then to think like the opponent, the techno-spies themselves. Since the global Internet allows the Netspionage agents easy access to networked systems anywhere on the world, it is vital that corporate managers understand they will inevitably be dealing with citizens from other countries, as well as those of their homeland.

Business Information

The raw material of the Information Age is information and the refined ore is knowledge. Each of the following categories should be considered as potential targets. As difficult as it is for corporate managers, as well as security and law enforcement professionals, they need to think like the "bad guys." This is especially important in dealing with techno-spies since what they seek may often not be the asset that is of greatest financial value to the business, or the asset with the highest street value in traditional sense. If their motivation is to harm the corporation, for example, short selling the company's stock, then they may not steal information to sell at profit, but may merely release the most embarrassing information found in computers and networks, so the targeted corporation's reputation will be damaged. This damage can be done using the information gleaned from the target while on the Honey Pot Web site.

Access to Other Networks and Systems

Perhaps one of the least obvious and potentially most significant reasons to target a specific business or government agency is the particular locus it occupies on the Internet. To managers accustomed to thinking of their business or government agency as a purely physical entity in the stream of commerce, it may be difficult to accept that the web of electronic connections, which constitutes the Internet and electronic business, may result in undesired attention. Even if the business or agency itself has nothing of special value, the Internet connections it maintains and the information that flows between the corporation and other businesses may be the cause for undesirable attention from techno-spies and other miscreants.

Safe Harbor and Staging Base

In some circumstances, the inadequate security at a location will make it a convenient staging area for operations against another, ultimate target, located in another corporation. Such situations are more likely if the intervening corporation has extensive Internet connectivity with large or high profile corporations with valuable digital assets. This is a serious risk for corporations extending their network to vendors in the form of extranets. Unless security standards are enforced for all participants in the extranet, they may create an unmarked back door that can allow the techno-spies direct access to the corporation's most valuable digital assets with possibly no need to first circumvent existing security systems.

Vendors

The existing relationship between a vendor and its corporate customers may provide a convenient way to gain information concerning a primary target. Vendors' Internet connections create the risk that outsiders and other customers may gain unauthorized access to the corporation's sensitive information. Another possibility is that the Netspionage agents may use Internet connections to access sensitive information concerning the targeted corporation stored at the vendor's location. The techno-spies may also gain initial entry to the vendor's network by invading other customers connected to the vendor's network. This "transitive property of vulnerability" can dramatically extend the risk to information far beyond the visible relationships of traditional business operations.

Corporate Dead Drop

If a corporation's systems are poorly protected, they may find that although they are not the direct target of a Netspionage agent, their servers may be used as a convenient place where the fruits of a crime are stored.[24] For example, the servers may be used to temporarily store source code or other digital property.

---

[24]See Mitnick's reported use of accounts on the Well to allegedly store the source code taken from Shimomura's systems.

Proprietary Technology

Obvious targets of Netspionage agents include valuable digital technology (binary software or source code) developed by the corporation for it's own use or as potential new product or service. There have been cases where software companies allegedly have lost the next generation of their source code to a techno-spy that invaded the company network.

Business Plans and Strategies

Typically the information that the techno-spy will target will answer questions such as, "What is the corporation planning to do? Where will it invest? Who will lead the effort? What is the expected amount of the investment? What is the expected (or required) return on investment? Who will benefit?" Techno-spies may also seek documents (including spreadsheets, presentations, and databases) on any servers that describe reorganization plans, labor relations plans, contract negotiation strategies, and litigation strategies. These materials could significantly help the opposing parties prevail over the corporation.

Research and Development

This information is an obvious target for exploitation. Once inside a corporation in either a physical or virtual sense, the techno-spy will probably target the servers and systems that contain information concerning new products in research. Related topics such as investment priorities, plans to enhance current products, and acquisition plans could all be immediately useful to a wide range of potential sponsors of the Netspionage attack. Sponsors could include stock analysts to foreign competitors to organized labor seeking an upper hand during contract negotiations.

Employee Files and Human Resource

Human resources computer systems provide access to potentially valuable information about the people who work at the company. Information desired by the techno-spy includes: salary, bonus plans or other compensation, stock option allocations, performance counseling or disciplinary files, employees home addresses, home telephone numbers, social security, and other key identifiers (i.e., drivers license, vehicle license, and access card information). Competitors may be able to use this information to find the most vulnerable, underpaid candidate for a recruiting pitch or use the information to impersonate an employee.

Facility Buildings Plans

Any information that could assist competitors in understanding the source of competitive advantages of a business corporation may be targeted. Floor plans or blueprints of a particular device or equipment layout that allow competitors to deduce unique business processes not common in the industry will be targets. Plans, documents, or reports that indicate the presence, operation, or limitations of physical security measures (e.g., alarms, sensors, and CCTV/monitoring systems card access systems) may be sought. This information is important when associated with high value components, raw materials, or finished products, especially if the purpose of the Netspionage attack is to support traditional crimes like burglary, theft, and robbery.

New Products

Marketing plans and supporting materials may provide timing, key investments, target accounts, or other milestones that could be used by competitors to thwart introductions, delay acceptance, or otherwise diminish market success or acceptance of current, new, or improved products.

Inventions

Lists, databases, or compilations of invention disclosure documents that identify the inventors or provide key technical insights could allow competitors to anticipate direction, capability, or intentions of the corporation; develop alternative products; or emphasize shortcomings or limitations of the improved products or services. If these materials are accessible on an internal web server they could perhaps be obtained by a Netspionage agent working internal to the business or who successfully invaded the network through an existing relationship. The U.S. government databases storing information on pending patents decisions and other related sensitive corporate information may be a prime target for the Netspionage agent. Under these circumstances, the corporation may never know that it had lost some of its future crown jewels.

Financial Conditions

Current or forecasted financial activities, status, or conditions of the corporation, investments, etc., could provide potential acquirers or competitors insight as to strengths or weaknesses of the company. Quarterly performance estimates of publicly traded corporations obtained in advance of the public announcement of the results, could allow investors to trade more successfully in the corporation's securities.

Production

Sometimes systems and servers contain details about the products manufactured by the company. The engineers or technical staff operating such systems may not fully appreciate the value and importance of the contents, or may believe that no one could steal the contents without a formal engineering or scientific background. The fact is, a techno-spy does not need to know how to use the stolen materials, only how to take all essential elements to complete the assignment.

Summary

When operating in the black zone, principles such as ethics and legal issues no longer apply. In today's Internet-based global marketplace, there are many techniques and software products that can be used by the Netspionage agents against multiple and vulnerable corporate targets.

9

Case Studies of Netspionage

True Cases of Netspionage

The small but growing number of cases that are presented and discussed in this chapter cannot, by the nature of the incidents, be considered definitive. After all, it rarely benefits any corporation to have the public, shareholders, citizens, and competitors become cognizant of the nature and extent of losses associated with breaches of security that are characteristic of successful Netspionage. Also, corporations that have already crossed the ethical line and used these techniques do not want to advertise their success. After all, there are others upon whom they may wish to wreak havoc. For all these reasons, successful Netspionage attacks are expected to largely remain in the shadows. However, there is every reason to believe that the reported cases and elements that have already surfaced in various media reports through other medium represent the "tip of the iceberg." When a case does become public, it deserves careful scrutiny and should be viewed as a "straw in the wind," an indicator that demonstrates how this concept is developing.

The public records are supplemented by several incidents of which the authors have personal knowledge based on extensive contacts. These have been deliberately sanitized to avoid disclosing the affected corporations. However, each incident presented is real and provides additional examples of the potential for Netspionage.

Our assessment, considering the sample of cases below, is that they forecast a dark and dangerous future for corporations that assume that everyone will engage in roughly similar norms of competition. Although clever terms like "co-opetition" and "ecosystems" may sound appealing to academics and Sunday op-ed business page writers, such relatively benign developments, regardless of how much desired, are very unlikely. Barring a fundamental change in human nature, it is much more likely, that ethically flexible managers will adjust their techniques to the limit of public tolerance for results over ethics, and usher in the full flowering of the age of Netspionage.

The case studies that follow are taken from public records and news sources. The basic facts of the cases as disclosed in public sources are presented and analyzed for their implications. In discussing Netspionage, one finds corporate management turns a deaf ear and doesn't believe that such incidents classified as Netspionage actually occur. They want proof before they commit resources to defend against Netspionage attacks. Well, the below-cited cases are real and should provide sufficient proof for the corporate management skeptics.

Bloomberg and Reuters: Did They or Didn't They?

The facts in this case remain murky and have never received a full public disclosure. The press reports issued at the time the matter was initially pursued (late 1997 and early 1998), contain many elements that justify a careful study of the allegations. The allegations in this case help frame what could be the prototypical Netspionage effort of the new century. Reuters, is a world-renowned news and information provider headquartered in the United Kingdom. It is a leading provider of financial information and associated services. In the late 1990s, it was losing market share and therefore revenues to an "upstart rival" from the United States. The Bloomberg Company, founded in 1981 by Michael Bloomberg, developed an information distribution strategy for clients that revolutionized the business world. By providing "Bloomberg terminals" for subscribers to its business information services, it linked customers more tightly to the company and began providing an increasing range of real time information, such as the latest stock market reports from around the world. The company grew rapidly beyond its New York base and soon was making over $1 billion annually. In response, it appears that Reuter's executive management in the United Kingdom authorized a project to attempt to regain market preeminence by developing a new computer system of their own that would have features and capabilities superior to the Bloomberg product. Such a response is exactly what one would expect from any business confronted with a new rival. Such ripostes are part of the dynamic nature of capitalism, where competition is the basis for business and drives much of the technological advancement. However, what is alleged to have happened next is very different.

The press reports claim that Reuters in the United Kingdom authorized Reuters in the United States to undertake steps to enhance the design of the next generation Reuters' workstation. One of the enhancement steps appears to have been to set up a new division named Reuters Analytics. What happened next is much less clear. It is alleged that Reuters Analytics hired a computer consulting company, called CRV, to perform some specialized research. A former Bloomberg employee reportedly founded the computer consulting company, which was based near the Stamford, Connecticut headquarters of Reuters' Analytics. What was initially alleged was that CRV then hired a technical expert who then remotely entered Bloomberg networks and obtained proprietary source code(s) for the Bloomberg product(s) without authorization.

The press reports go on to say that the efforts continued over some period of time and that Bloomberg monitored and documented the results of these intrusions with the assistance of the FBI. A grand jury then apparently began looking into the incident and the FBI even dispatched agents to England to interview senior executives and review documents to determine whether they had knowledge or involvement in this effort.[1] Three executives, including the head of the Analytics unit, were placed on leave when word of the grand jury investigation was released, leading to speculation that there may have been serious improprieties.

It is important to emphasize that this case was never resolved at trial. It was quietly dropped for unknown reasons[2] after a yearlong investigation. However, consider that if these allegations had been proved, the Reuters company and responsible managers or executives could have possibly been prosecuted under the 1996 Economic Espionage Act. The Act made it a Federal felony, punishable by large fines and long jail terms to steal the proprietary information of a U.S. company. Although the incident was not resolved, it is believed that it is a very instructive scenario. So let's reprise the critical issues as we see them.

Key Allegations

- A formerly dominant market leader
- Large foreign corporation with significant resources
- Losing market share to new U.S. rival (possibly creating a revenge mindset?)
- Executive sponsor commits to significant efforts to reestablish dominance
- Digital product included financial information delivery via custom software and hardware
- Alleged theft/misappropriation/taking of an entirely digital product (proprietary source codes)
- Possible use of a deniable third party to buffer the sponsor against allegations of wrongdoing

---

[1]Reuters Shares Fall Amid Probe of Allegedly Stolen Bloomberg Data, Dow Jones Online News, 01/30/98.

[2]U.S. Kills Probe of Reuters' Use of Bloomberg Data, B2 *Wall Street Journal*, 7/16/99.

- Third party may have employed a hacker to penetrate defenses at a target

Commentary

Since this case was never resolved at trial, it is not possible to know the truth of the charges and counter charges made by the parties. However, the case is worth careful study. For our purposes, we will assume the truth of the allegations, but only for the purpose of assessing the incident for implications. What may have happened is that local managers and executive in the United States extended a battle plan developed at headquarters in the United Kingdom far beyond the intended scope to include activities that may have been illegal. Although Bloomberg stated that "we believe that Reuters . . . obtained improper access to the Bloomberg system,"[3] Reuters claimed that "the focus of the investigation was not on whether it had tried to break into Bloomberg central computer to extract proprietary code, but on whether it had hired a consultant to breach his subscription agreement with Bloomberg and transmit data about bonds and stock. . . . "[4]

Reverse engineering publicly available products is well-accepted practice in both the law and business, but it assumes that the provider of the product makes it generally available to the public. However, if the product were software that is located behind firewalls and labeled as property of another company, the software would obviously not be accessible for reverse engineering. Obtaining a copy does not deny the possession and use of the original copy of the software to the legitimate owner, but it could represent theft or misappropriation of the contents, which would be a crime in both the federal and state laws of the United States.

The most interesting aspect of this incident was that so many people refused to believe it was even possible for one company to try to take the property of another in such a stealthy and underhanded manner. Although "gentlemen may not read other gentlemen's messages," the pressures of global competition may drive otherwise responsible and reasonable executives to resort to extreme measures. In effect, Reuters said as much ". . . the company announced that pressured employees may have misinterpreted company policy and stolen information from the company's fast-growing rival."[5] ("Misinterpreted synonymous with "plausible denial?")

---

[3]Ibid.

[4]Ibid.

[5]Ibid.

Attempts to gain additional information from other sources have not been successful. Neither rival has provided materials to support its position in the matter, so readers must draw their own conclusions. Perhaps the law enforcement authorities made serious procedural or technical errors that fatally compromised the investigation, perhaps there simply was no conclusive evidence to support the allegations, or there was an "out-of-court settlement." Regardless the most important lesson to draw from this case is that many things are now possible, and it's just conceivable that some corporations may choose to cross the line and steal information from rivals especially if employees may misinterpret company policies under the pressure of competitive circumstances.

Sladekutter and Labwerks[6]

The facts in this case provide another warning to managers and executives. Completely opposite the preceding case where the parties are giants in their industry, the companies involved in this incident were relatively small firms located in the United States. The facts as provided are very instructive. The key person in this matter was a former Sladekutter employee who apparently became Chief Technical Officer at Labwerks. Although he initially worked for Sladekutter full time for almost a year, he subsequently became a consultant. During this transitional period of several months, he apparently worked part time for both Sladekutter and Labwerks. During this interim time, he periodically used Sladekutter's computers to access Labwerks' systems.

The judge in this case found that Sladekutter "gained unauthorized access" to Labwerks computer system by using a combination of the former employee's name and social security number. Once they successfully hacked in, Sladekutter apparently copied both e-mails and the names of Labwerks' major customers. A detailed log of computer activity demonstrated that unauthorized entry into the system came from "sladekutter.com," and occurred after the hacker made multiple unsuccessful attempts to guess a password. Once they had customer information, Sladekutter subsequently contacted the customers and threatened them with legal action if they employed Labwerks in what they claimed was work in violation of a non-compete agreement Sladekutter had with the former employee.

As one might imagine, the judge was not amused at such actions. In the opinion of the court, the respondent's actions were not justified and were in violation of the Federal Wiretap Act. One is hard pressed to imagine under what theory the Sladkutter staff pursued their actions. Perhaps the technical staff believed they were allowed to engage in the

---

[6]The *Legal Intelligencer*, Injunction Issued for Hacking Away Competitor's Customer Base, 2/22/99.

intrusion activities in some variant of the hot pursuit concepts under which police sometime pursue fleeing criminals across geographical or jurisdictional boundaries? Or maybe they just felt sufficiently wronged and believed that a little intrusion into another company's e-mail system was trivial compared to the offense they believed the former employee had committed. Perhaps they believed that the intrusion would go undetected, and they could do what they wished regardless of the legalities; that it was only a problem if they were caught. Regardless, the judge in the case ruled against the respondents and ordered them to cease their attacks, return the e-mail messages they had taken, as well as to contact the customers and inform them of the results of the hearing. The words of Peter A. Santos, the attorney representing Labwerks, succinctly summarized the findings in this case, "The court has said in no uncertain terms that it will not tolerate one business breaking into another business's computer system. It's illegal, and it will be stopped."[7]

Commentary

Although the corporations involved in this case are relatively small, the implications of the case are very significant. One should reasonably expect a degree of common understanding of the legal framework for resolving disputes between corporations. However, one company was apparently willing to engage in actions that were clearly improper, even shocking to most outside observers.

As almost everyone now understands, the electronic businesses of the 21st century will involve every nation on every continent. How much more likely is it that disputes and competition between corporations on opposite ends of the planet, from different cultures, languages, and ethical systems will result in similar or even worse excesses? Will such incidents be viewed as criminal events, or merely "bad form?" Will the perpetrators receive sanctions, or merely be seen as savvy businesses engaged in sharp business practices, especially if their efforts bring increased prosperity to the local economy at the expense of some far off foreign multinational corporation? How will the aggrieved parties seek and obtain redress when the consequences of the intrusion incident may have been the loss of a multimillion or multibillion dollar contract to provide goods or services? And what if the source of the intrusion is not merely an indigenous business competitor, but the military or intelligence service of another nation or a transnational crime cartel? The permutations are nearly endless, and we expect all of them to occur with increasing regularity in the electronic business environment.

---

[7]Ibid.

Law Firm Sued for Hacking

In yet another example of one corporation accusing another of hacking, we move now into the legal arena. This case also demonstrates how it may be necessary to closely manage and supervise the technical staff, or risk serious problems for employers, especially when the actions are inferred to be authorized by the management.

In September 1999, Dig Dirt, Inc., a company that specializes in providing research services to law enforcement and large companies, filed formal charges claiming that a Washington, D.C., law firm, Steptoe & Johnson LLP, tried to hack into its systems more than 750 times.[8] What makes this accusation especially ironic is that members of Steptoe & Johnson have served on presidential committees dealing with the Internet and various security issues.

The complaint claims that a Steptoe employee hacked into the Dig Dirt system by using a password and Internet account that actually belonged to a small business. It seems that a Steptoe employee may have obtained the account information when he helped set up the small company's computer system. The filing states that Steptoe & Johnson used the stolen account to post-critical messages in various Internet forums.

Commentary

The case is important for several reasons. As far as we know this is the first time a large law firm (Steptoe ranks in the top 100 law firms in the United States with annual revenues of over $100 million) has been accused of hacking into another corporation's computer systems. It is also one of a small but growing number of cases where accusations of hacking have been publicly filed by one business corporation against another.

The implications of this case are troubling, even corporations whose management are above the temptation to engage in technical intrusions may have employees who may cross the line. Perhaps the final adjudication of the case will confirm the statement of one individual close to the matter who claimed that the described actions indicated the perpetrator was "somebody [who] seems to know enough to get in trouble but not enough to cover their tracks."[9] Whether the alleged intrusions and actions were in any way encouraged and abetted or completely unsanctioned by managers of the law firm will be very interesting. Perhaps the law firm merely had a rogue employee on their payroll who engaged in unauthorized and illegal activities, or perhaps the law firm had a Netspionage agent on payroll that will be allowed

---

[8]Computerworld Online News, "Investigator/publisher charges D.C. law firm with hacking," 11/11/99.

[9]Ibid.

to "take a fall," since the corporation is required to "disavow" their actions. Lastly, it is entirely possible there is some other reasonable explanation to be revealed when and if the matter ever reaches a trial.

The previous two cases provide important precedents for the evolution of Netspionage. The technical skills exist in many places that could be used to hack into a target corporation's computer systems and networks. Some employees, whether sanctioned by management or operating entirely on their own, may be tempted to use these skills to achieve questionable business objectives. Monitoring and controlling the technical employees, including all regular, temporary, and contract staff, to ensure they do not engage in inappropriate activity is essential to protect the reputation and image of major corporations against the actions of potentially rogue employees. Of course, if management does authorize, direct, or encourage the activity of such employees, they should be prepared to face the consequences if they are discovered, which may not be all that terrible given the current state of the law as the next case demonstrates.

Amazon and Alibris

An online bookseller and Internet Service Provider was fined $250,000 for intercepting e-mail sent by Amazon.com and other competing Net book retailers. The company reportedly extracted information from the e-mails that were intercepted and created a list of the best selling books.[10] The company, Alibris, pled guilty to almost a dozen charges alleging the company illegally intercepted e-mails and also copied customer lists after hacking the competitor's servers.

Commentary

The press reports note that the spying began at a company called Interloc, which merged with Alibris in May 1998. However, the illegal activity apparently continued after the merger, and it was alleged that top executives of Alibris knew about it and approved it.[11] In January 1998, the systems administrator for the ISP allegedly modified the e-mail software so that it intercepted and copied all the e-mails sent to customers from Amazon.com, Bibliofind.com, and Advanced Book Exchange. According to the prosecutor, Interloc intercepted and copied thousands of e-mails. The company may have intended to extract information from the e-mails to create a list of the book dealers' most pop-

---

[10]DA nabs online bookseller for Internet snooping, IDG News Service\Washington Bureau, 11/30/99.

[11]Ibid.

ular book orders. The systems administrator of Interloc also allegedly hacked into the servers of Shaysnet, Megatron Data, and CrockerCommunications—and gained access to customer lists from these ISPs. What Interloc intended to do with the customers lists they obtained from these other ISPs is not known.

It seems that a single company was responsible for illegal Netspionage actions directed against six competing companies. This incident is a classic case of Netspionage in the private sector and demonstrates how one individual in the information systems department may have been responsible for multiple intrusions and violations. One might infer that the responsible system administrator was operating under "hacker ethics," so the computers and networks of anyone competing with the company was a legitimate target for penetration and intrusion. Of course, on the other hand, maybe the technology staff was only following management's orders and attempting to acquire sensitive information from competing corporations in order to execute a particular business strategy. Since the company denied any intention to do such things it is difficult to know the truth. What is clear is that they were very active in using technology in ways that were definitely outside the "white zone."

Argentine Hacker

A 23-year-old Argentine man returned voluntarily to the United States and pleaded guilty to hacking into U.S. university and military computer networks, where he reportedly obtained access to sensitive but unclassified research files on satellites, radiation, and energy-related engineering. He was sentenced to three years probation and a $5,000 fine.[12]

Commentary

The existing treaties between the United States and Argentina did not allow Ardita to be extradited to the United States to stand trial for illegal wiretapping and unauthorized penetrations of computers and networks. Although he was sentenced under a plea agreement to three years' probation and a $5,000 fine, the agreement allowed him to serve his probation in Argentina.

This case received significant media coverage when it occurred as a sensational example of a non-U.S. hacker penetrating primarily government systems. One lesson to be drawn from this case is that intruders are able to access systems with sensitive information from many places outside of North America and Europe. However, the much more

---

[12]Argentine Pleads Guilty to Hacking U.S. Networks; Wiretap Led Authorities to Arrest, Special to the *Washington Post*, 5/20/98.

important lesson to be learned is that in dealing with incidents of Netspionage is that the results of a successful prosecution are likely to be very disappointing.

In this example, a national government was able to track down, with the aid of a court-ordered wiretap, an international hacker. Had it been a full-fledged techno-spy, there would have been little satisfaction in knowing that after all this effort, only a small fine and a probationary period is levied. After all the problems this person caused he would never have faced a U.S. court if he had not voluntarily come to the United States. Perhaps this case, and others that have been prosecuted by governments, is teaching corporations that self-help may be a better choice than relying on law enforcement agencies.

Canadian Companies Victimized by Hackers

A report published in the Counterintelligence News and Development Volume 3, September 1999, the Canadian Secret Intelligence Service, (their equivalent of the U.S. CIA) stated that an unnamed foreign government ordered its intelligence service to obtain specific business intelligence. The intelligence service contacted computer hackers to help achieve the objective, which resulted in the loss and compromise of numerous computer systems, passwords, personnel, and research files of two companies.[13]

Commentary

Netspionage by official agencies may nonetheless involve the use of common computer criminals/hackers. By using members of the cyber under-culture to achieve their objectives, the foreign government sponsors of a Netspionage effort gain increased deniability in the event that the operation is ever discovered or publicized in the media. Although it may be extreme, to some another advantage of using hackers is that they may be terminated "with extreme prejudice" if necessary. As a chilling example, many believe that at least one of the German hackers who helped the Russian KGB search out "Star Wars" information in the early 1980s was allegedly killed by the KGB. This may have been done to prevent him from disclosing to Western investigators the full extent of the earliest publicly discussed example of Netspionage.[14]

---

[13]http://www.nacic.gov/cind/Sep98.html, Counterintelligence News and Developments, September 1998.

[14]For discussion of this matter see *The Cuckoo's Egg* by Cliff Stoll.

Russians in the Moonlight Maze

In the fall of 1999, the finest example of Netspionage yet emerged from the world of defense and national security. In what was officially dubbed Operation Moonlight Maze, it has been alleged by U.S. officials that over a period of more than a year, a wide ranging and systematic collection campaign was directed against U.S. Department of Defense unclassified network systems and their contents. The intruders "plundered vast amounts of sensitive information."[15] The targets included "unclassified computer networks at Department of Energy's nuclear weapons and research labs; at the National Aeronautics and Space Administration; numerous university research facilities; and defense contractors."[16] The worst aspect of this incident may not have been the actual information lost as much as the fact that after intense efforts, U.S. government officials were apparently not able to determine the identities of anyone involved with the intrusions, or whether the objective was espionage or some other purpose.

Although individual identities are unknown, circumstantial information leads a reasonable person to believe that the operation could have been at least based in Russia, whether it had official support is an open question. The fact that at least some of the attacks were traced to Internet servers located very close to Moscow and that the intrusions occurred on weekdays between 8 a.m. and 5 p.m. Moscow time—but not on Russian holidays, is to say the least, very suspicious. At least one nameless U.S. official went even further ". . . it's our belief, that it's coming from Russia and that it may be a sponsored [intelligence] activity."

Although the U.S. public has become accustomed to the typical media reports about hacker attacks defacing Web pages or shutting down sites with computer viruses and other malicious codes, these intrusions were different. "They weren't shutting down systems. They were taking file listings, looking to see what's in people's directories."[17]

Yes, the difference is dramatic. In place of the crude language and swashbuckling bravado that characterizes the antics of the largely adolescent boy hackers, Moonlight Maze amounted to an electronic vacuum cleaner operated by another or others on the other side of the planet. The ability to sift through terabytes of data stored in poorly protected computer systems, find the nuggets of valuable military, political, economic, technological, or other information and transfer it to the control of outsiders is the very essence of a well-orchestrated Netspionage attack. It must be exhilarating to the techno-spies. Working in the air conditioned comfort of their regular offices or cozy

---

[15]*LA Times* Yearlong Hacker Attack Nets Sensitive U.S. Data, Thursday, October 7, 1999.

[16]Ibid.

[17]NASA Inspector General Roberta Gross quoted in ibid.

warmth of a rustic dacha, perhaps enjoying a shot of favorite vodka to celebrate each small victory over the ineffectual American systems administrators, one can imagine it must be very satisfying to the Netspionage agents and their sponsors.

At least one U.S. intelligence officer has recognized that the Internet has changed the spy game forever, "You can sit anywhere in the world now and run an espionage operation. You find the name of a scientist at a nuclear lab, for example. Get his credit ratings, his bank statement, his school records, his mortgage, his insurance, his hospital records."

Once in possession of such useful data, the techno-spy may supplant more conventional agents in approaching the target and probing for weaknesses in online chat rooms or web forums. Or, if the situation is right, the scientist could be approached directly by e-mail or manipulated during chat sessions into disclosing the targeted information.

It's also possible that all these activities may have been directed by Russian organized crime (sometimes called the mafiya) trying to search out valuable but unprotected commercial information. This hypothesis is supported by the fact that some of the files reportedly compromised include pricing, contract, and bidding documents.

It seems that the United States was not much better prepared to respond to this latest incident than it was back in 1998. Back then, the obliquely named Operation Solar Sunrise was the code name for an all-out effort by the FBI to hunt down the perpetrators of over 500 system penetrations that occurred at more than 90 different facilities, bases, and companies. Since the timing of the intrusions coincided with one of the periodic increases in military tension in the Middle East directed towards Iraq, it seemed possible that the Iraqi's or someone sympathetic to them was starting an all-out cyber-war against the United States. After nearly six weeks of investigation, which represents an extremely long time on the Internet, the attacks were traced back to a teenaged Israeli who called himself "Analyzer" and two 16-year-old California boys. The young men arrested in Israel and California hardly seemed the cyber-espionage masterminds that had been described in early media coverage of the intrusions. On the other hand, if it took six weeks for the FBI and military security resources to track down three teenagers, the question naturally arises as to how much chance does the United States have in late 1999, in running to ground the possible Russian perpetrators of Moonlight Maze?

For the past two decades there have been a series of reports showing that information systems security of both military and civilian agency computer systems was substandard. In spite of the recent hyperbole concerning dire threats from terrorists, information warfare and defending critical U.S. information infrastructures the most recent GAO report on federal government information security, which was released at the same time as the details concerning Moonlight Maze, disclosed that 22 agencies had major security vulnerabilities.[18] In light of these conditions, it is only surprising that it took someone, possibly the Russians, until 1999 to move effectively into the many gaps and use a full scale Netspionage attack to take everything they could that was not protected. Now that the entire world has seen the example of how effective Netspionage can be in Moonlight Maze, we would be amazed if other opponents and competitors of the U.S. government and businesses didn't follow the successful example and pursue every opportunity to commit Netspionage.

The Mafiya's Role

The Citibank case is another example that we believe provides valuable insight as to how Netspionage operations may unfold in the 21st century. What has been publicly released in the media and court filings indicate that in late 1996 one of the leading U.S. banks became the target of a well organized and executed series of network and computer system attacks. These attacks, which originated in St. Petersburg (formerly Leningrad), Russia, had the apparent objective of transferring out funds to accounts and locations controlled by the Russian *mafiya*. Andre Levin, the technical mastermind of the incident, was apparently assisted by two nontechnical associates in a scheme that lasted over 11 months and resulted in unauthorized transfers of $11 million, of which all but $400 thousand was recovered by authorities. Although Citibank apparently employed commonly accepted information security tools and techniques, and was assisted by both the FBI and U.S. Secret Service, the attacks continued for a long period of time.

At least one press report speculated that one or more inside accomplices, a.k.a. moles, might have assisted Levin. The use of such auxiliaries to scout the internal systems environment would be a logical extension of contemporary hacker techniques and is a key component of Netspionage attacks. For example, in the mid-1990s, the well known hacker magazine, *2600*, reportedly advised subscribers to seek jobs as janitors or night security guards in order to better obtain unrestricted physical access to facilities where they sought to penetrate computers and networks. As almost every information security professional understands, good protection for information assumes that a secure physical environment exists at the perimeter and inside the corporation. When hostile intruders or their associates have physical access to network and system hardware, it's almost impossible to compensate for such access with purely technical security measures.

If there actually were internal accomplices assisting the external attackers, they would likely have performed some or all of the following tasks:

---

[18]Ibid.

- Document internal security measures
- Identify specific individuals with requisite access privileges
- Determine User ID and password standards and practices
- Internal network scanning to identify target host vulnerabilities
- "Sniffing" internal networks to capture password packets
- Obtain documentation for bypassing or neutralizing application security measures

The Citibank case had a happy ending. Levin was ultimately lured to the United Kingdom on a pretext, extradited to the United States, and convicted in a U.S. court. However, the case demonstrates once again that even a corporation with substantial resources devoted to information systems security may be victimized by sophisticated techno-spies in the era of Netspionage. Eternal vigilance may be the price of liberty, on the Internet; it will also be the price of electronic business.

There had been a rumor that Levin conducted the attack against the bank because his family was being held hostage by members of the mafiya. After they were rescued and reportedly sent to the United Kingdom, Levin agreed to give himself up for prosecution.

The Temp Who Took the Software

In the fall of 1998, the Kodak Company experienced one of those unfortunate incidents that have served to highlight the vulnerability of leading corporations to Netspionage. The facts in this incident are very interesting. A temporary employee was nearing the end of her work assignment at Kodak in Rochester, New York. What is alleged is that she attempted to send key source code of a next generation digital camera via e-mail to her sister, who was reportedly employed by Xerox Corporation in California. Fortunately, the employee was not very technically sophisticated, for the multi-megabyte file was simply attached to a common e-mail message and sent out through the e-mail gateway. The company was very fortunate that the sheer size of the file attachment apparently caused the e-mail gateway to clog and crash. The second piece of good luck happened when the e-mail system administrator apparently was curious as to the cause of this disruption. In examining the log files and reviewing the contents of the files, the administrator apparently noted the unusual content and notified someone in management who quickly initiated a much broader investigation. The employee was arrested for attempted theft of trade secrets but claimed that she was only transmitting the camera source code to her sister "for safekeeping."[19]

---

[19]Kodak Staffer Fired over Espionage, *ComputerWire*, July 1998.

Commentary

The reported facts in this case should raise security red flags for any corporation making products that use software to manage and control hardware, which includes a number of consumer electronics. The first and most disturbing question is how did a temporary employee gain access to what was most probably one of the crown jewels of this corporation? However strange this might seem, it is a real problem that managers in many corporations seem to rarely appreciate. The economic advantages of using contingent staff, like temporary employees, are often fully appreciated, but the need to modify business procedures to address the security risks created by the rapid turnover of temporary staff often receive little or no attention. It seems reckless, but most American companies have no practices to screen the assignments provided to such contingent staff. What this means in practice is that almost anyone may be hired by the corporation, and they may be assigned to work anywhere within the corporation. Typically we find temporary employees filling in for even the most sensitive administrative positions, for example, replacing the CEO's secretary while the secretary takes a vacation, or supporting a project manager bringing a breakthrough product to market. Although most people are honest, using contingent or temporary employees in such roles is often taking an unnecessary gamble on an individual's character. After all, if the corporation puts a temporary employee into such a position the result is a person who knows they have a short tenure being exposed to sensitive information that they may be able to use to great personal benefit. It's simply a very poor bet to assume a person will pass the opportunity to make a lot of money at the expense of a corporation for which they probably have no emotional attachment nor any shared economic interests.

The 1999 American Society of Industrial Security— PricewaterhouseCoopers "Loss of Proprietary Information" survey[20] established that nonemployees with trusted access are one of the major causes of loss of information. In that sense, the Kodak case is a perfect example of what can go wrong if temporary employees are given unfettered access to company sensitive information and information systems, or if they are able to circumvent existing safeguards. What is worse, the same survey noted that temporary and contract employees rarely receive background investigations, which dramatically increase the risks of hiring temporary staff with troubling issues (such as prior convictions for felony thefts, assaults, or other problems). It also shows that an opponent who is considering Netspionage has favorable odds of inserting a techno-spy inside the target corporation to perform any number of useful tasks.

---

[20]Survey documents available online at http://www.pwcglobal.com/InformationLoss.

Calling Cadence: The Silicon Shuffle

This case serves as another warning that corporations must do much more to protect their key digital assets against theft and misappropriation via the technological means used in Netspionage.

It seems that a group of people who were previously employed at Cadence (a successful producer of design software) formed a company to compete with Cadence. Over a short period of time, they recruited away from Cadence a number of the people responsible for new software products. However, these resignations did not go unnoticed. After losing several key people, the lawyers for Cadence sent a formal letter to their counterparts at the start-up company, Avant, warning that any further recruitment of Cadence professionals by Avant would result in litigation for unfair competition. Avant would be accused of employee raiding, which is an illegal practice when it is done to adversely impact an opponent's ability to compete. So far, however, the situation parallels any number of situations where a nimble start-up company largely composed of alumni of an established corporation apparently seek to better their previous employer in the marketplace.

However, what happened next was the crux of the criminal allegations against Avant. One last member at Cadence resigned. Cadence claims that prior to resigning his position, this person uploaded proprietary source code from Cadence products to his personal e-mail account. The person then resigned employment with Cadence and hung out his shingle as a software consultant, coincidentally consulting on a project for Avant.

Court filings by the prosecutors claim that the source code taken from Cadence was copied and used by Avant as a portion of their product. The claim was that the copying was so complete that it even included the comments provided by the Cadence programmers in the actual product released by Avant.

One of the factors that makes this case so interesting is that unlike similar cases of alleged misappropriation or infringement, which are commonly pursued as civil suit, criminal charges for theft of trade secrets were filed against the Avant corporation and key executives by the local prosecutor. As anyone familiar with the American legal system knows, there are very serious and far-reaching differences between a civil litigation by one party against another and a criminal prosecution by the "state" on behalf of "the people." Whereas successful civil litigation typically results in payments and other measures to make the plaintiff "whole," a conviction at a criminal trial may result in large fines and imprisonment.

Needless to say the trial has stirred significant debate in Silicon Valley where innovation and business thrive on the alumni of established corporations. On the one hand, supporters of the prosecution see it as essential to support the intellectual property rights of corporations against the depredations of unethical and highly mobile employees who may deprive owners of the rightful returns on their investments. On the other hand are those that worry that criminal prosecution casts a chill over every employee's right to pursue a career, seek new employment, and maximize their personal economic situation, while coincidentally creating new wealth to the benefit of the larger society. It is not the purpose of this book to take a position on such controversial issues. However, what this discussion does highlight is the many aspects to consider in safeguarding the most important assets of high-technology companies. In most high-tech corporations, the most valuable assets are in digital form and may be scattered in multiple unprotected locations throughout the enterprise. This means they could very easily be subject to scenario's similar to what is alleged to have happened at Cadence.

At the time of this writing, the matter has not been formally settled in court in spite of a lengthy investigation. There have been at least two grand juries that have charged Avant for criminal theft of trade secrets. Regardless of how this case is ultimately resolved, it has raised many important issues that will be debated for years.

French Spies

In the world of economic and industrial espionage, the French have earned their place as one of nations that are recognized experts in obtaining key information. It should surprise no one that they are already engaged in full-scale Netspionage. In the early 1990s, U.S. counterintelligence agencies warned American executives that the French government has a special operations group, Service 7, that specializes in "Black Bag Operations" directed against commercial rivals. Reportedly, these French government agents break into the hotel rooms of visiting business people and copy anything that might be useful. The portable computers and media brought by these business people are their prime targets. The reason traveling computers are priority targets is because a successful operation often provides access both to the current contents of the hard drive, as well as a backdoor into the corporate network. The backdoor is obtained because senior executives typically save their passwords in remote access software. Once the User ID and password combination has been copied from the hard drive, it may provide French competitors everything they need to pass right through the firewall masquerading as the authorized user.[21]

Once inside the corporate network, the agents could copy, modify, or delete sensitive e-mails and other key files to which that account had access. They could also possibly install other software to capture other User ID and password combinations, attempt to crack existing securi-

---

[21]Time, 5/28/90; NewsWeek, 5/4/92.

ty safeguards, and generally spread their access tentacles throughout the target corporation. Not too shabby for a couple of minute's work duplicating a hard disk drive in a laptop system.

According to a leading French magazine,[22] France also systematically eavesdrops on American and other countries' telephone and cable traffic via a network of listening stations and passes commercial secrets to French companies competing for lucrative contracts. The DGSE, which is the French equivalent of the U.S. CIA, allegedly operates electronic communication intercept outposts in France and in several overseas locations such as French Guyana in the Western hemisphere and New Caledonia in the South Pacific. One senior official in the DGSE was quoted as saying, "This is the game of the secret war. Our job is to do as they [the Americans] do, and to be just as good at it."[23]

The German intelligence agency reportedly shares the spoils of political and economic secrets obtained by these French assets. In return, the Germans allegedly share with the French whatever their interception stations in central Asia manage to obtain.[24] Together these efforts constitute a Franco-German alliance that is attempting to rival the Anglo-American collaboration on intelligence matters.

Commentary

The threat of government sponsored Netspionage from advanced information age nations with sophisticated capabilities is perhaps the most serious problem for large companies who compete against an indigenous "national flag" business. Without even realizing it, they may be covertly attacked through a wide array of sophisticated collection techniques.

This is also a prime example of how the U.S. governments past history of opposition to strong encryption for commercial purposes may have inadvertently helped U.S. competitors. If French intelligence is able to intercept a fax, telephone, or other electronic transmission that has been sent in clear text (unencrypted) or copy an unencrypted laptop hard drive, they have no problem translating the contents and passing it on to the French companies that could benefit. As more information moves over the Internet and associated networks, the advantages of monitoring the international communications of global companies becomes even more valuable. Given the propensity of managers and executives to make telephone calls and send e-mails to discuss

---

[22]French "spy on U.S. business in new secret war," Le Point (translated at www.infowar.com), June 1998.

[23]French "spy on U.S. business in new secret war," Le Point (translated from French), June 1998. www.nacic.gov/cind/SEP98htm, Counterintelligence News and Developments, September 1998.

[24]http://www.nacic.org/CIND/sep98.html.

problems and opportunities, the interception undoubtedly provides substantial information that helps French firms defeat their competitors. One must remember that most information driven nations appear to be involved in such tactics.

Taiwan, Republic of China

A Taiwanese hacker broke into the real-time pricing systems of 20 brokerages, including some of the most established houses in Taiwan, and used the stolen market data over 12 months to earn over $303,000. The information stolen included transaction data, account numbers, and records of big investors.[25]

Commentary

The suspect was reportedly an unemployed law graduate from the National University in Taiwan. In addition to the money he made by selling stocks short based on his knowledge of the positions taken by the major brokerages, he is also alleged to have blackmailed brokers who had sent out false information about various stocks. Allegedly, he threatened to go public with the information concerning their duplicity, according to other press reports.

"Perhaps this case will persuade management at other Taiwan companies to invest in training their systems engineers to implement better security precautions," commented an industry veteran. (We doubt that will happen.)

PRC and Taiwanese Hackers

A hacker in the National Taiwan University BBS "Hacker-or-Cracker" chat room claimed that while he was using the Chinese hacker program "Netspy," someone using an IP address registered to a Chinese mainland intelligence organization in Hunan Province attempted to attack his system.[26]

Commentary

There is a certain delicious irony in a situation where a hacker advises those who use a popular software hacker tool that the code may intro-

---

[25]Hacker Raids Taiwan Stock Brokerages for 12 Months,
http://www.internetnews.com/intl-news/archives/0,1068,6,00.html, International News Archives, 3/23/99.

[26]TAIWAN, TAIPEI, 3/22/99 (Newsbytes).

duce a back door into the hacker's systems. For years hackers have been releasing modified executables into the Internet on various download sites. These modified versions of games, utilities, and other software introduced vulnerabilities that the hackers could use to gain control over systems that had installed the modified software. Now it appears that mainland Chinese intelligence may have used the same technique to try to monitor hackers from Taiwan.

Chinese Snoop Program

The picture.exe plants a Trojan on a target computer and then tries to copy and transmit any AOL passwords along with any URL recently visited to an Internet Service Provider (ISP) in the Peoples Republic of China.[27]

Commentary

In this incident we have an example of how malicious code may be used in a random Netspionage attempt to capture useful information. Such shotgun attacks are crude and represent an early stage of development of Netspionage. What this incident demonstrates is that the capability for Netspionage is global and the Chinese are very active in building a capability to engage in such actions. Although this incident was not serious in itself, it is one of an increasing number of exploits that utilize covert communications between the potential targets and the Netspionage agent through the Internet. It is also another in a number of incidents where the technology for Netspionage has fingerprints from China.

The Online Spies from the PRC

China doesn't need to use spies to obtain precise details and sketches of America's most modern thermonuclear weapons, ballistic missiles, and reentry vehicles. Anyone with an Internet account or library card can get some of the military secrets that China is accused of stealing from Los Alamos.[28]

Commentary

Over the past several years, Chinese government agencies and technical academies have tried and succeeded repeatedly to access allegedly var-

---

[27]CNN/fn "New Trojan Horse Program Warning Issued," 1/7/99.

[28]On Internet, Anybody Can Be in the Spy Game, *Los Angeles Times*, 5/16/99.

ious unclassified online commercial databases. Some of these databases contain materials extracted from U.S. Congressional hearings, magazines, and other publications. When brought together, they provide very useful information that could be very helpful to potential adversaries. Although the contents may be only estimates, such information could be very useful to the Chinese or any other nation-states. However, since the Chinese have been unwilling to pay for the subscriptions they have been denied authorized access to the information by the owners. (Are they gaining unauthorized access?)

The concept here relevant to Netspionage is that there is now so much information available from so many sources on the Internet. This flood of sources has made it almost impossible for security organizations in both the government and private sector to keep up with all the ways that sensitive information may be accessed, aggregated, and lost or stolen. "The computer revolution, which has given society enormous benefits, has also made possible a revolution in espionage."[29]

The radical and extensive nature of rapid technological change has made protection doctrines from the Cold War obsolete. The greatest threat to sensitive and defense information is no longer human agents but the Internet intruders safely operating keyboards from their homelands, techno-spies among the temporary staff, and Trojan horse software targeting systems and information. These are much greater threats today to a corporation's sensitive information and will become even more so in the future.

The Case of the Missing Desktop Computer

The security officer of a high-technology company located in California relays the following incident: In the early 1990s, shortly after the manager began working for the company, he was contacted by a manager of a workgroup in one building. Over the course of the preceding week, about a dozen desktop microcomputers had been examined by unknown person(s). In each case, the authorized users claimed they had shut down their systems prior to ending the workday. When they returned, in some cases the computers were powered on, in some files or folders were opened or had apparently been moved or rearranged from the previous desktop configuration.

There did not appear to be any motive for such actions. There was no commonality in subjects of files accessed or opened among the computers and there was nothing sensitive or valuable on the specific systems that were affected. The manager requested placement of surveillance cameras in the general area, but was overruled by the human

---

[29]Ibid.

resources director. A request for access control software from the supporting information technology group was also ignored.

The next weekend, someone stole a desktop unit. This system did contain something valuable; the quality control protocols for several of the companies major products. If someone had these electronic documents and an understanding of the company manufacturing processes, they could duplicate the quality, features, and functions of these products. These elements were the source of competitive advantage for this company in their market.

About two years later, the security manager engaged a retired Soviet block intelligence officer to provide assessment of the company's risks from Russian and Chinese espionage. The former Soviet agent (who worked for U.S. government intelligence agencies following his defection to the United States) advised the security manager that during the same time (1992) that the theft occurred, the specific technologies in the company's products were top priorities for Russian intelligence as dual use defense and commercial products. About a year after the former Russian advised about the priority, the security manager was contacted by a law enforcement agency working a case where the suspect was employed by the company and was an expatriate Russian with suspected ties to former KGB intelligence operations. Coincidence? Not very likely, however, no arrest was ever made for the technology theft.

Commentary

Leave it to the Russians to provide us another fine example of the many ways to conduct Netspionage. As elegant as a sophisticated software intrusion may be, one can accomplish the same objective by directing an internal agent in place. Physical access to the potential information targets allows that agent to search systems and steal the physical computers that contain the desired information. Such thefts may be the method of choice if the contents are too voluminous to fit on portable media, or if the techno-spy lacks the skill or sophistication to probe for the information using software tools and techniques. The downside of physical theft and the reason it will be avoided in most cases is that it tells the corporation that they have actually lost something, which could trigger a serious investigation that might result in the compromise of the Netspionage agent.

Summary

The cases noted are just a few of the many that seem to be occurring all too frequently. Based on corporate management's current attitude, the Netspionage agents and techno-spies will continue to enjoy success plying their trade, especially against U.S. corporations. Why? Because it pays, and the chances of getting caught are rare and rarer yet is the chance of being successfully prosecuted. In summary, for the Netspionage agent, it is like "taking candy from a baby."

Section III: Protecting What You Have from Those Who Want It

Now that you understand the new information-based environment detailed in Section I, and the threats and techniques that may be used against your corporation as stated in Section II, Section III will discuss what you can do to mitigate the risks to your vulnerable sensitive information.

Chapter 10: Defending Against Netspionage

This chapter will discuss basic, cost-effective, and common sense processes that can and should be in place to defend one's competitive advantage or market share. Both technological enhancements and human-procedural changes that can toughen the organization's perimeter and dramatically increase the potential to deter, detect, and rapidly respond to known or suspected incidents will be presented.

Chapter 11: Operational Security and Risk Management Techniques to Mitigate the Netspionage Threat

This chapter discusses proactive methods to perform a self-assessment that can help determine the level of vulnerability of a corporation to *Netspionage*.

Chapter 12: The Best Defense May Really Be a Good Offense and Other Issues

There is an increasing belief that corporations cannot depend solely on law enforcement or other government agencies to protect them from Netspionage and techno-spies. Some have begun to attack their adversaries in retaliation or even before their adversaries are able to attack them. This new form of vigilantism and ramifications will be discussed as well as the role of the hacker as a business' new hired gun and defender.

10

Defending Against Netspionage

"Perimeter" defenses evolved within the Department of Defense to "defense in depth" and "layered defense" (see Figure10–1). Those same approaches are applicable within the corporation. In fact, it must be done if the corporation is to fend off Netspionage agents and techno-spies. Remember, it is a war, a business and economic war.

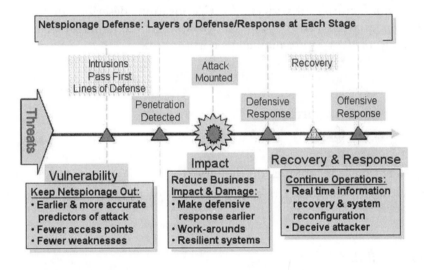

Figure 10–1 A protection process that can help mitigate Netspionage attacks.

Since most businesses are profit and shareholder value-oriented, cost-benefits must be taken into consideration. After all, security is normally a business overhead cost and as such is a "parasite" on the profits of the corporation. In other words, some of the profits are sucked away to provide for security. However, now those corporations are so dependent on connections to global networks in order to buy and sell in the global marketplace, and thus more vulnerable to Netspionage, information security is now an essential enabler for business survival.

Corporations have no choice but to allocate resources to the security functions, for without providing those resources—well, Section II's case studies showed some examples of what can happen. In order to allocate the minimal amount of resources necessary to obtain the minimum security needed to ensure a prudent sensitive information protection program, corporate managers should ask their staffs or hired consultants some very basic—*and specific*—questions. By specific, we mean not just the general threats, e.g., you have an Internet interface, therefore, you are vulnerable. Yes, that is assumed. However, what the corporate manager should want to know is also specific to their corporation.

These should include the questions stated below. Each question should be asked and answered from the perspective of each of the following four business environments as it will give the corporate manager a good perspective of the entire global marketplace and warfare situation: (1) Corporations, in general, doing business in the global marketplace; (2) Corporations in the corporate manager's business group, e.g., manufacturing of widgets; (3) Corporations described in 1 and 2, and headquartered in the same nation-state as the manager's corporation; and (4) Corporate manager's corporation.

Threats

- Are there any threats?
- What are they?
- Who are they?
- What basic techniques do they use?
- How do you know? (General answers, best-guesses should not be accepted)

Vulnerabilities

- How sensitive is the information?
- How valuable is the information?
- How vulnerable is the corporation's sensitive information?
- How vulnerable are the corporation's information systems?
- How do you know?

Risks

- What is the level of risk to the sensitive information?
- What is the level of risk to the information systems?
- How do you know?

Current Protection

- How well are we currently protected?
- How much is that costing?
- Is it necessary? Why?
- Is it adequate? Why? Why not?
- If it is not adequate, what must be done to make it so?

Options

- What are the options?
- How much will each option cost?
- What are start-up costs?
- What are the recurring costs?
- What threats are mitigated and by how much?
- What vulnerabilities are mitigated and by how much?
- What risks are mitigated and by how much?
- Explain how you made these determinations and your level of confidence in them.

In order for anyone to answer the above questions, there normally must be research, studies, and analyses conducted. Some of these studies take time, and yes, funding. Remember that you need a protection program that meets at least the minimal needs of the corporation at least cost. So, it is prudent to use the quality and process improvement approaches.

As the saying goes, "When I go slow, I go faster." That means that if you take your time, do it right the first time with a plan, understanding and some patience, you can build a more cost-effective, dynamic information protection program in less time for the long term. It's like building a house. If you pour the concrete for the foundation without first identifying the type of soil, how well it is compacted, etc., and then to compound the problem not wait for the cement poured for the foundation to properly dry before putting up the building frame, the house will not be stable, may become unstable and will be weak. It may even collapse. Don't waste the "profits" of the corporation by building a poorly constructed protection program. Such a program not only is not cost-effective, it may give everyone a false sense of security, cause complacency, and ironically, it may make the corporation's sensitive information more vulnerable to Netspionage.

This is an ongoing, dynamic effort as the environment changes, the value of information changes, the information systems change, and the corporation also changes. Intrusion detection systems, corporate and personal firewalls, encryption, anti-virus software, training, hardened routers and operating systems, biometrics, and other approaches are employed to protect the information-based environment not just at the perimeter, but throughout the corporation. That includes all its locations around the world. These are all part of a basic program. However, the best advice from consultants, information technology specialists, and information systems security professionals, is that one must take a holistic approach. Although security devices are necessary in most instances, but how do they fit into the total protection program? Trying to piecemeal security is costlier than establishing the entire program over time as a logical approach, and using such security measures and devices as building blocks of the total defensive shield.

The Challenge of Defense

The very first question to be answered should be "what will be protected?" There is no simple answer for most corporations. There is a wealth of digital assets ranging from customer lists, product designs, product specifications, marketing plans, patent applications, and the list goes on almost forever. And, of course, the assets may be manifested in so many different media, forms, and formats from databases to word processing documents to e-mail messages to web-based streaming video. In some companies, the attitude has been that everything is confidential and understandably the attitude of security and technical staff has therefore been that everything must be protected.

If the corporation implements a uniform set of strong security measures to combat Netspionage, it risks being both ineffective and inefficient. The inefficiency may arise from spending too much money and other scarce resources over protecting assets that don't deserve the degree of protection they receive. Ineffectiveness may develop if too little is invested securing the most valuable and important assets. Corporate managers should consider the wisdom of one of the most famous generals in Western history, Frederick the Great, who admonished, "He who defends all, defends nothing!" The lesson here is that whether one is allocating infantry and cavalry or information systems security personnel and audit reduction software, there will almost always be more possible assets to be attacked than can be defended by fixed, positional defenses. The key is to protect the resources that matter most against the vulnerabilities that are most probable.

Focus on the Basics First[1]

Protecting the corporation's sensitive information is a challenging task. However, from a management perspective, one does not have to know the details of installing security software or how every security process or mechanism works. Leave that to the techies.

From a management perspective, certain basic information protection principles should be understood and applied.

Sensitive information protection is based on three basic functions:

- Controlling physical and logical access to the sensitive information
- Individual accountability for that sensitive information and identifying the people who have access to it
- Audit trails, both physical and logical, that show a history of who accessed what sensitive information, e.g., who, where, when, why, what, and how

The goal of a sensitive information protection program should be to: Establish and maintain an innovative sensitive information protection program that minimizes Netspionage risks at least impact to costs and schedules, while meeting all of the corporation's and customers' requirements.

The objectives of such a program are to:

- Minimize the probability of sensitive information protection vulnerabilities
- Minimize the damage if a vulnerability was found and exploited
- Provide a method to efficiently and effectively recover from the damage

The Value of Information

In order to establish and maintain a cost-effective information protection program, one must identify the information that requires protection.

---

[1]It is beyond the scope of this book to provide a detailed plan for protecting sensitive information. There are many specific books on the technical topics such as TCP/IP. There are also good management-specific books on information protection. Some of the information from this chapter was taken from Dr. Kovacich's book, *Information Systems Security Officer's Guide: Establishing and Managing an Information Protection Program*, also published by Butterworth–Heinemann, which was the number one selling information systems security book for Butterworth–Heinemann in 1999.

How to Determine the Value of Information

Determining the value of a corporation's information is a very important task, but one that is very seldom done with any systematic, logical approach.

The consequences of not properly classifying the information could lead to over-protection, which is costly, or under-protection, which could lead to the loss of that information, thus profits.

Determining the Value of Information

To determine the value of information, the corporation's management and staff must first understand what is meant by information; what is meant by value. The management and staff must also know how to properly categorize and classify the information; and what guidelines are set forth by the corporation for determining the value and protection requirements of that information. In addition, how the corporation's management and staff perceive the information and its value is crucial to classifying[2] it.

Why Is Determining Information Value Important?

As alluded to earlier, if the information has value, it must be protected; protection is expensive. One should only protect that information that requires protection; only in the manner necessary based on the value of that information; and only for the period required.

One might ask, "Does all the information of a company or government agency have value?" If the corporation's management and staff were asked that question, what would be the response? The follow-on question would be, "What information does not have value?" Is it that information which the receiver of the information determines has no value? When the originator of the information says so? Who determines if information has value?

These are questions that the corporation's management and staff must ask—and answer—before trying to establish a process to set a value to any information. As you read through this material, think about the information where you work, how it's protected, why it is protected, etc.

The value of the information may be determined by the holder of the information. Each person places a value on the information in their possession. That information that is necessary to successfully complete their work is very valuable to that person. However, it may not be very valuable to anyone else. For example, to an accountant, the accounts payable records may be very important and without them, the accoun-

---

[2]In the context used here, the term "classify" has nothing to do with classification as it relates to national security information such as Confidential, Secret, and Top Secret.

tants could not do their job. However, for the person manufacturing the company's product, the information has little or no immediate value.

Ordinarily, the originator determines the value of the information, and that person categorizes or classifies that information, usually in accordance with the established guidelines.

Three Basic Categories of Information

Although there is no standard categories of information, most people agree that information can logically be categorized into three categories:

- Personal, private information
- National security (both classified and unclassified) information
- Business information

Personal, private information is an individual matter, but also a matter for the government and businesses. A person may want to keep private such information about themselves as their age, weight, address, cellular phone number, salary, and their likes and dislikes.

While at the same time, many countries have laws that protect information under some type of privacy act. In businesses and government agencies, it is a matter of policy to safeguard certain information about an employee such as their age, address, salary, etc.

Although the information is personal to the individual, others may require that information, but at the same time, they have an obligation to protect that information because it is considered to have value. This information could be used to approach, influence, and even possibly blackmail an individual to provide sensitive corporate information.

National Security Classified Information is one of the most important categories of information that must be safeguarded by all in the interest of national security. It is mentioned here briefly because the process used to place a value on that information goes through more stringent analyses than the personal, private information, and business information.

National security, classified information is generally divided into three basic categories:

- Confidential—loss of this information can cause *damage* to national security
- Secret—loss of this information can cause *serious damage* to national security
- Top Secret—loss of this information can cause *grave damage* to national security

There is also national security information that is not classified, as that stated above, but requires some lesser degree of controls and protection because it has value, but less value. These include:

- For Official Use Only
- Unclassified but Sensitive Information
- Unclassified Information

Business Information also requires protection based on its value. This information is sometimes categorized as:

- Company Confidential
- Company Internal Use Only
- Company Private
- Company Sensitive
- Company Proprietary
- Company Trade Secret

The number of categories used will vary with each company. However, the less categories, the less problems in classifying information, and also, possibly less problems in the granularity of protection required. Again, a cost item consideration. The corporation's management and staff may find that Private, Internal Use Only, and Proprietary would meet the needs of the corporation.

This corporate information must be protected because it has value to the company. The degree of protection required is also dependent on the value of the information during a specific period of time.

Types of Valued Information

Generally, the types of information that has value to the business and which requires protection include: All forms and types of financial, scientific, technical, economic, or engineering information including, but not limited to data, plans, tools, mechanisms, compounds, formulas, designs, prototypes, processes, procedures, programs, codes, or commercial strategies, whether tangible or intangible, and whether stored, compiled or memorialized physically, electronically, graphically, photographically, or in writing. Examples of information requiring protection may include: research, proposals, manufacturing processes, pricing, and product.

Determining Information Value

Based on an understanding of information, its value, and some practical and philosophical thoughts on the topic as stated above, the corporation's management and staff must have some sense of what must be considered when determining the value of information.

When determining the value of information, the corporation's management and staff must determine what it cost to produce that information. Also, to be considered is the cost in terms of damages caused to the company if it were to be released outside protected channels. Additional consideration must be given to the cost of maintaining and protecting that information. How these processes are combined determine the value of the information. Again, don't forget to factor in the time element.

There are two basic assumptions to consider in determining the value of information: (1) All information cost some type of resource(s) to produce, e.g., money, hours, use of equipment; and (2) Not all information can cause damage if released outside protected channels.

If the information cost to produce (and all information does) and no damage is done if released, you must consider, "Does it still have value?" If it cost to produce the information, but it cannot cause damage if it is released outside protected channels, then why protect it?

The following is an example: A new, secret, revolutionary widget built to compete in a very competitive marketplace will be announced to enter the market on January 1, 2001. What is the value of that information on January 2, 2001? Remember, information, to have value, to be useful, must get to the right people at the right time. Information is also time-sensitive.

Business Information Type and Examples

Types of Company Internal Use Only Information

- Not generally known outside the company
- Not generally known through product inspection
- Possibly useful to a competitor
- Provide some business advantage over competitors

Examples are company telephone book; company policies and procedures; and company organizational charts.

Types of Company Private Information

- Technical or financial aspects of the company
- Indicates company's future direction
- Describes portions of the company business
- Provides a competitive edge
- Identifies personal information of employees

Examples are: Personnel medical records; salary information; cost data; short-term marketing plans; and dates for unannounced events.

Types of Company Sensitive Information

- Provides significant competitive advantage
- Could cause serious damage to the company
- Reveals long-term company direction

Examples are: Critical company technologies; critical engineering processes; and critical cost data.

Questions to Ask When Determining Value

When determining the value of your information, you should, as a minimum, ask the following questions:

- How much does it cost to produce?
- How much does it cost to replace?
- What would happen if I no longer had that information?
- What would happen if my closest competitor had that information?
- Is protection of the information required by law and if so, what would happen if I didn't protect it?

Baseline Protection Measures

The security measures identified below are recommended because they have over time proven to reduce the risk of Netspionage and other forms of information theft within a corporation. They are commonly used by many corporations to protect critical and sensitive information.

Training and Awareness

Design and implement an information security awareness program using a customized training curriculum. Insure all new hires receive an information security orientation. Ensure all current employees receive some form of general refresher or job-specific training every 12–18 months.

Create and distribute a handbook and/or an online reference document on the corporation Intranet that is accessible to professional employees as part of the overall training and awareness program. Contrasted with value of the information assets the staff creates and use, these vehicles are very good investments. An additional advantage of the internal web server is the ability to ensure everyone in the corporation can receive current Netspionage defensive information through the web server and internal e-mails.

The corporation must invest in procedures and training that will allow the systems administrators to create and maintain a secure application and operating system foundation.

Classification and Marking of Information

All sensitive and valuable information should be marked in hard copy and electronic forms with the indication of proprietary rights. Adding the word "proprietary" to any existing classifications (such as "Corporation Confidential") communicates directly the corporation's ownership rights in the information.

ID Badges and Facility Access Controls

Implement a state of the art integrated access control system (one that records access and is tied into alarm and Closed Circuit TV surveillance cameras) at building entries and perimeter areas to ensure only corporation staff have easy access to the corporation's area and buildings. Consider using "time of day" restriction and definitions of access control zones to exclude unauthorized personnel from sensitive work areas.

The corporation should consider implementing a building-based access control model so that employees (whether regular, temporary, or contractors) receive a standard access profile based on their common job assignment. If they have no business need for default access to a particular building, they should not be able to use their access cards to enter the building. The focus must be on using access control measures to help screen out unauthorized access to areas, like the research and development laboratories, and all information technology nodes to deny easy access to the large quantities of highly sensitive materials such areas typically contain.

Vendor and Contractor Nondisclosure Agreements (NDAs)

Create a customized Nondisclosure Agreement for every contractor, consultant and vendor. Consider creating a blanket nondisclosure agreement for every site visitor. The visitor NDA may be used to inform the person of prohibited activities and the fact that they may be subject to search upon ingress and egress of the facility and that specified items (e.g., cameras, tape recorders, transmitters, etc.) may not be brought into the facility without specific authorization.

Every vendor should have an NDA that will describe the specific areas or types of information to which the employees of the vendor may or will have access. This NDA document should be included in any contract. A formal vendor clearance process should be developed that considers the criticality of the product or service provided, the nature of information to be shared with the prospective provider, and the nature of the vendor's existing business and corporation relationships.

Controlled Destruction of Materials

Every self-service copy room and reprographic/printer area provide either a local shredding/destruction device or a secure trash bin to store overflow or discarded sensitive output awaiting destruction. The bins should have one-way doors that allow materials to be deposited but not removed. Replace any strip shredders with criss-cross shredding devices to enhance destruction of sensitive documents. Provide utility software similar to Norton disk-wipe, East Tech Eraser, or equivalent capabilities to those departments and users who generate significant quantities of highly sensitive and confidential digital materials.

Employee Nondisclosure Agreements (NDAs)

All employees should sign a standard confidentiality/nondisclosure form and a copy should be placed in some sort of files, preferably the employee master file. Consider developing and using a customized NDA for departments or groups that create or handle information associated with breakthrough products. Departments or groups that create such custom NDAs should be required to provide a copy for the employee's master file. This will allow a terminated employee's access to be tracked throughout their employment history. If this information is placed in some sort of database system, it will also allow investigators to easily identify all employees who have had authorized access to critical information.

The language of project and product nondisclosure agreements must be explicit concerning who can have the information, who cannot, and how to add others who have a legitimate need for the information. In product and project work teams the security briefing should once again reinforce those with legitimate need for access, and the adverse consequences to the team and the project/product of unauthorized disclosure of the critical information. Since risk of disclosure is greatest at the individual level between friends, classmates, and family members, all these examples must be explored during the training and briefing process.

Published Formal Policy

Create a formal, written policy document signed by the most senior executive management and distribute a copy, either in hard copy or via e-mail, to every employee. Such a simple and direct communication combined with other significant changes in the corporation's approach to protecting information and digital forms of intellectual property will begin the process of creating a culture of security. A policy from executive management sets a clear direction for future efforts. Such a policy is also important to begin distributing ownership of the information security function among all employees.

Formal Security Procedures

The corporation should create and maintain formal security procedures that implement the corporation's sensitive information protection policy. These procedures and standards should be updated as new protection technologies and techniques are deployed, such as enhanced access controls, secure fax, and other measures.

Proprietary Information Protection Orientation

Create a new hire orientation that is positive and encourages a sense of ownership of information security by all employees. One cost-effective means to begin the process is with a customized video production that is supplemented by other documentation and periodic awareness materials.

Internal Audits/Self-Inspections

Management at every level of the enterprise must be trained and encouraged to understand the importance of complying with information security standards and recommendations. Areas that repeatedly fail to achieve minimum compliance with security measures should be sanctioned. Those that excel consistently should be singled out for special recognition and praise by senior management. Departmental inspection criteria and schedules must be coordinated with the responsible security department/manager/team to ensure consistency throughout corporation facilities.

Property Removal System

Actual approval authority for removing most items should reside with the employee's senior manager or director. Procedure should be developed that address the release/removal of the most critical "crown jewels" documents and other sources of critical information.

Controlled Storage of Sensitive Information

Areas containing large amounts of highly sensitive information and documents will be prime targets for espionage agents. They should be compartmentalized in a manner that prevents personnel with general access privileges from access. Consider uses of guard patrols to verify secure status of containers, intrusion alarm systems to detect unauthorized access attempts, and CCTV to record activities in the area. These measures become very important when dealing with areas containing large quantities of "crown jewel" information.

Secure Networks and Computer Systems

Information systems security products should be installed and maintained in order to help mitigate the Netspionage threats. These products should be fully implemented and updated versions purchased, as they become available. Often, security devices are not fully implemented and upgrades are not purchased; thus leaving a false sense of security as these devices will not indefinitely protect the sensitive information in their current configuration.

Exit Interviews

The corporation should create listings of nondisclosure agreements and other documents that indicate the technology and sensitive information that was accessed by terminating employees. Terminating employees who are joining competitors must be briefed concerning their responsibilities to continue to protect corporation information. It may also be very useful to conduct a focused analysis of other electronic activity records such as e-mail and telephone call logs. In some cases it makes sense to forensically examine the employees computer to determine if there has been any systematic efforts to transfer the corporation's key information materials in advance of the resignation.

Travel Procedures

The corporation should provide every overseas traveler with specific security recommendations that may be applied by installation staff, support personnel, and managers while traveling. The information that may be provided by the corporate travel office directly to the employees should also include a 24-hour emergency number to call in country and in the United States if anything suspicious or serious happens during the trip

Monitor E-mail and Internet Use

If the corporation has access to sophisticated information technology staff, they may choose to create a customized program to perform filtering functions. Others may elect to purchase commercial products that provide necessary functionality.[3] An effective filter program for monitoring and surveillance of e-mail should block messages and

---

[3]Please see http://www.softek.co.uk/mimesweeper/ for details of an example product.

attachments that may contain sensitive proprietary information. These materials may be found by searching for specific key words or phrases such as product names, project code names, or other descriptive words. It may also be wise to block messages (or at least create a log) of all messages that exceed a specific size or are addressed to inappropriate destinations (for example, to known competitors or perhaps foreign countries known to be actively seeking the corporations key technology).

The filter may apply to e-mail sent externally via the e-mail gateway or internally between various departments or workgroups. In some cases, it may be necessary to archive e-mails to provide copies to support prosecution or litigation against individuals responsible for theft or misappropriation of proprietary information.

Need-to-Know (NTK) Principle

Corporate information that has been identified as sensitive should only be made available to those individuals that have a management-approved need for that information in order to accomplish their assigned tasks.

Prepublication Reviews

A knowledgeable management and/or legal person must review every technical publication or presentation by any corporation employee prior to any release to outside magazines, trade press, or participation in any seminar. This should also include materials prepared for courses at colleges and universities when the materials concern products, services, or details of the corporation. Individuals who will be speaking at trade shows and seminars should, in addition to having their presentation materials approved, be briefed on how to handle and report common collection methods such as flattery, criticism, and other techniques such as the ever popular "honey trap." So named by the former East-bloc intelligence services, the trap uses the promise or potential of sex to gain access to targeted information.

Independent Audits

The corporation should obtain independent audit services to provide periodic reporting to executive management. These services should include both operational audits and inspections of security operations at each site. The audits should also schedule and conduct in depth technical audits and reviews of a prioritized group of critical application systems to ensure the systems function properly, and provide adequate protection of corporation information and other critical assets.

Secure Fax

There are many vendors that provide systems for secure transmission of confidential information. The corporation should establish mechanisms for secure fax transmission that will allow highly sensitive documents to be transmitted without possibility of compromise. As a minimum, strong encryption products should be employed.

Secure Voice

The corporation should consider itself a very likely target for interception by competitors and foreign nation-states. The selection and use of some form of secure voice system using strong encryption is a must.

Media Procedures

As part of the overall corporation's processes to mitigate Netspionage, management must ensure appropriate attention is given to the risks of media contacts. Intelligence staff and Netspionage agents may misrepresent themselves as press. A Netspionage technique is to e-mail targeted individuals within a corporation and pose as a media representative. Corporate policy, procedures, and employing training should all address this issue.

Web Logging and Filtering

The corporation requires software programs that can block access to inappropriate sites and log for reporting purposes the access and web activity of individual users. Pattern analysis of the activity may disclose unusual activity that could pinpoint possible techno-spies or other illicit activities.

One of the problems with unfettered access to the World Wide Web is that it opens the corporation to a wide range of new technical threats. It is important to control access to Java, cookies, ActiveX, and other sources of malicious code and unauthorized activity, or run the risk these active tools will themselves steal information or facilitate unauthorized access by techno-spies.

The corporation's Web site should be protected and controlled through a process that ensures sensitive information will not be posted.

Telecommuters Netspionage Protection

A corporation should establish a test protocol to provide technical assessments of telecommuters' home systems.[4] In addition, it may be prudent to provide the home and remote users a form of cryptography and at least a rudimentary personal firewall[5] to reduce their vulnerability. As telecommuting becomes ever more attractive in most major urban areas globally, expect the challenge of establishing and securing these proliferating remote nodes against techno-spies to become an integral part of leading corporation's programs to safeguard their key information.

Netspionage Tiger Teams and Incident Response Teams

Establish a team of skilled employees to form a proactive tiger team and incident response team. This team should establish operational projects to play the part of Netspionage agents and determine what sensitive corporate information they can obtain using Netspionage techniques. In addition, this team should form the basis of an incident response team in the event a Netspionage attack was identified.

Summary

Defending against the Netspionage agents and techno-spies is an ongoing effort that requires a holistic approach to protecting the corporation's sensitive information. The corporate manager must understand the environment in which the company is competing, the threats, vulnerabilities, and risks related to the business environment.

The corporate manager must also know what information needs protection and the information that does not need protection. Therefore, it is imperative to identify that information requiring protection using a logical, objective, and analytical approach. One must focus on the basics first and build on those baseline protective measures.

---

[4]One interesting approach to dealing with this risk is a site sponsored by Gibson Research Corp. (http://www.grc.com). The site offers a free service called "ShieldsUP!" which tests an individual PC's Internet connection to determine if there are exploitable vulnerabilities.

[5]See http://www.networkice.com, for example of home defense software.

C   h   a   p   t   e   r

11

Operational Security and Risk Management Techniques to Mitigate the Netspionage Threat

Operations Security (OPSEC)

Remember that managers of corporations that have implemented global networks and are moving into the world of electronic business should first identify the assets that are truly vital to the enterprise, that are the source of obtaining or sustaining the current or future competitive advantage(s) enjoyed by the corporation. Alternatively the most critical information may be characterized as those assets, the unauthorized loss, modification, or disclosure of which would allow competitors or other opponents of the corporation to frustrate the corporation's initiatives.

A tight focus on what may be called the "crown jewels" of a corporation is one way to begin prioritizing the informational assets of the enterprise. Finding and securing the "crown jewels" can benefit from a program originally developed by the U.S. government to combat the loss of sensitive and classified information during military operations, Operations Security (OPSEC).

OPSEC applied to corporations doing business in the global marketplace is a process of identifying critical information and analyzing the corporations' actions and responses:

- Identify those actions that may be subject to (or are known to be) observable or detectable by the intelligence systems and collection methods and techniques used by competitors. More information on OPSEC can be found at the Web site of the OPSEC Professionals Society (http://www.opsec.org).
- Conduct analysis of friendly activities to find the indicators that competitive intelligence systems might obtain that could be interpreted or pieced together to derive critical information in time to be useful to competitors.

- Select and implement protective measures that eliminate or reduce to an acceptable level the vulnerability of the corporation's actions to competitor exploitation.

The OPSEC process consists of five distinct actions that are applied sequentially:

1. Identification of critical information
2. Analyses of threats
3. Analyses of vulnerabilities
4. Assessment of risk
5. Application of appropriate protection measures to manage risks

When applied to countering the risks of Netspionage, OPSEC begins by focusing on the identification of the most significant "crown jewels" of the corporation. Once there is some consensus as to what comprise these assets, the analysis must also consider the computer systems, networks, and the various media in which these assets are resident throughout their lifecycle. For example, a crown jewel asset for a particular corporation may be a customer list.

This list may begin life as a series of e-mail messages sent via the Internet from sales representatives to an analyst. The contents are entered into a database or Web site. These inputs are then compiled into a summary, which is then distributed to select managers in the sales corporation via attachment in an e-mail message or made available via a URL on a special area on the internal Web site. Although each individual e-mail message is valuable to the competitor, it is the compilation into the database that creates the crown jewel, and the loss of the contents of this database is deemed by this corporation's management to be critical.

Analyses of Threats

Threat analysis should include consideration of the means available to an opponent if they target a specific crown jewel element. In the example above, some of the threats that should be considered include:

- Capture of the e-mail messages as they are sent to the company analyst
- Direct penetration of the Web site or database via cracking attack by a Netspionage agent exploiting any weaknesses in configuration or maintenance of the application itself or the underlying server operating system
- Redirection of e-mail messages by adding an unauthorized recipient as a: bcc (blind carbon copy) to the outbound messages as they are distributed

- Guessing, cracking, or stealing the passwords used to control manager access to the web/database

Netspionage Risk Management Program

The objective of a corporation's risk management program should be to maximize sensitive information protection from Netspionage attacks at minimal protection costs.

What Is Risk Management As It Relates to Netspionage?

In order to understand the Netspionage risk management methodology, one must first understand what risk management means. Risk management is defined as the total process of identifying, controlling, and eliminating or minimizing uncertain events that may affect the protection of something—in this case, sensitive corporate information.

It includes risk assessments, risk analyses (to include cost-benefit analyses), target selection, implementation and test, security evaluation of safeguards, and overall review.

Netspionage Risk Assessments

The process of identifying Netspionage risks, determining their magnitude, and identifying areas needing safeguards is called Netspionage Risk Assessment. In other words, you are assessing the Netspionage risk of a particular target.

The risk assessment process is sub-divided into threats, vulnerabilities, and risks.

Threats: Manmade or natural occurrences that can cause adverse affects to systems and information when combined with specific vulnerabilities. For example:

1. Natural threats include such things as fire, floods, hurricanes, and earthquakes.
2. Man-made threats or threat-related matters include such things as unauthorized system access, hacker/cracker/phreaker programs, the Netspionage agents or techno-spies themselves, theft of systems or services, denial of services, attack software, and destruction of systems or information.

Vulnerabilities: Weaknesses that allow specific Netspionage agent and techno-spy threats to take advantage of the weak points in the corporation's business environment to cause adverse effects to systems storing, processing, or transmitting sensitive information that make it easier to gain access to that sensitive information. For example:

1. Lack of timely implementation of software patches;
2. Services that are not required on the system are enabled;
3. Lack of access controls; and
4. Anything that weakens the security of the systems and the information they process, store, and/or transmit.

Risks: The chances that a specific threat can take advantage of a specific vulnerability to cause adverse affects to systems and information that would compromise sensitive information. For example, if you do not have audit trails on your system, the system contains company information that would be of value to others; what are the chances someone would try to steal that information? Without the audit trail logs, you would not know if someone had tried to penetrate your system, or worse yet, whether or not they succeeded!

Assessments: Assessments are an evaluation of the threats and vulnerabilities to determine the level of risk to your systems and/or sensitive information that the systems store, process, and/or transmit.

Assessments are usually done through a qualitative or quantitative analyses, or a combination of the two. It is the measurement of risks.

Qualitative analyses usually use the three categories of risk as high, medium, and low. It is an educated best guess based primarily on opinions of knowledgeable others gathered through interviews, history, tests, and the experience of the person doing the assessment.

Quantitative analyses usually uses statistical sampling based on mathematical computations determining the probability of an adverse occurrence based on historical data. It is still an educated best guess, but primarily on statistical results.

Netspionage Risk Analyses
Analyses of the risks, the countermeasures to mitigate those risks, and the cost-benefits associated with those risks and countermeasures make up the risk analyses process. Basically, it is risk assessments with the cost and benefit factors added.

Vulnerabilities must be eliminated or the risk of their exploitation knowingly accepted by management. The risks may be mitigated by application of additional protection measures or management may choose to accept a risk for a limited duration or for a limited population of assets if there is some compelling reason. Management should never accept risks for an indefinite time for an unlimited population of systems, as that is tantamount to writing off the asset to outside exploitation. In the example noted above, the most likely attack would be against the Web site password, perhaps by technical probe. The purpose would be to determine if it was misconfigured, but most likely by social engineering the holders of the password to convince them to release it to the unauthorized outsider masquerading as an authorized person who has forgotten or never received the password.

Risk Management Process Goals

The goal of the Netspionage risk management process is, of course, to provide the best protection of sensitive systems and the sensitive information they store, process, and/or transmit at least cost consistent with the value of the systems and the information.

Remember that the purpose of protection and security measures is to manage, not to eliminate, risks. Managers are in business to deal with the uncertainty that arises in the course of daily activities. Loss of critical informational assets is another risk that must be managed.

Defense in depth is required for the computer and network systems. The most common misconception is that a firewall will secure your computer facilities and additional steps don't need to be taken. A firewall is just one component of one security model. Additional or alternative components or layers should be added to create an effective security model within your corporation.

Using multiple layers in a security model is the most effective method of deterring Netspionage agents' use of computer systems and network services. Every layer provides some protection from intrusion, and the defeat of one layer may not lead to the compromise your whole corporation. Each layer has some interdependence on other layers. For example, the intrusion detection systems and the incident response plan have some interdependencies. Although they can be implemented independently, it's best when they're implemented together. Having an intrusion detection system that can alert you to unauthorized attempts on your system has little value unless an incident response plan is in place to deal with problems. The most important part of overall sensitive information protection program is the security policy. You must know what you need to protect and to what degree. All other layers of the security model follow logically after the implementation of the corporation security policy.

Managing and Reducing Netspionage Risks

A key element of an effective Netspionage protection program is that it must integrate the existing protective functions into a seamless perimeter. This means that all the protection functions of a typical corporation including physical/corporate security, information systems/network security, law and human resources departments in particular must align their efforts. By establishing both a formal and informal Netspionage attack response process (see Figure 11–1), mitigating such attacks can be improved.

The starting point is assumed to be a basic protection program that uses integrated security measures to safeguard the enterprise assets. An ongoing monitoring and surveillance program augments this baseline program and addresses both internal aspects coupled with attention to external factors that could drive the threat. The risk of a Netspionage incident is not static, it is a dynamic variable that will fluctuate in part based on business cycle elements and in part on the ripeness of new products and new technologies for exploitation. Varying the degree of watchfulness, in effect adopting a process of heightened alert for periods of increased risk and of basic vigilance at other times based on the inputs received from the monitoring and surveillance systems. When appropriate preventive measures are in place that are likely to detect an effort to collect information via network systems and if they do, this should trigger a formal incident response effort.

Reducing Risks of Netspionage

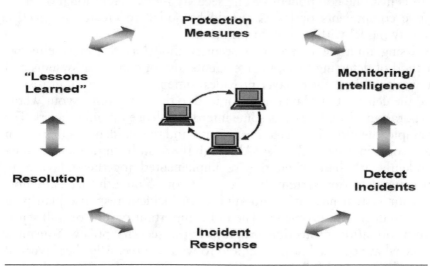

Figure 11–1 A graphic representation of a process to reduce the Netspionage risks.

The response element should include a combination of internal and external assets capable of determining the facts in a legal and expeditious manner. Whereas investigations in the physical world may proceed at a deliberate pace (hours, days, weeks, or longer) in cyberspace the investigation must move at Internet speeds, which means minutes, hours, and days at most. The reason such speed is necessary is because some key information may well be perishable, residing in the temporary storage buffers of ISPs or temporary files at intervening sites or individual computer systems. Timely notification to disinterested third parties, such as Internet Service Providers, is needed to ensure they do not destroy sources of potentially valuable evidence.

The best possible resolution of an incident of known or suspected Netspionage may include arrest and conviction of the perpetrator(s). However in some circumstances, it may be more desirable to turn it to a counterintelligence operation. It may be that an attempt that is detected early enough could be misdirected or mislead in a way that will feed to the opponent inaccurate, incomplete, or misleading information (misinformation) to confound the opponents analysts. After all, if the intrusion was detected quickly and done properly the intruders may believe that they have avoided detection by the target. Playing to this belief, the intruders may be subtly deflected or attracted to a source of sanitized information, perhaps in one or more "honey pot" servers with impressive sounding names that may be counted on to attract intruders, e.g., perhaps strategic information servers or global marketing server.

Regardless of the outcome, it is vital that every case of known or suspected Netspionage should be carefully analyzed and weaknesses in security, operations, and procedures that facilitated the security breach should be addressed. Which leads once again to the beginning of the cycle where enhanced protection measures are implemented and await the next onslaught of Netspionage agents and techno-spies.

Program for Managing Netspionage Risks

The following points should be considered in building a framework for managing risks arising from Netspionage. Note that in many ways the operational and procedural protection measures are as important or more important than purely technical measures. This is true because the computer and network systems that are implemented by the corporation must provide uses that benefit the productivity of human beings. Since there must be a human in the loop to use the processes in place, the computer network systems must be managed with a combination of technical, procedural, and operational safeguards.

It must be emphasized that preventing, detecting, and responding to Netspionage is a dynamic process that will change as rapidly as new technologies are implemented. Keeping up with the rapid pace of these changes is essential if the corporation is to defend its key assets against this pernicious threat.

Understand What Needs to Be Done

First, it is important to understand that preventing any possibility of Netspionage against a corporation is probably impossible in the near term. The reasons are many and include, but are not limited to, all of the following:

The attacker/intruder has the choice of timing, means, methods, techniques, and tools. The "bad guys" always get to make the first move. They may choose to launch a purely technical attack or fashion a combined operation that uses internal and external Netspionage agents as well as software tools that are tailored to the target's systems, network, and applications.

The uncharted complexity of the extended virtual corporation, which may include numerous business partners, customers, vendors, suppliers and others, any or all of which may provide additional access pathways. These external corporation connections may reach into the core of the target corporation, or they may simply be intermediate repositories of the targeted information. It has often been said that information systems and network security are only as strong as the weakest link. Ensuring that the security perimeter links were adequately strong for core business units was always challenging. Now that the security perimeter links may include a pool of changing second and third parties, it may now encompass the protection perimeters of perhaps hundreds of closely allied corporations. And, of course, one should consider how those parties interact with their contractors, suppliers, vendors, etc. . . . so the chain of transitive vulnerability may actually be quite long.

Given the fact that risk elimination is not feasible, it is more practical to develop a risk management strategy that focuses on identifying whether the corporation is at high risk to this type of threat. If found to be at high risk then it is useful to assess whether baseline protective measures already exist. If the corporation has not even implemented the basic protection mechanisms, an opponent will never be deterred and may need only to employ the most basic means of attack in order to fulfill the need to obtain targeted information.

Determining Whether or Not a Corporation Is at Risk to Netspionage

To begin, it is important to understand the difference between technical vulnerability, which is a function of systems and operations, and the risk probability that an adversary will elect to use Netspionage in lieu of or as an adjunct to other means of collecting critical information about your corporation. Although nearly every corporation now has some degree of reliance on networks and systems, not every corporation is "blessed" with the combination of key digital assets exposure, ruthless competitors, and operational risks that align to make Netspionage a highly probable risk.

What Must Corporation's Do to Reduce Risks?

The most fundamental and essential step is to conduct an information protection assessment that considers the new implications of Netspionage. The purpose of such an assessment is threefold:

1. Identify the full range of important digital assets of the corporation including intellectual property, sensitive proprietary information,

trade secrets—especially any digital assets that are unique to the corporation. Determine where they are physically located, how they are created, which computer systems, servers, and networks store, process, and transmit the assets throughout their lifecycle.

2. Create a value matrix of the digital assets and determine their relative contribution to the corporation's business. Stratify them to identify the top tier, the ones of greatest significance. We generally refer to those that are the most important by the term "crown jewels." Although there is no precise formula for determining when a specific asset qualifies for such status, most senior managers and executives of a corporation can reach a rough consensus as to the items they can all agree are "crown jewels." Subsequent steps in the assessment should then focus on managing and reducing the risks to these, the most significant assets.

3. Review the existing framework for safeguarding the corporation's most valuable digital forms of intellectual property including trade secrets and sensitive proprietary information using an interdisciplinary team that can evaluate technical, operational, procedural, and legal protective measures. Consider how well the existing array of protective measures will defend the most critical resources against the multiple technologies and techniques that will be used by techno-spies if they are assigned the task of obtaining them.

The primary objective of the review called for in the third purpose is to ensure that the corporation has invested sufficiently in the integrated technical and operational security measures as well as a complete legal and procedural foundation to prevent, detect, and respond to known or suspected incidents of Netspionage.

In those corporations that have a known or suspected incident where Netspionage or other technique has resulted in loss of digital forms of business secrets or other proprietary information a two-pronged response is necessary. First, management must ensure that it makes a serious effort to determine all the discernable facts concerning the incident. Too often there is a tendency to either write off an incident as an isolated event or as the result of simple bad luck. Although both may be true, the opportunity also exists to gain valuable insights as to strengths and weaknesses in the existing protective program. The insights gleaned from such a detailed analysis may help prevent a future, and perhaps even more serious incident. Second, management will be better prepared to make informed decisions concerning steps to actively enforce the corporation's rights through litigation or prosecution, if it is armed with a complete report of the incident. Of course, such an analytical process presupposes the corporation has mechanisms to identify, and report known and suspected incidents in timely manner such that investigative response is possible.

Management must also consider that in order to get assistance from the FBI to investigate an incident of known or suspected Netspionage under the auspices of the Economic Espionage Act (EEA) there are several key hurdles they must overcome. How does the corporation know an incident (crime) has happened? Is the information a trade secret, and if so, was it protected consistent with its status (did the corporation take reasonable steps commensurate with the value of the asset) have they calculated the value of the asset and any associated losses? Although ability to answer these questions is not a prerequisite for contacting the FBI, expect the agents to ask for these and other details early in any official discussion concerning an incident. The topic of how to respond to incidents, including proper investigation protocol, goes well beyond the focus of this chapter. Suffice to say at this point that although the corporation has many options when it knows or suspects an incident, do not expect any public agency to come in and act as the internal security team for the corporation. The company must be prepared to conduct its own inquiries and should only approach law enforcement when management believes there is reasonable basis for suspicion that an incident has actually occurred, and weighed the pros and cons of reporting the incident.

A Sample Netspionage Risk Assessment

One way to determine whether a corporation is doing enough to protect itself is to conduct a formal risk analysis. The following framework, although not intended to be all-inclusive, can help the security or other managers frame the issues in the context of their own corporation and begin to tailor protection measures to the most important assets in their company. A basic risk matrix and questionnaire follows.

Risk Matrix

The following risk matrix helps identify those corporations that may be at increased risk of Netspionage theft or other losses of trade secrets, proprietary information, and other key intellectual properties. For each of the risk factors, the person or team conducting the assessment should decide whether the description applies. If the risk is generally applicable, the response should be affirmative. Bear in mind that "yes" answers will be interpreted to indicate that more risk will affect the corporation due to the impact of this factor. The more "yes" answers, the higher the likelihood that Netspionage or other means of illicit information gathering will be attempted against the corporation. A summary of why each of these factors is important follows the checklist.

Corporations are assessed to be at high risk under the Risk Matrix (see Figure 11–2) if they answer yes to 50 percent or more of the questions. Those with eight or fewer affirmative answers should consider themselves at low risk. There is no common standard for judging the adequacy of a corporation's Netspionage protection program.

However, our experience tells us that corporations that ignore or accept risks increase the possibility that they will be victimized. Failure to act responsibly in this area could result in otherwise preventable losses, with attendant adverse consequences on the bottom line performance of the company, not to mention stockholder lawsuits.

Selected Risk Factors	Yes or No?
1. Operations in more than one continent	
2. Distributed and decentralized computer and network infrastructure	
3. Internet connectivity generally available to the workforce	
4. National / international media profile	
5. National Security Threat List industry	
6. Multinational operations contribute substantial revenues (40%+)	
7. High level of collaboration with competitors	
8. Multiple significant foreign joint ventures	
9. Two or more major domestic joint ventures	
10. Major acquisition/merger in last 12 months	
11. Recent or projected downsizing	
12. Workforce turnover exceeds industry average	
13. Workforce is composed 40% or more of contractors, temporaries, consultants	
14. Operations or presence in High Risk Areas	
15. "High Tech" product(s) comprise significant portion of annual revenues	
16. Breakthrough product(s), and/or services	
17. Benchmark level business processes	
18. Top 10% industry rank	
19. No competitive intelligence program	
20. Extensive reliance on computers in product design, development, delivery	
21. Knowledge based business	
22. Limited physical security program	
23. No formal protection of proprietary information program	
24. There have been prior attempts in the industry to steal secrets	
25. Past attempts to steal the corporations information	
26. R&D is substantial portion of Revenues or Total R&D exceeds industry average	
27. Partnering is a major aspect of the business	
28. Overseas business partners	
29. Manufacturing is totally or in significant part outsourced	
30. No formal information systems security program	
31. Significant e-business or e-commerce operations	

Figure 11–2 A questionnaire to conduct a limited risk survey.

Descriptions

1. *Operations in more than one continent*: Global corporations are by definition operating in different continents where there are likely to be differences in culture, ethics, and standards of business conduct and staff loyalty that often result in different attitudes and methods of handling and protecting critical information.

2. *Distributed and decentralized computer and network infrastructure*: Allocating computing and network systems to individual business units complicate systems administration and makes it difficult to achieve and sustain a consistent uniform and reliable standard for security measures.

3. *Internet connectivity generally available to the workforce*: Providing Internet access to all staff members makes it easy for them to upload sensitive information or to download hacker software, tools. They are also able to accidentally or deliberately transfer key digital assets to unauthorized or inappropriate locations and persons.

4. *National/international media profile*: Prominent corporations that receive media coverage become more visible to opposition managers who plan collection efforts. The media coverage itself may assist in targeting if it discloses specific locations, individuals, or even systems for exploitation if they are identified as the source of the desired information.

5. *National security threat list industry*: The FBI has identified a series of technologies in which the United States leads the world. Companies in these industries have and will be targeted by both commercial and national foreign intelligence agencies for both economic and industrial espionage.

6. *Multinational operations contribute substantial revenue (40%+)*: Multinational operations indicate a corporation that has substantial presence in one or more foreign countries, which in today's global economy is very common. Unless there are rigorous internal network and operational security measures, these locations may provide access points that will be penetrated by foreign intelligence agents or techno-spies to gain access to the corporate "crown jewels."

7. *High level of collaboration with competitors*: The situation where competitors may be collaborators in some products or market segments or in which competitors share common suppliers for key subassemblies or components. The risk here is that the opponents will exploit the close and continuing relationship between the parties to obtain access to information that is not included in the authorized relationship. The classic example of this is where the competing corporation has a contract with Division 1 for product A and uses its liaison staff stationed at the Division 1 location to seek critical information concerning product B produced by Division 2. In the past such collection would probably have relied upon lunch conversations or after-hours wandering. In cases where common suppliers exist, the staff may be queried or convinced to provide periodic reporting on the information they obtain concerning the target corporation.

8. *Multiple significant foreign joint ventures*: Joint ventures carry with them the risk that the partners in one area may also be competitors or allied with competitors in other areas. In cases where employees of the joint venture have physical access to the facilities or electronic networks of the core corporation there is a good chance they may exploit the access to seek out information for other purposes.

9. *Two or more major domestic joint ventures*: When corporations have many major joint ventures it tends to exacerbate the challenge of safeguarding the crown jewels of the enterprise against an influx of outsiders. Whether granted physical or virtual access these outsiders may share common interests for only a short time. However, they, like the foreign joint venture partners described above, may either be competing with the core corporation in other areas or they may be closely allied with other corporations who are in competition.

10. *Major acquisition/merger in last 12 months*: In the frenzy to grow and survive in a global marketplace, mergers and acquisitions are a fact of contemporary business life. From personal experience, we can testify to the psychological turmoil and instability that such events create for staff of the affected corporations. Even when there really are compelling business advantages to the merger, they inevitably change everything: status, responsibility, power, and influence, and thus create increased uncertainty about the future. Such uncertainty can lead employees, even those at relatively senior levels, to conclude that they are justified in taking or selling key assets, including perhaps the digital resources that have significant value.

11. *Recent or projected downsizing*: Downsizing and outsourcing even the term "right sizing" are a common result of the mergers and acquisitions and represent an ultimate form of change. An end to the employment relationship due to cutbacks or layoffs to eliminate redundant employees or other efforts to drive costs out of the value chain by transferring responsibilities to other corporations. When people lose their jobs, many tend to adopt lifeboat ethics and will take whatever they can in order to keep themselves afloat.

12. *Workforce turnover exceeds industry average*: A turnover rate that exceeds the industry average indicates the company has difficulty in sustaining employee loyalty, which increases the possibility that the mobile workforce will take along whatever valuable and useful information to which they have had access during what may have been a short period of employment. It also means an unethical competitor willing to insert a Netspionage agent into the real or virtual corporation may have many opportunities to do so.

13. *Workforce is composed of 40% or more of contractors, tempo-raries, consultants*: A larger contingent workforce has several con-sequences that are favorable for Netspionage. As with high turnover, it facilitates placement of penetration agents under the cover of temporary or contract staff into the target corporation. It also means there is more chance that existing security protocols may be unknown to the temporary or contract staff, or they may lack motivation or sufficient experience to identify or report suspi-cious or unusual events.

14. *Operations or presence in high-risk areas*: High-risk areas are those places in the world where there has been a substantial break-down in general social order. Local law enforcement may be cor-rupt, ineffective, or nonexistent. In such locations, incidents of every type are likely to be more common, and the penetration of systems and computers will be no exception.[1]

15. *High-tech product(s) comprise significant portion of annual rev-enues*: High-technology products by definition derive significant portion of their value from the technology features. These features increasingly derive their functionality from software and other dig-ital techniques. These digital elements are the very ones that are at greatest risk of theft using Netspionage techniques since they may be copied and transmitted most efficiently.

16. *Breakthrough product(s), and/or services*: Breakthrough products, those that incorporate revolutionary new features, functionality, or offer an order of magnitude improvement over alternatives, are natural candidates for Netspionage. The commercial profitability that may be achieved by stealing someone else's breakthrough has been motivation for industrial thievery at least since Eli Whitney stole the secrets of the cotton gin and brought it to the fledgling United States.

17. *Benchmark level business processes*: Benchmark level business processes means that the corporation is one that is considered to have best in class processes such that it will be considered to be the trendsetter for the industry.

18. *Top 10% industry rank*: Top 10 percent industry rank demon-strates that the company has products or services that have allowed it to attain a preeminent position. However, when a com-pany is number one, there is increased chance that the management of one or more of the others may be tempted to use extreme means to attain parity. This is especially true in situations where the com-pany has displaced a long-standing industry leader. Such former leaders may have managers willing to accept greater risks in order to regain the lost glory of their former position.

---

[1]"High Tech Criminals Flourish in Developing Nations," Inter Press Service reported on WJIN Web site http://www.wjin.org.

19. *No competitive intelligence program*: The absence of a competitive intelligence program contributes to corporation blindness. Unless the managers of the company are well informed and current on competitors, they may not notice anomalies or suspicious circumstances that could indicate loss or theft of key information assets. An ethical competitive intelligence program helps defend the corporation by identifying discontinuous leaps in competitor capabilities that could indicate sudden acquisition of key information perhaps stolen from the company.

20. *Extensive reliance on computers in product design, development, delivery*: Extensive reliance on computers in product design, development, and delivery means the key elements of the product will be in digital form(s) in many stages of the product lifecycle. The failure to ensure consistent protection in many environments could result in increased vulnerability to Netspionage attacks.

21. *Knowledge-based business*: Knowledge-based business is when products or services rely on the skill and experience of the individual employees.

22. *Limited physical security program*: Limited physical security program indicates incomplete or inadequate measures have been taken to control access to facilities and resources owned and/or operated by the corporation. At a minimum, the company requires strong controls on visitors and off-hours access to those areas that contain the sensitive proprietary information, trade secrets, and the information systems and network components that support them.

23. *No formal protection of proprietary information program*: No formal protection of proprietary information program means the company does not have a program that is focused on identifying and securing the sensitive information of the corporation against loss, theft, and disclosure, regardless of media.

24. *There have been prior attempts in the industry to steal secrets*: There have been prior attempts in the industry to steal secrets means that in the past five years there have been at least one or more incidents within the industry to steal business secrets. The incidents need not have been publicized, but are probably known to managers and executives in many companies in the industry.

25. *Past attempts to steal the corporation's information*: Past attempts to steal the corporation's information describes situations where the managers know, even if they cannot prove it in a court of law, that the company has lost sensitive information to competitors.

26. *Research & Development is substantial portion of revenues or total R&D exceeds industry average*: R&D is substantial portion of revenues or total R&D exceeds industry average means the company creates lots of new digital intellectual property.

27. *Partnering is a major aspect of business*: Partnering is a major aspect of the business thus more individuals have access and control over the crown jewels of the business.

28. *Overseas business partners*: Overseas business partners may cause additional risk, as their loyalties may be contrary to those of the other partner(s) of other nationalities.

29. *Manufacturing is totally or in significant part outsourced*: Manufacturing is totally, or in significant part, outsourced, thus more at risk to nonemployees.

30. *No formal information systems security program*: No formal information systems security program means that you won't even know when you are attacked, and if attacked no process for responding.

31. *Significant e-business or e-commerced operations*: Significant e-business or e-commerce operations means greater risks in the global marketplace because of greater visibility and access possible by Netspionage agents.

Risk Management Evaluation

The following questions will help clarify whether the corporation is exercising reasonable diligence in protecting trade secrets and digital forms of intellectual property:

1. Has the corporation performed a formal review and risk analysis that addresses the potential for network enabled attempts to steal digital forms of sensitive information?

2. Did the review include valuation of sensitive information?

3. Have the existing protection and security measures been sufficient and tested to ensure the corporation has not experienced any known or suspected losses of sensitive information to unauthorized access or use of computers, networks, or systems in the past three years?

4. Does the corporation include specific contractual requirements or obligations in the terms and conditions presented to key customers or business partners to protect the corporation's digital forms of sensitive information?

5. Does management take active steps to safeguard current operations to reduce the risks of network-enabled thefts or misappropriation of digital forms sensitive information?

6. Has the corporation taken special steps to reduce the potential for loss or compromise of sensitive information that could prevent or impede the production or development of critical new products or services?

7. Does the corporation's insurance (general insurance, separate proprietary information, or intellectual property protection policy) provide coverage for digital forms of sensitive information (investigations, infringement, counterfeit, litigation, etc.)?

8. Does the corporation have policies and procedures that address the identification, protection, and proper destruction of all electronic storage media containing sensitive digital information and other valuable proprietary information?

9. Is someone specifically assigned responsibility for developing and enforcing policies, standards, and procedures to protect the corporation's key digital assets to include sensitive information?

10. Has the corporation considered the impact on sensitive information protection in all projects that involve additions, modifications, or extensions to existing computer and network infrastructures?

11. Does the corporation have procedures for tracking and responding to all known or suspected attempts to obtain sensitive information and other confidential proprietary information?

12. Do corporation mechanisms for tracking and responding to known or suspected attempts to obtain sensitive information integrate all available sources of incidents' information, e.g., are network and system incident tracking, monitoring, and reporting mechanisms integrated with physical, legal, and operations incident data in one incident tracking and response system?

The above set of questions is not exhaustive, however it provides a foundation, which readers may adapt, refine, or extend. The objective of this effort is for corporate management to craft a self-assessment process for evaluating the corporation's overall vulnerability to Netspionage and other forms of information theft. The deliverable from this exercise should be a report that provides meaningful information to senior management concerning the corporation's degree of readiness to prevent, detect, and respond to situations that may involve the theft of the critical digital assets of the enterprise. In each of the above questions the "yes" answers and supporting justifications are considered efforts to manage and reduce risks, while "no" answers indicate a risk that is not effectively addressed.

It is important that the person responsible for evaluating the protection program of the corporation create a framework that can be adapted to deal with the wide range of assets, resources, and threats that are created when digital assets are operated in the global networked environment.

The risk profile self-assessment should be completed with senior or executive management at every primary location where the corporation creates, stores, or processes key digital assets. It is vital in this process to include representatives of the corporation law department or

General Counsel's office. Although corporation lawyers are important, they must not be the only executives consulted.

For each of the 12 questions, summarize the answers in the report. If the majority of the Risk Matrix answers are "yes," and the majority of Risk Management Questionnaire answers are "no," then the corporation is at significant risk of a Netspionage attack. In that case, one should take at least immediate steps to reduce the potential for loss of sensitive information.

Summary

OPSEC and a proactive, common sense Netspionage risk management program is required in order to mitigate the risks of Netspionage. Basic and cost-effective techniques can, and should, be used. You must know the global marketplace, your competition, the threats to your competitive edge, and the risks. Then one can make logical and cost-effective decisions to safeguard the corporation's sensitive information from others. Methods to perform a self-assessment can help proactively determine the level of risk to your corporation to Netspionage attacks.

12

The Best Defense May Really Be a Good Offense and Other Issues

To summarize thus far, the world is rapidly changing due to technology leading to today's global marketplace. Competition amongst corporations is becoming so fierce it can be called business warfare. Governments see that world power requires economic power. Thus, many are supporting their national corporations any way they can. International treaties and laws cannot keep up with these changes, especially when hindered by the politics of the nation-states. So, the global marketplace is ripe for Netspionage.

For a corporation that is competing in the global marketplace that would appear to be bad enough, but it gets worse. When these corporations are attacked, they often call law enforcement for help. There is an increasing belief that corporations cannot depend on law enforcement or other government agencies to protect them from Netspionage agents and techno-spies, nor do an adequate job of investigating such matters. Although many, at the national level especially, talk a good game, they can't deliver. While at the same time, U.S. local law enforcement officers often say "it's a federal matter, call the FBI."

So, here we have it; corporations fighting for a competitive advantage or maybe their survival in the global marketplace. They are being attacked, while law enforcement is outgunned and outmaneuvered, and prioritizing their resources against drugs and violent crimes. What are corporations saying about all this? Well, as Winn Schwartau stated in his new book, *Cybershock*, when discussing the recurring theme amongst many top corporations—and government agencies, "We're mad as hell, and we're not going to take it anymore." So what's the answer? Many are turning to the old United States "Wild West" response to lawlessness—vigilantism.

Hired Guns and Vigilantes

The inability of law enforcement around the globe to effectively combat Netspionage attacks in our information-driven world leaves the defense of valuable information-related assets to the corporations themselves.

Some corporations in various countries are doing little to prevent these attacks. Then when they are successfully attacked, they turn to some outside hired-gun to investigate the incident and/or fix their problems. Looking at some of these so-called experts selling their services, one wonders who the real bandits are in this information age.

More than ever, corporations are turning to these hired guns without thoroughly checking their experience level and background. Some may be convicted hackers who are felons. Can they be trusted? Some probably can while others probably cannot. How do you know the difference? The corporations often don't verify the credentials of the consultants they hire. Some may work for several competitors at the same time. However, they do not see any conflict of interest in these multiple contracts. They sell their services just as the snake oil salesmen of the old "Wild West" days in the United States or the old fashioned used car salespeople.

In many information age nations of the world, businesses in particular are relying on what was formerly their external accounting firms to take care of their sensitive information protection needs and defend the corporation against Netspionage agents. Why does the external firm make the leap from accounting to security to Netspionage and techno-spy prevention? It's simple, there's money in it.

For the last several decades in the United States and other nations of the world, the slow economy coupled with increased computer power leading to more automation, caused the reengineering, process improvement restructuring, and mass downsizing. "Downsizing" is another word for getting fired, but sounds nicer. So, if you weren't directly involved in building the corporation's "widget" product, you were downsized.

This meant that those individuals classified as "unnecessary" overhead were let go, to include many security and audit personnel. Allegedly, in the United States, the federal government's Securities Exchange Commission (SEC) looked at many of these stockholder-owned corporations and said that the stockholders interests were not being protected.

Executive management did not want to rehire these auditors and security people. They decided that since the accounting firms were already "safeguarding" the interest of the stockholders through their accounting-audits, why not let them also do security functions such as information systems security—amazing how little management knows about the differences between auditors and security personnel.

These international accounting firms were not the type of firms to turn down the extra money. Thus, they begin by using primarily auditors and information technology people to do information systems security. If Netspionage agents and techno-spies attack the corporate networks, these same people are rushed in to defend the corporation. If you are a corporate manager, have you ever wondered why your corporate systems continue to be vulnerable and successfully attacked? Maybe, the wrong people were hired to do the wrong job. Thus, businesses are now being charged, at great expense, for this additional service. Are these firms doing an adequate job?

The main problem with these types of hired guns is that the partners whose backgrounds are those of accountants and auditors are still directing them. Sorry, but it's two different professions requiring different experiences and techniques. Audit controls do not equal security controls, and security controls don't equate to preventing Netspionage (although they do have some processes and techniques in common).

Why are they doing this and why do they fail to hire the right people? It is simple. These partners do not want to abdicate their power or share it with others. They look upon information systems security (InfoSec) people and high-technology crime investigative professionals as only "cops with badges and guns." So, they fail to hire the right people. If they do hire the right people, they fail to support them. Also, when a big client needs help developing a sensitive information protection program, they go instead of sending the real professional. Not only can they then do their marketing, but they also can charge the client more money. And what does the client get? A large bill and a generic program lacking a realistic and client-tailored proactive approach. Then there are those who hire firms employing "ethical hackers." Oh please! What does that mean anyway?

Are these hired guns worth the money—usually not. To catch a Netspionage agent or techno-spy one must think like one. Accountants, InfoSec people, and auditors don't understand the mind of the spy. They know controls and compliance. Some can't imagine how to circumvent a system, yet they are expected to recommend controls that prevent Netspionage agents from doing just that.

In addition, to establish, implement, and maintain a successful sensitive information protection program, one must also understand the business processes, culture, information communication channels, the employees, the personalities of the key people, and the like. This is not something that can be learned or truly experienced in 30 days or a six-month contract. It can only be learned by an employee who works in that business environment day after day. You want a quick and dirty fix, you get it but it probably doesn't solve the systemic problems. For the long term, it is also more costly. One wonders if some of these consultants would be selling used cars if we were not in the information age.

So, what is a corporation to do? There appears to be a growing number of businesses and government agencies who have found that they cannot rely on the "local sheriffs and their posses of hired guns" to adequately address their problem. Therefore, some are defending their information assets by hiring and/or employing a different breed of hired gun—the bounty hunter. These folks are hired to seek out and counterattack those that have attacked the corporation. This vigilante approach may be expected to grow as attacks on businesses and government increase. Not a bad idea—pay someone to track down and deal with the miscreants attacking your system, or is it?

Most of those in the criminal justice system of a nation frown upon vigilante techniques. Those using such techniques are chastised for taking the law into their own hands. One dictionary describes a vigilante as ". . . independent of the law working to suppress crime." The key is "to suppress crime." Others argue that one must let law enforcement do it. One must work within the criminal justice system. However, we all know that it is not working very well, and while working within the system, businesses and government agencies are being attacked with relative impunity. Do the ends justify the means? That has been debated by scholars for decades. However, businesses and government agencies don't have decades. They only have nanoseconds.

So, what's the answer? Some believe that it's actually very simple. Hire good people as corporate employees with the expertise necessary to defend and protect the corporate digital assets, and give them the support and tools to do their jobs. There's some very good security hardware and software available today. That coupled with good policies, procedures, awareness program, and risk analyses—back to the basics—and your chances of being successfully attacked are greatly reduced. And if attacked, strike back? Is it time to go back to the ancient concept of an "eye for an eye?" Is it worth it? Maybe it is if you're going to rely on Internet, intranets, and the global information infrastructure for your e-commerce, and the future success of your business in the global marketplace.

Today, this is a controversial subject and, of course, any smart corporation will not discuss it or admit to anything related to attacking in self-defense, and well they shouldn't. At least in the United States, they would undoubtedly be the topic of national and local news for doing so, not to mention many lawyers suing them in the name of some poor innocent Net surfer who was the subject of an unprovoked attack by this massive corporation. No one can win those battles.

There is sufficient evidence to believe that the U.S. military, whose computers in such targeted places at the Pentagon have been under global attack for years, have already started to counterattack. Allegedly, when the "Electronic Disturbance Theater" attacked the Pentagon systems, they were the target of denial of service attacks.[1] Of course, that is what some sources have said, as the Pentagon folks

---

[1]www.nwfusion.com.

aren't talking. There are indications that corporations are quietly doing the same thing or worse.[2]

Winn Schwartau believes that corporations are developing "hostile perimeters: if you don't belong here, we're going to knock you back—hard—and maybe into unconscious." He states *we are beginning to see offensive products make their way to corporate tool kits. But in any case, the legal challenges that coexist with Hostile Perimeters and counteroffensive defense are daunting. The astute company will examine every aspect of its posture before marching down the slippery slope of vigilantism.*

An informal survey conducted by Mr. Schwartau disclosed that 44 percent of the respondents said that corporations should respond by counterattacking their attackers; while 30 percent did not, and 26 percent stated "maybe/sometime."[3] A CNN quickvote poll published January 12, 1999, asked, "What should be the proper response to a cyber attack?" Eighty-two percent of the respondents (6,334 votes) stated to retaliate in kind; 15 percent (1,153 votes) said that the attack should be reported to law enforcement; and 5 percent (269 votes) said to ignore the attack.

According to one source, a 1999 survey in Australia identified 65 percent saying they supported/condoned vigilantism.

Here's one of the major challenges to counterattacking as a defensive measure: When a government agency or business computer system is attacked, the response to such an attack should be based on the attacker threat. Who is the attacker? What does the attacker want? Is the attacker an ordinary hacker, phreaker, cracker, or just someone breaking in for fun? Is the attacker an employee of a business competitor, in the case of an attack on a business system, or a terrorist, or a government agency-sponsored attack for economic reasons? Is the attacker a foreign soldier attacking the system as a prelude to war?

These questions require serious consideration when information systems are being attacked, because the answers dictate the appropriate response. Would a nation-state attack a country because of what a terrorist or economic spy did to a business or government system? Would a corporation attack another nation-states' computer systems that were being used by the attacker? What would be the response of that nation-state, especially if the corporation did business in that country? To complicate the matter, what if the attacker was in a third country but only made it look like he/she was coming from your potential competitor? How do you know?

---

[2]More information on this topic can be found in Mr. Schwartau's new book, *Cybershock*, Thunder Mouth Press, 2000.

[3]See www.infowar.com; www.nwfusion; www.cnn.com.

Hackers: Freedom Fighters of the 21st Century, Netspionage Agents, Techno-Spies, or Defenders of the Global Corporations, and Other Thoughts

What about defending the corporation and its employees from the power of those governments who may want to take away the freedom of the foreign corporation to do business in a free global marketplace. Well, there are some who believe that maybe the hacker will be the 21st century equivalent of the freedom fighters of the 20th century.

Most security and law enforcement people look upon hackers as the archenemy of the 20th and 21st century. This view is also supported by the news media. In their interest to sell, sell, sell, the news media have made the term "hacker" synonymous with anything from juvenile delinquents to mass murderers and even linked them to the information age equivalent of the nuclear bomb in their ability to destroy the information-based world as we know it. New draconian laws have been written in countries around the world to support the investigation, apprehension, prosecution, incarceration, and, in some cases, execution of these "vicious and violent" threats to societies and mankind itself.

The original definition of the term "hacker" and the original goal of the hacker, basically a computer enthusiast whose goal is learning all they could about computers and making them the most efficient machines possible to support mankind and his search of knowledge, has sadly been manipulated, modified, destroyed, erased, and/or deleted. Let's separate hackers from the Netspionage agents, techno-spies, basic criminals, and others that defraud users, damage, steal, and otherwise destroy systems and information for fun.

To understand this, let's look at what is happening today and the trends that forecast tomorrow. There are miscreants, juvenile delinquents, and wannabe's out there causing us some grief. The folks changing Web sites are like the graffiti writers defacing the walls and highways of our cities. The only difference is that these guys with the paint can't afford a computer, only paint spray. Others are stealing and destroying computer-based information, modifying it, and denying access to the systems that store, process, and transmit that information.

The corporate manager may think that all those attacks are a government problem and don't impact the corporation. It's not a business problem. However, it is when they are stealing your corporation information by passing through the weakly defended government systems to attack your systems while remaining anonymous through the government site. On the other hand, where your system is the weakly defended system that they are going through to conduct Netspionage on government systems, you are involved.

Wait! That's not bad enough. We also have the United States government and other civilized, information-based nations using these threats as an excuse to gain more power, more control over our lives.

The U.S. Secretary of Defense was quoted a year or so ago, allegedly said that "if Americans want more security they will have to give up some of their freedoms." Wait! It gets worse. Look at Intel's Pentium III chip that can allegedly provide government agents and others the chip serial numbers of a user's computer without their knowledge, and thus allow monitoring, tracing, and trapping of user's communications.

Also, look at similar activities by Microsoft, Novell's balanced approach, and don't forget this does not include the alleged classified contracts and programs that government agencies have with vendors for providing covert backdoors. And we won't discuss the encryption fiasco with the FBI trying to protect us from—who was that again? The FBI Director wanting ISP's to give them information about users at their request. Oh, but you say a search warrant is required, probable cause, etc. Some judges are more liberal and pro-law enforcement than others. In other nations, it is easier yet. Add to all this the newest President Clinton push to allow theft of encryption keys and passwords by covertly conducting searches of a corporation or person—of course with a search warrant. However, search warrants are easy to obtain with a little judge shopping. Even if done legally, how can a corporation that was the subject of a covert search be assured that the corporation's encryption keys and passwords are safeguarded and don't end up in court records for example. If the case is not prosecuted, the security of your systems has still been compromised—and worst of all, you don't know it.

The excuse being used by the federal agencies for more power and control is the protection of the information infrastructure of a nation. Wait a minute! Isn't most, if not all of that, privately owned? Look at Russian's SORM, and alleged Chinese attacks against a U.S. Web site devoted to the Falun Gong sect. If true, then has China attacked the United States? It certainly has attacked a legitimate association or business on United States' soil. Can China do the same to a foreign corporation they don't like or one that they want to squeeze some concessions from? Who will stop them? Will the United States government support your corporation and its fight against China if such an event occurred? Look at the government track record and especially current administration's track record in dealing with other Chinese threats, and you should have serious questions.

Do the Chinese have such plans? One never knows. However, their history and every indication noted in their writings on information warfare makes one believe that they will do anything to anyone that furthers their cause. Remember that a communist form of government believes that what supports communism is morally right and what doesn't support communism is morally wrong. You may be thinking that this is old Cold War rhetoric. We wish it was so, but our research indicates otherwise. The corporate manager who doesn't believe this is not only naïve, but also taking risks because they will not support information protection programs that meet the threats. Thus, the corporation's sensitive information will incur an increased level of risk.

Look also at other nations' attempts at spying on Internet users, monitoring and controlling the Internet and their citizen's use of it. This includes the communications between your customers, suppliers, and associates, and your corporation.

In the United States, the Clinton administration plans to create a government-wide security network of electronic obstacles complete with monitors and analyzers to watch for potentially suspicious activity on federal computer systems. Who will define "potentially suspicious activity?" Add to that Janet Reno, the U.S. Attorney General, pressuring other nations to restrict, curb, and/or otherwise control encryption products. The reason is obvious, to allow the government to read other people's e-mail. What would that mean for your corporation's mail? It means your encrypted, sensitive information can be read by government agencies, and probably others.

As we all know, everyone has a price. What if some government bureaucrat had access to that sensitive corporate e-mail and for a price, provided it to your competitor? You may say that the competitor would never accept it because management would know that such action was illegal. That is not a deterrent, and if the competitor was a foreign business, the laws may not apply. If they did apply, how could they be enforced in a foreign country?

As we all know, government employees do not all stay in government service forever. What better way as an entrée to employment with your competitor than to give them possibly years of information gleaned through reading your e-mails, after all, your former employees probably already do it.

President Ronald Reagan once called the Nicaraguan rebels "freedom fighters," while their government called them criminals and terrorists. The same dichotomy holds true throughout the world. Those in power want to keep it and make the rules. Those that are left out of the governmental process want their voices to be heard; thus, conflict. As the nation-state begins to have less importance, its employees will fight to keep their power and conflicts will rise at the expense of personal liberties. The global hacker community, although often misguided as to worthwhile objectives in their attacks, are at least beginning to establish better communication lines amongst themselves.

The hackers of the world are using the Internet to communicate and attack systems on a global scale. Many of the attacks are aimed at totalitarian governments, government agencies, political parties, against the slaughter of animals for their fur (by attacking and defacing at least one furrier's Web site), all of which can be considered politically-motivated attacks. These are the worst kind and most feared by nation-states. The mounted attacks by global hackers, based on a "call to arms" by hackers, against the government of Indonesia's Web sites is an example of what they can do and more importantly what is yet to come. These same forces can be used as a "hired gun" by your corporation, your competitor (maybe both at the same time), government agencies, political groups and associations. All it takes is finding the right person with the right experience, with the right motivation, at the right price. Should your corporation use vigilante tactics and hire bounty hunters? It is something to think about. Note: John F. Quinn suggests that one may want to use OPSEC principles to weight the risk of a cyber-vigilante operation.

Summary

Strikeback (cyber vigilantism) and vigilantism will increase if government and law enforcement don't effectively support the business community with business friendly legislation, proactive protection, and investigation. No corporation is willing to have its Internet and e-commerce-related vulnerabilities aired in court because it will lead to loss of investor and customer confidence and may lead to shareholder lawsuits because the company wasn't diligent in following best practices. Therefore, there will be a reluctance of corporations to report Netspionage to law enforcement, further exacerbating the problem.

As with nuclear weapons used as a form of deterrent, in the future, counterattacking information weapons systems may be the basis of the deterrent. However, one must be very careful. While at the same time, corporate management must remember that it is bad enough being attacked, but it is worse to be attacked and not know it until it is too late. The key to fighting Netspionage is the establishment and maintenance of an aggressive sensitive information protection program. All these factors must be weighed before counterattacking through vigilante tactics and the hired bounty hunter.

Section IV: Based on Where We Have Been and Where We Are Now, Where Are We Going?

This section provides a short overview of the possible things to come based on the trends of the past. Someone once said, "You don't know where you are going, if you don't know where you've been." In this book, we have looked at the past and the present. Hopefully, that view provides some trends to indicate where we are going.

Chapter 13: Future of Technology

Based on today's technology, there are trends that indicate the technology changes that will be taking place and impacting businesses on a global scale in the 21st century. This chapter will look at those trends and make some "best guesses" about what this 21st century technology will look like and how these trends will impact the potential vulnerability of corporations to both legal competitive intelligence as well as Netspionage and other forms of espionage.

Chapter 14: Business, Crime, and Security in the 21st Century Global Marketplace

This chapter will project into the future and envision the early 21st century business environment incorporating technological changes, social changes, and governmental changes.

Chapter 15: Future Netspionage

This chapter will look at the early 21st century drivers for Netspionage, and discuss the new dangers and their impact on businesses, society, national, and global economies. How, why, and where the well-equipped Netspionage operative will exist and their likely contribution to future conflicts between nation-states and businesses will be explored.

Chapter 16: Businesses and Governments Agencies—Shared Responsibilities

This chapter will discuss the adversarial relationships between United States' businesses and government agencies, and how this has hampered our ability to compete globally. We will suggest what must be done in a joint, cooperative effort to help win the global economic war that is already increasingly intense.

Chapter 17: Epilog: We're All in This Together

Final comments by the authors on the entire topic of Netspionage, and the critical importance of an integrated information collection and protection program to survival and success in the next 20 years of business to gain and sustain the competitive edge for corporations.

C h a p t e r

13

Future of Technology

High-Technology, Pushing Us into the Future[1]

As alluded to throughout this book, technology, which in this era is based on telecommunications and computers, is the driving force of practically every device, piece of equipment, machine, and the like. These technological devices have within them a brain, and that is the microprocessor. It is in fact the computer.

The microprocessor runs the processes of our government agencies, businesses, and it often seems that they also run our lives. This little silicon chip is the central processing unit of all computer life as we know it. It has grown exponentially in power and flexibility while at the same time, it has exponentially decreased in size and price. This trend is expected to continue for the foreseeable future. Pundits have said and continue to say that this little, silicon chip computer will soon be reaching its physical limits.

They say that miniaturization can only go so small and eventually heat factors and other factors known only to God and physics majors will cause the chip to hit a technological advancements brick wall. Such may be the case. Yeah, right, and people aren't supposed to fly, humans can't go to the moon or survive in space.

As with any topic, there are always different, and usually opposite, opinions. If this pessimistic view were to be believed, then we will shortly be reaching that brick wall. If that happens, what is the worst case scenario? The power of the chip would probably not stop the further development of the "sugar cube" storage devices, more memory, faster telecommunications, and continuously declining prices. However, if such a brick wall was hit, would high technology progress stop? No, it won't even slow down because as chip mak-

---

[1]This chapter includes excerpts taken from our book, *High-Technology Crime Investigator's Handbook: Working in the Information Environment*, also published by Butterworth–Heinemann.

ers are cranking out those little beasts, their research and development folks coupled with university laboratories, think tanks and the like are looking for new materials to replace silicon. So, progress would, and will, continue.

Maybe such a breather in this fast-paced development would be a good deal for all of us. Time could be taken to make computers user-friendly and write bug-free software code. We could take time to concentrate on putting the computers to better use in a more focused effort to actually relieve people of more of life's burdens while at the same time increasing everyone's quality of life. Is that realistic? No, because the technology industry, in order to survive, must continue to improve. The chip race between the leading chipmakers is similar to a space race or drag race. Everyone is looking for more speed more power. On the optimistic side of breaking the physics or physical brick wall, there are those who continue to find innovative ways to get more speed and power out of those little chips.

Amoebae Power!

The future may also bring us biological computers. For example, it is rumored that some are even looking at using electrically charged amoebas or other methods that can allow a direct interface with the human brain! Such incredibly advanced computers could perhaps store the entire history of the human race on a single chip. Who will determine what is contained in that history? What are the social ramifications of such dramatic extensions to personal information access? What happens if a criminal or a terrorist embeds a virus, logic bomb, or other malicious software in a computer extension attached to your brain?

If you remember from your biology classes, amoebas are little one-celled animals that like to especially hang out in water. As long ago as the 1970s, some have thought of electrically charging them—positive charge for the binary "1" and a negative charge for the binary "0" digit. Is this possible or fiction? We won't know until it happens.

However, in the United States, this may not be possible because these little buggers may fall under the umbrella of some lawyer or animal rights activists who make it their personal objective to protect these "sweet little creatures" from the evil of humans trying to use them as slaves. Sound far-fetched? Think about it, and when you hear of the formation of the "The Society for the Rights of the Amoebae," remember that we told you so.

Since information is power, who will decide what goes in those brain-attached storage devices full of information? Who can afford them? If information is power, will only the rich and powerful be able to have these devices? What will that do to our social structure? Does that mean that children, prior to leaving the hospital or laboratory after being born, will have such a microprocessor embedded in their body and surgically connected to their brain? Will this, at birth, then give them total knowledge as we know it with their only learning need is to learn how to properly use and access the information? Imagine the new knowledge that can come from starting off at that level at birth and then expanding from there.

In the United States, we are quickly reaching the point that not having access to a computer connected to the Global Information Infrastructure (GII), Internet, and National Information Infrastructure (NII), immediately places an individual at such a basic disadvantage that it might be seen as a violation of one's civil rights. Today, some are beginning to call this computer gap between the have-and-have not society the "digital divide." Even though it is estimated that only about 40 percent of the population have a computer, that number is quickly rising. As that disadvantage grows, a computer with appropriate Internet accesses may be dispensed to those who can not afford one.

Integration of Today's Technologies Tomorrow

The key word is integration. When discussing integration, one can look back and see that these have been logical steps in the evolution of high-technology. It seems that it is almost inevitable that these high technology devices would expand their scope of options as the microprocessors became more powerful, smaller, and cheaper.

The entire business of high-technology fueling the fire that created the GII, Internet, NII, intranets, cellular telephones, pagers, and private branch exchange was, is, and will be done for one very simple reason: to communicate information in one form or another. One form or another means transmitting information in the form of voice, video, and data.

In the future, this will all be integrated into one portable, wireless device, as technology is able to improve on bandwidth and correct other deficiencies that limit our ability to share information in a totally integrated form at high speeds. We are in the crawling stages of this integration process, but the 21st century will see us quickly move to walking, jogging, and then running at speeds only talked about in science fiction novels.

While all that is going on, our cable televisions will be sold as completely integrated units with the built-in intranets and Internet accesses—actually, GII accesses, to include telephones. After all, we can now make telephone calls via the Internet, albeit not as clear and user-friendly as we would like, but it is getting better. With mergers and talks of mergers between Internet corporations such as America Online (AOL), and content companies like Time Warner, we see the beginning of the future. The Internet is about communicating information through e-mail and Web sites. Time Warner is about entertainment. Combining the Internet and entertainment fields will change the way we communicate and are entertained.

We see other hints of major communications changes coming now in the form of integration of services from several devices into one. One now wears a watch, often carries a pager and cellular telephone. We now see the pager and cellular phone devices being integrated into the cellular phone. However, these are not the large, bulky cellular phones available at a big price only several years ago. These new cellular phones are now digital, the size of the pagers. As the global personal communications services (PCS) come online and their costs come down to wired-phone levels, there will be a tremendous, exponential increase in their use by the ordinary citizens of the world. Already one cellular telephone corporation has predicted that by 2002, there will be as many cellular phones in the world as wired telephones.

The "wireless age" is already upon us and with it the increased use of technology allowing mobile electronic communications from any place on earth to anywhere. Wired telephones will soon be a thing of the past as we each will have our own telecommunications number regardless of the device we are using, just as we in the United States each have our own, unique social security number. Wireless technology is already being used extensively in other parts of the world such as for telecommunications in Asia. Why build a wired telecommunications infrastructure at great expense when wireless systems in the future will be faster, cheaper, more flexible, and more modern? For example, try building such a wired system across more than 17,000 islands that make up Indonesia.

However, that is not even close to what is coming. We already are beginning to see this new cellular phone-pager be incorporated into watches. In the not too distant future, watches as we know them will not exist. They will be information devices that provide the time, monitor your health, e.g., vital signs; as well as provide satellite-supported voice, video, and data from anywhere in the world to any place in the world.

According to Perry Luzwick,[2] "I studied how do you bring the Internet to the former Eastern European countries to support capitalism, free markets, and democracy? Doing the cities was easy, as was the countryside. In the near-term, use wireless because it's fast and reinforces the democratic movement now. People in the countryside would need wireless—primarily driven by the geography and cost per person. Density in the cities made it very profitable. But especially in the cities, capacity (bandwidth) was a problem. And in the long run, it was

---

[2]See http://www.shockwavewriters.com.

cheaper to have a high capacity fiber backbone that supported ped-abits."

These new devices will also include mini-televisions for teleconfer-encing, geo-positioning features, and will no longer need batteries. The new ones, in the short term, may be solar powered with the ability to store that power for extended periods of time. So when you are sitting outside eating lunch, your wristband or wearable information system will be getting its solar food for the next several days—and it may be just that, if we can figure out how to best keep an electrically charged amoebae fed.

One of the greatest technological advances that will soon be com-ing is solving the problem of powering these devices. Solar power and batteries have improved, but there have not been any major break-throughs that would equal those of the computers. That will be com-ing. There may even come a day when we power our portable, body-strapped devices with our own body heat or from another source of power—our brains.

In order for the consumer to reap the full advantage of such rela-tionships, we all need more bandwidth. Audio has helped push us in that direction, and MP3 is the newest craze by helping to fire the flames of our audio technological revolution. While video is behind by proba-bly a few years, there will be an explosion of that capability in the not too distant future. The current delay is due to video requiring probably about 10 to 20 times the bandwidth of audio. Then there is the matter of storage space needs. How much storage space do you need to down-load and store a full-length feature film? Right now, it's too much, but very soon it will be trivial.

We have seen the beginning of the storage capacity issue being solved. Now, buying a home computer with about 18 gigabytes of stor-age capacity is about the norm—and it's relatively cheap. New storage devices will make storage so cheap that systems' makers and integra-tors may just give it away depending on your needs—give or take a few zillion bytes. The sugar cube size storage devices will be large in com-parison to the storage devices of the future. Those devices will allow us to access or possibly intuitively know all the information that's stored in all the libraries of the world. We already see indications of the minia-turization of storage devices when we look at today's digital cameras with the Sony memory sticks, compact flash memory cards, and IBM 340MB microdrives.

If we look back at the computers of the 1940-90s, they weren't close to being user-friendly, but that will also change. You will be shop-ping online at the various information stores and purchase your home information system—television, telephone, GII access, videoconferenc-ing, and oh yes, the future version of the home computer. The home computer, desktop, personal computer, or whatever you choose to call it, will not be built after one or two more decades, if that long. True, miniaturized information and knowledge systems will replace them.

You may ask, but how many remote devices, mice, and keyboards will we need to operate it? The answer is none—well, maybe one. The input device will be your voice. Is this more science fiction than science fact? Not at all, in fact they are all being researched, developed, prototyped, or being sold right now, but in their more primitive state.

You won't have to reprogram or make any changes to your home information and entertainment system to get the information that you want access to while you continue to desperately try to deny that same access to your children. This future system will scan you and based on specific biometrics to include your physical profile, and voice identification, it will automatically configure itself according to your previous instructions.

Just as we now have PDA's, notebook computers, desktop systems, with workstations tied into servers, wide area networks and the like, these new integrated devices will have us re-thinking what we mean by such things as pagers, computers, cellular phones, wired phone, radios, and watches. Those will be old outdated terms for our information wrist device or whatever name the manufacturers dream up, and usually the first to market sets the standards. For example: Do we say we will copy a document or do we say we will "Xerox it?" Do we use a "PC" (the personal computer term coined by IBM) or a stand-alone, microcomputer? The rapidly changing technologies will cause businesses to either adapt or die. Today's pagers, cellular phones, and the like are destined to go the way of the carbon paper.

Those of us that are optimistic about the advances in technology that will occur in the future do not see any problems that cannot be overcome. Maybe it is based on the faith in the collective mind of mankind, but whatever it is, it is driving all of us into the future at literally the speed of light—and no, there are no brakes.

Enhanced technology will continue to support the drive to global tele-medicine where the best specialists in the world will be in a position to medically assist anyone, anywhere, at any time. However, with this enhanced use of the Internet may come tele-medicine murders. These could be accomplished by changing medical test results, the automated dosages of prescription drugs, and denying tele-medicine services. Security and law enforcement specialists will be involved in conducting murder investigations where the crime scene will be tomorrow's equivalent of the Internet.

Robotics and True Artificial Intelligence

We have barely begun to grasp the possibilities of what robots can do for humans. In the future, computers will do most labor-intensive jobs.

Even now, there are machines being built to do farming. While the field is being plowed, farmers could spend their time in more productive ways, saving a great deal of time and making farming more cost-effective. Robots as our doctors will be as commonplace as they are now in the assembling of automobiles. They will become our sentries and also our soldiers as humans use them more and more for hazardous and routine intensive duties.

Artificial intelligence is a field that had not lived up to its potential in the past, but will in the future. As we begin to unravel the mysteries of the brain while at the same time developing more powerful and sophisticated microprocessors and information systems, the two will come together to the point only dreamed of in past science fiction movies. As these robots begin to learn from their experiences, we may truly reach a time when they become our adversaries. However, the less pessimistic side is one where we combine the best of both worlds through the use of human-like artificial body parts. Then we will see the true evolution of technology for the benefit of the human race. The days of *Star Trek* technology are truly in our future.

The Microbots Are Coming!

Microbots, these extremely tiny robots will begin an exponential growth for use in medicine, hazardous areas, and of course espionage by techno-spies. In fact, they may become the techno-spies. As we all know, research and development that has driven us through this portion of the technological revolution was well financed by the U.S. government, e.g., the first computers, Internet. Therefore, it stands to reason that the U.S. government and other governments are well into classified research and development of these tiny creatures. And probably as with many past government sponsored technological devices, the microbots will also eventually find their way into our business and personal lives.

So miniaturization will continue, as well as mobility, flexibility, integration, lower costs, and increased communication and information collection. This will all lead to one of the most important decisions that mankind will ever make in 21st century, and second only to whether or not to clone humans. The question is whether we will want to have a microbot with human programmed software code integrated with our brain. Regardless of our answer, we will use them to clean out our arteries, repair failing internal body parts, and the like. The advanced high-technology that will do that is being researched today. From a Netspionage viewpoint, can these microbots also be subverted to serve the Netspionage agents' purposes?

Communication between humans and machines is something that we continue to develop with technology. The future holds promises that will enable us to transcend the language barriers. When that happens, we may not agree with each other, but we will at least understand what we say to each other. Language translation software will continue to improve to the point where there will be instantaneous translations of various languages to our own and vice versa. This will take place regardless of the form of communication used. If we choose to go the way of the microbot-brain connection, we will be able to speak those languages. Thus, true one-on-one human communications can take place unhindered by the language barrier.

Will 1984 Come Again?

There will be many obvious and hidden dangers due to technology. Most information-based societies seem to be willing to give up some freedoms in return for more security. Technology will help provide more security, but at a cost in terms of personal privacy and possibly personal freedoms. Technology now allows us to track automobiles and other property. We can pinpoint the location of a cellular phone call. Advancements in photographic and other technologies allows us to view objects here on earth from outer space as though they were right next to us.

Identification chips can be embedded in the skin of animals to identify their owners. Because of the fear of kidnapping, small electronic tracking packets can now be inserted in the backpacks and other items that are used by children or others. There may come a time when such devices can be embedded under the skin.[3] It may first start with the military to embed their medical history and also to pinpoint their position. A great capability for the field commanders in order to determine the location of their troops in the field and how to properly deploy them. However, in the wrong hands this type of technology can be a devastating weapon. Most loss of freedoms and human rights begin with the excuse that something is being done for our own good, to increase security of the nation and ourselves. Will this be another one of those excuses?

Summary

It is obvious that the technological trends to make microprocessors and everything that they are used for, smaller, more powerful, totally integrated and cheaper, will continue. This, coupled with the ever-increasing bandwidth, multimedia, and personal communications systems will provide for a micro-portability only dreamed of and shown in science fiction movies.

---

[3]See http://www.digitalangel.net for exactly this kind of product.

The need to have such devices in order to work, shop, and access information will require that everyone be guaranteed such a system as an inherent right as a citizen of an Information Age nation. Without such devices, the government will be depriving the citizens of everything from due process to the right to work. The Internet, NII, and GII, that now seems still a novelty in so many ways, will be in truth one of the mainstream methods of working and communicating.

The development of more sophisticated information systems that are able to understand and react to normal human speech will become commonplace. This technology will be a major break-through that will allow previously computer illiterate individuals to use the power of the computers, networks, and the Internet to work, play, and communicate. This will allow poor people and others who could neither afford a computer, nor learn how to use one, to become better educated and valuable members of societies with less effort. Those changes will require us to make some very serious decisions that have great, and maybe grave, impact on the human race.

The world will still be a dangerous place because we are still human and are not progressing as fast as the technology we are building. *The Matrix*[4] may not be more than a half-century away.

---

[4]*The Matrix* is a science fiction movie where the man-made computers have taken over the world and control the human race.

14

Business, Crime, and Security in the 21st Century Global Marketplace

Fasten Your Safety Belts as We're in for a Rough Ride

What will the 21st century business environment be like? The assumption is that it will be more chaotic—the world changing ever faster with increases in competition, nation-state changes, social changes, more techno-crime, and the inability of anyone, nation-state or society, to apparently stop or slow down any of the rapid changes.

The Future Global Changes that Impact Businesses

The global changes brought on by the Internet, GII, and NII will continue to impact, in a positive and negative manner, the interactions of nations, societies, and businesses as well as their very existence. As we noted earlier, the rapid changes brought on, in part, by the Internet, GII, and NII will cause increased communications on a global scale—also a necessity for a global marketplace. New nations once thought of as "third-world" will begin to flex their technological muscles. For example, "Nations such as India want to be a global power, they believe they are a regional power now. Places like Bangladesh are booming because they're riding the software production wave."[1]

Brought on by the "Three Revolutions," nations will be torn apart with ever-increasing chaos and rapid disintegration into factions that will use the Internet, GII, and NII to communicate their grievances, desires, and try to build a world consensus in their favor (see Figure14–1). The nation-states will use the Internet, GII, and NII to justify their controls, government policies, etc. The breakup

---

[1]According to Perry Luzwick. See http://www.shockwavewriters.com.

of the old Soviet Union, and the old Yugoslavia are just two examples of what other nations may face in the 21st century.

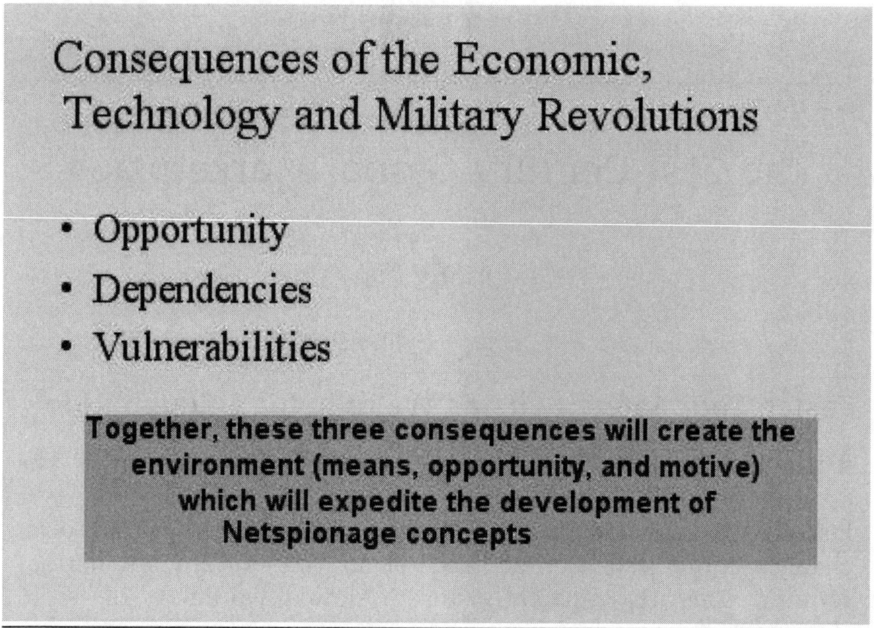

Consequences of the Economic, Technology and Military Revolutions

- Opportunity
- Dependencies
- Vulnerabilities

Together, these three consequences will create the environment (means, opportunity, and motive) which will expedite the development of Netspionage concepts

Figure 14–1 The consequences of the technology, economic, and military revolutions.

The "economic domino" effect that has taken place throughout the world validates the interlinking and interdependencies of nations. With the expansion of the Internet, GII, and NII commerce, these dependencies will play a more crucial role in the global order. Netspionage and techno-spies will continue to grow in support of a nation's and businesses' objective of becoming an economic power because they can operate effectively in the global information era.

The economic power and influence of global corporations will exert greater and greater influence over governments and societies of the ever-weakening nation-states.[2] The global business giants will usurp the power of the smaller nations. The need for government's support for social programs will diminish as that slack is picked up by the businesses who in turn receives tax-exempt status and other benefits in the smaller nations that they will control.

One must also look at the new forms of businesses taking shape on the Internet, GII, and NII: . . . *At the dawn of the 20th century, you had trusts—interlocking, powerful, quasi-monopolistic corporations that Teddy Roosevelt muscled into oblivion. By mid-century, you had conglomerate—international assemblages of unrelated, slow-moving busi-*

---

[2]*The End of the Nation State* by Kenichi Ohmae published by The Free Press in 1995. Also, completely separate book with the identical title originally published in France by Jean-Marie Guehenno, published by University of Minnesota Press, 1995.

nesses squirming under one big thumb. (Think ITT. Think GE.) Now, as the millennium turns, a new corporate animal is evolving, and the implications are enormous. Call them EcoNets—the economic networks of the future . . . [3]

Asia's economic woes will lessen, and the Asian nations will gain renewed strength as the dominant, economic region of the world, which will be led by China. The financial and intellectual resources of Singapore (Chinese), the intellectual resources and technology of Taiwan (Chinese), integrated with the cheap labor, natural resources of China, including the financial power of Hong Kong, will ensure the domination of Chinese as a global economic power above and beyond national borders. For example, in Indonesia alone, it is alleged that the Chinese make up only about 4 percent of the population but control more than 70 percent of Indonesia's wealth. Thus, the Chinese in Indonesia became a scapegoat for the Indonesian economic woes.

Such ethnic violence will continue to grow on a global basis due to religion and race. Factions, ethnic groups, religious groups will increase their presence on the Internet, GII, and NII and sub-Internet. Some of these links will be closed, encrypted links to be used only by those within the selected group, e.g., Chinese businesses, Moslem businesses, Jewish businesses, others. Global corporations in foreign lands may be attacked because they are seen to represent an adversarial nation. The attackers may be incited by their global competitors whose corporate headquarters resides in that same nation.

Governments will continue to use the Industrial Age legislative processes in vain attempts to control those portions of the Internet, GII, and NII that impact their nation, and to continue to try to control e-business through laws and regulations. Much of their attempts will adversely affect corporations' ability to effectively compete in the global marketplace causing businesses to move to other nations that they can control and intimidate.

Governments will continue to fail in their efforts to control the Internet, albeit some small successes may occur here and there. As Internet commerce increases, governments will not be able to avoid the temptation of taxing it. However, this will lead to serious disagreements among nations. Some nations will integrate the Internet, GII, and NII environment into the normal course of commerce throughout their nation, while others will treat it as a unique environment and make new laws that are specific to it. Regardless, laws will be used to support the individual nations in their quest for global and economic power.

---

[3] *Red Herring* magazine article, AND NOW, ECONETS, Some Internet incubators are morphing into economic networks—call them EcoNets. They could become the conglomerates of the 21st century, Peter D. Henig, February 2000, p 96.

Future Social Changes

The people of all the nations who have Internet connectivity will become more sophisticated in using it. They will have ever-increasing, massive amounts of information at their disposal, allowing them to become more knowledgeable on global matters, businesses, and their products. They also will become more aware of those throughout the world who have similar and different views.

The Internet as a massive, personal communications pipeline will provide the means for people to communicate globally as never before. Such massive one-on-one communications will be the driving force that will affect governments, businesses, and societies to such an extent that governments and businesses will develop extremely sophisticated techniques to influence communicators and consumers.

Future Mergers, Partnership, Associations, and Acquisitions

The future will see dramatic increases in the formation of massive, globally oriented businesses (see Figure 14–2). The "bricks and mortars" businesses are beginning to realize that they won't be able to compete if that can't compete globally, and they can't compete globally if they are not on the Internet and GII.

Privacy and Encryption

The issue of privacy (or the lack thereof) will continue to be discussed on one hand, while government agencies heighten their Internet monitoring activities with the other hand. Unfortunately, privacy issues will continue to run contrary to the needs of businesses, societies, and individuals. They will be given no more than lip service. This will be done so governments can continue to try to maintain power. At the same time, some nations seeing the benefits of secure business encryption will allow any encryption. These nations will see the benefits of strong global businesses as more beneficial than the governments' desire to read other people's e-mail. There will be a shift of global businesses' headquarters and facilities to such nations, who may also offer tax incentives to encourage such moves.

Encryption will continue to become more sophisticated while the issue of key management overhead costs, prohibitions of exporting of effective encryption methods will continue to be debated on a global scale. Nations' security agencies will require and continue to obtain access to encrypted communications via "key escrow" and "backdoors," but on a massive scale. There may be unsuccessful attempts to outlaw encryption that does not meet a given nation's standards.

Other nations with less sophisticated technology will require that technology in order to allow Internet communications to transit their nation. Some will prohibit any encryption under the banner of national security interests. Their concern, and excuse, will be the use of encryption by factions whose purpose is to bring down the current government.

NEW YORK (CNNfn) - In a stunning development, America Online Inc. announced plans to acquire Time Warner Inc. for roughly $182 billion in stock and debt Monday, creating a digital media powerhouse with the potential to reach every American in one form or another.

With dominating positions in the music, publishing, news, entertainment, cable and Internet industries, the combined company, called AOL Time Warner, will boast unrivaled assets among other media and online companies.

The merger, the largest deal in history, combines the nation's top Internet service provider with the world's top media conglomerate. The deal also validates the Internet's role as a leader in the new world economy, while redefining what the next generation of digital-based leaders will look like.

Figure 14–2 The first major Internet "bricks and mortar" business merger.

These vulnerabilities will be exploited by other nations and Netspionage agents who will become more sophisticated in decrypting communications due to more and more effective computers and massive chaining of computers to break encrypted messages.

The Internet security answer for transmission of business information will continue to be encryption. Encryption today seems to be in a similar position as the locksmiths of the 1800s. Then, knowledge of locks was unknown except to the experts. Criminals needed keys to break in and concentrated on obtaining keys. With the invention of powerful explosives, keys were no longer needed. The criminals just blew the locks off.

The same may be true in the future with encryption, but as we have begun to see, encryption works because the chances of guessing the right key is, statistically at least, almost impossible. However, what if a person guessed it—even guessed it the first time? Also, the more tries at "guessing" the encryption key, the better your statistical chances of getting it right.

The real problem with encryption is key management, just as we have password management problems today. Also, with more powerful

and cheaper computers, techno-spies are finding that they can sometimes identify encryption keys through brute force attacks on weak
algorithms.

Encryption can prevent, with some degree of success, the ability of
someone to read our mail. However, it cannot prevent denial of service,
that is a growing threat.

The Internet will continue expansion to individuals, businesses, and
government agencies throughout the world, and will do so exponentially. There will be more reliance for contract negotiations and formal
contract agreements through the Internet, thus paving the way for some
serious legal issues and contract frauds.

Copyright Issues

Copyright violations on the Internet will continue unabated with more
and more information being made available on a massive scale. Thus,
the "software police" and others will be so overwhelmed that they will
only attempt to investigate and prosecute those cases that provide good
public relations for the agency and are violations on a massive scale.
New, consumer-oriented technologies will allow the consumers to stay
one or two steps ahead of the laws and software police.

These issues will continue to only be a concern of a few of the most
mature Information Age nations such as the United States and the
United Kingdom. Other nations, to include the rest of the European
Union, East European nations, Asian nations, and other nations will
provide only token assistance. This will be done in order to rapidly, and
cheaply bring their nations into the Information Age through the use of
free copyrighted information.

Increased Business Risks Due to the Global Connections

As businesses become more dependent on their interfaces to global
networks as the backbone for their businesses, there will be greater and
greater risks to their businesses.

There are many reasons why these risks have been created. They
include:

- Global economic competition where Netspionage, industrial and
  economic espionage, can be conducted with little risk of being
  caught
- Further decline of the mainframe systems, increase in LANs and
  WANs, and the creation of client server systems—all of which rely
  more on the users to protect the systems and information than a
  professional staff of systems personnel

- The "Maginot Line" mentality of managers and some information systems security professionals who look at access control software, firewalls, and passwords as the only security needed
- The focus on customer service by management and network staffs as the highest priority, as well as that technical staffs being unfamiliar with their security role will continue to allow successful Netspionage agents, techno-spies, hackers, and others to access the business networks for their own purposes
- Limited security technology will continue to always be a step or two behind the attackers
- Lack of management support to provide better security as a higher priority

Business Will Face Increased Fraud and Other Crimes Due to Increased E-Commerce

Internet crime will rise dramatically as electronic commerce (electronic business) increases over the years. The following estimates[4] are provided so that the reader understands that with this much money in the system, it is too good a target to ignore (1997 compared to 2001):

- Financial Services: $1.2 billion to an estimated $5 billion
- Apparel and footwear: $92 million to an estimated $514 million
- PC hardware and software: $863 million to an estimated $3 billion
- Event ticket sales: $79 million to an estimated $2 billion
- Entertainment: $298 million to an estimated $2.7 billion
- Travel: $654 million to an estimated $7.4 billion
- Books and music: $156 million to an estimated $1.1 billion
- Business-to-business sales: $8 billion to an estimated $183 billion

Electronic commerce is already on the Internet, GII, and NII. It is too large for the criminals to ignore. Billions of dollars through millions of transactions will be conducted each year. To have electronic commerce, one must have sellers, customers, and infrastructure to transfer goods, services, and money securely. Security will continue to be enhanced, thus providing reasonable, cheap, simple transaction security. This will happen exponentially and cause a rapid expansion of the Internet, GII, and NII for electronic business.

Internet criminals will become more sophisticated as the computers become more sophisticated. Threats to these valuable business and

---

[4]*BusinessWeek*, "Our Annual Report on Information Technology, doing business in the Internet age," June 22, 1998.

public assets are increasing while the public demands more time spent pursuing violent crimes, allowing less time to be spent pursuing techno-criminals.

The enactment of international laws will lag behind the technology making it extremely difficult to identify, apprehend, and prosecute Internet criminals across national boundaries. Some successes will of course occur, e.g., international fight against child pornography. However, the more sophisticated, financially-based, Internet crimes will grow in number due to the lack of the capabilities of security professionals to prevent them and the lack of capabilities of the law enforcement professionals to investigate and apprehend the techno-criminals.

Security and Law Enforcement

Law Enforcement's response to the rapid evolution of the Internet, GII, and NII techno-criminals has been slow. In large part, this is because of the prevalence of other, some say more serious crimes in such nations as the United States. So, the public's priority has been to use the limited, budgeted resources for fighting gangs, drugs, and violent crimes. Netspionage, high-technology crimes, and frauds are considered victimless, and thus receive a low priority. This priority order will continue for the foreseeable future.

Law enforcement officers are hampered in investigating such attacks due to nonexistent laws, lack of jurisdiction, difficulty in getting cooperation from law enforcement officers of other countries because of politics, different laws, etc. For example, what may be illegal in Indonesia may not be illegal in the Netherlands. Therefore, extradition would not be possible, since the citizen of the Netherlands violated no law of their home country. The investigation processes of techno-crimes are complicated enough. When they are internationally accomplished, it is almost impossible to bring these criminals to justice. Law enforcement efforts to forge an effective response to the proliferation of Internet, GII, and NII crimes will continue to be thwarted by the international criminals, international law inadequacies, lack of jurisdiction, lack of budget, and lack of skills. Use of highly skilled private investigators, bounty hunters, and vigilantes by businesses to respond to serious crimes will be the norm.

The Impact of Information Warfare on Future Business

Information warfare will play an increased role in 21st century warfare. Civilized nations today have less tolerance for violence, human death, and suffering. The use of computers and networks to fight the information wars of the future will become more common as they offer cheap, rapid, and powerful weapons of mass destruction.

Electronic and computer weapons to destroy an adversary's information infrastructure, and thus their economic power, will take on more importance. The use of the Internet, GII, and NII by military forces and techno-terrorists will continue to increase as a nation's adversaries become more dependent on information systems and the Internet, GII, and NII for their political and economic power.

The roles of the military, security, and law enforcement professionals will become more important than ever before. They will be used extensively to support the governments in power to maintain that power. The military soldiers will become more technologically sophisticated and the revolution in military affairs will continue to increase the military's dependence on technology, thus also making it more vulnerable to a nation's adversaries who practice information warfare.

These information wars will drag businesses in to the fray, causing massive loss of not only business, but also sensitive information and the businesses' critical information infrastructure.

Four Major Challenges for Corporate Managers and Information Security Officers for the 21st Century

In looking at current trends, one can find these trends indicate that there will be many challenges to the corporate managers and security officers who are charged with protecting the valuable information assets of the corporation. Among them are:

- The continued increase and globalization of Internet, NII, and GII, and their connections to the businesses' and government agencies' intranets for electronic commerce
- The increasing threats of Netspionage
- The increasing threats of techno-criminals
- The concern and potential threats of information warfare

Summary

The Internet, GII, and NII of the 21st century will continue its rapid growth and expansion on a global scale. It will play a major role in changing nations, societies, business, and technology; as well as changing the responsibilities of corporate managers, security and law enforcement professionals. By looking at current trends, one can anticipate many changes yet to come. At the same time, business and security professionals can only be sure of one thing: they and their professions must also rapidly adapt, or they may cease to have employment in their chosen profession. Furthermore, their professions will require more global business management and more technical skills than ever before.

15

Future Netspionage

Sun-tzu: Past, Present, and Future—He's Still Right

In the beginning of the book was a quotation from Sun-tzu.[1] It was relevant when he wrote it; it is relevant today, and it will be relevant in the future. It is basic and an integral part of military warfare, economic warfare, and business warfare. In fact, the entire book, *The Art of War*, is relevant to any conceivable type of warfare. When it comes to spies, he said:

Advance knowledge can not be gained from ghosts and spirits, inferred from phenomena, or projected from the measures of Heaven, but must be gained from men for it is the knowledge of the enemy's true situation . . . Thus there are five types of spies to be employed: local spies employed from the local district; internal spies employ their people who hold government office; double agents who employ the enemy's spies; expendable spies who are employed to spread disinformation with false information and have them leak it to the enemy; and living spies who return with their reports . . . Unless one is subtle and perspicacious, one cannot perceive the substance in intelligence reports. It is subtle, subtle! There are no areas in which one does not employ spies . . .

Let's dissect this paragraph and apply it to the future.

Advance knowledge cannot be gained from ghosts and spirits, inferred from phenomena, or projected from the measures of Heaven, but must be gained from men for it is the knowledge of the enemy's true situation . . .

As it relates to Netspionage, the use of technology by men must not be considered *the* answer to learning about the enemy's plans, their true intentions. In the past, the spies just used different tools and techniques. Ever wonder how the "spyglass" got its name? As we have learned from today's technology such as spy satellites, tech-

[1]Summary taken from Sun-tzu's *The Art of War*, New Translation by Ralph D. Sawyer, Barnes & Noble Books, New York, pp. 229–233, 1994.

nology can help, but it cannot read the mind of the adversary. If so, the invasion of Kuwait by Iraqi forces could probably have been prevented before it started. As in the past and present, so will it be in the future, learning the true intent of the adversary will still be a difficult task. Using Netspionage to access the plans of the competitor can provide a better road map but the human element will still be center stage.

Local spies employed from the local district

The local district may be considered the network that is used by your business integrated with your customers' and suppliers' networks. We have seen the beginning of the future when it comes to the total integration of that process. Your adversary will have many more ways to penetrate your network and steal your business' sensitive information. Remember the weakest link theory is no longer a theory when it comes to Netspionage. Your competitor may enter your network from the network of your suppliers or even your customers. In fact, in today's and tomorrow's business environment, your competitor on one contract may be your team member on another. Most businesses normally give their team members carte blanche in their facilities and for the most part on their network. They are treated as though they were employees. Thus, their access is much the same as an employee.

Most businesses will continue to not differentiate their database information between contracts. Access may not be authorized under the contract, but it's all there in the massive noncompartmented databases. This problem will get worse in the future. Furthermore, the business will find that the information for the teaming contract can also be used by the teaming partners to their advantage as they compete on another contract. A trained Netspionage agent-analyst will know how to make that connection. A business won't have a choice but to share the information in order to get a lucrative contract. One can argue that any unauthorized use of the information as stated in the contract would be cause for a lawsuit. It's a violation of our licensing agreement, etc. Hopefully, it would be. However, what controls does your business have in place to monitor the use of that information by a team member and occasional competitor? Chances are, none and if some policies or procedures are in place, they are probably unenforceable. Unenforceable, that is, unless you employ Netspionage agents and techno-spies.

Internal spies employ their people who hold government office

This one is obvious and throughout our Cold War period, we have seen numerous cases of this from the U.S. Navy Walker case to the CIA's Ames case—and many more around the globe on both sides of the Cold War. This, of course, will continue and no type of security can keep these internal spies out of the networks where the sensitive, proprietary, and national security information resides. That is because these internal Netspionage agents have "authorized access" to the information. And with the GII, NII, and Internet interfaces, one can send the information to anywhere in the world in a nanosecond. This will become so much easier in the future as technology becomes increasingly wireless. Remember, there is a great deal of information on government databases that is very relevant to global businesses, e.g., plans for trade negotiations, tariff positions, and the like. As economic and business warfare heats up in the future, the Netspionage agents will be very busy.

Double agents who employ the enemy's spies

In the future as it is today, the Netspionage agents are in a position to negotiate deals with the management of their targeted business. In addition, if a Netspionage agent was caught, the business will usually continue to ignore the pleas from law enforcement to report such matters. This is because there would still be the matter of bad publicity, questions by owners and stockholders, as well as potential lawsuits by the competitor. The competitor will, of course, deny the charges and accuse the other business of jealousy because they are trying to steal market share through unfair competition, innuendoes, and the like. Successfully litigating such matters can get very nasty, messy, expensive, and the outcome is always uncertain. So, the Netspionage agent will usually be paid off by one side or the other and quietly go on to the next contract job. Sometimes the Netspionage agent may turn against his employer when caught by the targeted business, and in doing so, provide valuable information to that business. The information provided, if only the tasks assigned to the Netspionage agent, would tell the business a great deal. For example, knowing what information the adversary was seeking would indicate the state of the competitor's competitive advantages and disadvantages. As with other past and current spy matters, the future brings with it the same issues, just the playing field has changed from a physical field to a cyber playing field.

Expendable spies who are employed to spread misinformation with false information and have them leak it to the enemy

This classic tactic of the past and present will also continue into the future; however, it will be so much easier to spread misinformation due to ever-growing and massive communications links. With anonymous e-mails, postings online, chat rooms, one can easily spread misinformation. We see so much of it today with the "urban legends" (false statements, rumors), those tales that spread like wild fire via the Internet. There are even some Web sites that list urban legends. However, how does one know that those are not themselves urban legends? If the person who spreads such rumors is identified, prosecution is unlikely. In either case, the firm that hired this expendable Netspionage agent will be sure to adequately compensate the agent.

Living spies who return with their reports

In the future Netspionage agents will "return" through secure e-mail and through other networked enabled devices. The need to physically meet, the most dangerous time for any spy, is avoided. Interesting examples appear in the recent movie The Saint. Such techniques will be more commonplace in the future.

Unless one is subtle and perspicacious, one cannot perceive the substance in intelligence reports. It is subtle, subtle!

When all is said and done, and the Netspionage agent has completed the assigned tasks, it is still up to the receiver of the information along with the specialized analyst to derive meaning from the information. As has been the case throughout history, good intelligence reports are changed and misinterpreted for political or other reasons. Thus, the human element will still be the weak link in future Netspionage.

There are no areas in which one does not employ spies

In the future, one can say that there are no communications links, networks, or any other forms of technology-based communication where one does not employ Netspionage agents.

Nation-States and Competitors
Use of Netspionage Techniques in the Future

Economic and business warfare will increase in the future. With the continued improvements in global communications systems, competitors and nation-states will become more aggressive. Some will begin to use information warfare tactics borrowed from the military and intelligence agencies (see Figures 15–1 through 15–6). In fact, in some nations, they will be supported by their nation's military and other government agencies. One unnamed source stated, "How about Menwith Hill and other antennas turned on European countries since the Cold War enemies are gone?" That may be a further indication of use of government technology for economic gain. And one must not forget the U.S. submarine designed to link with underwater communication cables to listen in on all the cable communications—are they still in operation after the Cold War?

1984 Is Coming Again

June 1999 marked the 50th anniversary of the publishing of George Orwell's book entitled *1984*. Many people believed, and others still believe, that the book was a work of science fiction, while others

---

Netspionage Offensive Operations

- During future economic and business warfare in which Netspionage plays a role, it will be important to develop and refine Netspionage methodologies which can be used against a competitor (or nation-state)
- By identifying a competitor's GII interface, NII, and Internet in detail, mapping that environment against corporate strategies; and Netspionage attack tools, techniques and methodologies, one can prepare to successfully mount a Netspionage attack in support of the corporation's objective, e.g., to gain global market share advantage

---

Intelligence Collection Phase

- Collect and map the Internet nodes, links, groups, personnel, hardware, operating systems, applications software being used by the competitor's networks
- That information is analyzed to identify the vulnerabilities of the networks and what Netspionage tools to be used against them

These tools can be used to collect and read messages being transmitted through the network for subsequent use in the other phases of the corporation's plan, e.g., send misinformation, take over the network, or just deny use of the network.

Intelligence gathering   (Protection, Exploitation, Hacker War)

Pre-Hostilities   Time   Post-Hostilities

Figures 15–1 through **15–6** Gradual build-up of economic and business warfare hostilities through five phases.

Diplomatic Pressure Phase

- Network is monitored to determine the reaction of those on the network to the diplomatic pressure; read e-mail of others; increase e-mail correspondence using cover story or overt tactics
- This information could then be used as part of the psychological warfare part of diplomacy to gain economic advantage

Diplomatic pressures	(Psychological Operations - PsyOps)
Intelligence gathering	(Protection, Exploitation, Hacker War)
Pre-Hostilities	Time	Post-Hostilities

Economic Pressure Phase

- Use the network to collect information as was used during the diplomatic phase; release false economic-related information on targeted networks; change economic information of the competitor

Economic pressures	(Economic warfare)
Diplomatic pressures	(PsyOps)
Intelligence gathering	(Protection, Exploitation, Hacker War)
Pre-Hostilities	Time	Post-Hostilities

Posturing Phase

- Using Netspionage-gathered information, the network or selected portions thereof could be prepared for attacks as part of denial-of-service attacks or prepare misinformation to be inserted in order to get the competitor's country to act in a manner conducive to the corporation's objectives; send out false messages over compromised links

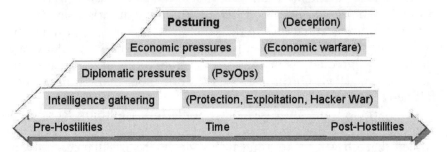

E-Business Combat Phase

- Initiate economic or business operational plan based on Netspionage-obtained information, e.g., send out misinformation; spoof and read transmission; deny use of the system

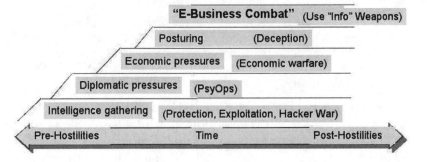

believe it represents things yet to come. In fact, some people that have read it from a futuristic viewpoint believe that Orwell may have been more of a Nostradamus than a writer of science fiction.

The reader may wonder what does this have to do with Netspionage in the future? Quite simply, Netspionage is an integral part of maintaining power and control, whether it is a business or government agency. It is an integral part of all future wars—information warfare, economic warfare, business warfare.

If what ol' George has written comes true, then you are going to be either a victim of those predictions or one of those that ensure that "Big Brother" is alive and well in the 21st century. *The Washington Times*, printed an article on June 15, 1999, titled, "Some futurists say beware, Orwell's future is at hand."[2] In the article, David Ross, a journalist and author, reportedly said that he, working with an Orwell scholar counted ". . . 137 predictions or indicators of the 'total surveillance future' envisioned in *1984*. Of those 137 indicators, more than 100 have been fulfilled . . ."

The article went on to say ". . . Some futurists think Ross is too negative. Peter Huber, in a popular 1994 book, *Orwell's Revenge*, argued that Orwell was wrong in his views of surveillance and computer devices necessarily being negative. Orwell may have been right in the details of the future, but he was wrong in how the technology would be put to use . . . personal computers in private hands impact freedom—even to overthrow "Big Brother."

Ross advised that citizens must "devise a plan to bypass government and corporations reassuring us that Orwell was wrong in his scenario . . . By the Internet and home phone lines, citizens themselves must identify threats posed by technology in the wrong hands . . ."

So, who is right? Let's look at some events that may be related to the "Second Coming of 1984" and the use of Netspionage and techno-spy techniques:

> Police will have 24-hour access to secret files (United Kingdom). E-mail code-busters to join crime fight. A 24-HOUR technical centre to help crack secret Internet and e-mail systems used by criminals in being set up by the computer industry and the police . . . (From SpyKing, June 1, 1999)

Note: Of course, police always say they will have a warrant. Yeah, sure, that's not hard to get. These tools, if available to police, will also be available to Netspionage agents. Besides, police retire and need a job. Their talents may be useful. After all, many go into the profession of private investigator and security when they retire or quit the force.

---

[2]The article is available from *The Washington Times*, document id PN19960616140061003, citation 2; Vol 20, No. 5, A; CULTURE, ET CETERA Section, author is David Goodman.

Also, we do hear of police in every country that take bribes and kick-backs. Maybe another example of what Sun-tzu calls the internal spy.

> *Big Brother is listening in Australia. In this Sunday investigation, Australia's spy-chiefs acknowledge for the first time this country's role in an international spying alliance that is monitoring the overseas phone, fax, and e-mail messages of every Australian—indeed, everyone on the planet . . .* (http://Sunday.ninemsm.com.au/sun_covtrans.asp?id=818)[3]

Note: All countries with this capability do this to some extent and share the information with other nation-states or corporations when it is in their interest to do so. Search the Internet for the keyword "Echelon." This is true government Netspionage in action. How much of the information gleaned is passed on to the nation's businesses to help them compete in the global marketplace? In the future, this will not slow down but speed up as technology becomes even more powerful, cheaper, and sophisticated.

> *Australian Computer Crime article . . . A court order had allowed police to implant a signal device on the thief's computer and for days it has been transmitting raw data to an outside receiver . . . They know his password, and a government agency has granted them access to the "key" to the military-strength encryption the thief uses to disguise instructions . . .* (SMH Saturday, October 24, 1998)

Note: It is interesting to note the long battle going on in the United States and other nations about the export of encryption products, yet, some agencies don't seem to have a problem breaking some military-strength encryption. Again, if the police have this technology, imagine what a Netspionage agent has.

> *The U.S. 1998 Wiretap Report is available: http://jya.com/wiretap98.htm. Total federal and state is up to 1,329 from 1,186 in 1997. Two requests were denied. That makes five denials in the last 10 years compared to 11,000 authorizations.* (http://www.infowar.com, May 5, 1999)

Note: So, when law enforcement say that they can't access your files, tap your telephone line, or fax without a warrant, look at these numbers. It is about as automatic as one can get. Furthermore, if, according to the FBI, major crimes in the United States continues to decline, why are the number of wiretaps increasing?

> *Singapore Telecom checks customers PCs . . . scary. Singapore's national telecommunications company has scanned more than 200,000 computers of its Internet customers without their knowledge as part of a plan to ward off hackers . . . Singapore Telecom, which is 80 percent owned by the government, . . . "We are merely protecting the interest of our customers," the report quoted Singapore Telecom*

---

[3]As with many Web sites, the information is volatile and may be not be available by the time this book is published.

chief executive officer for multimedia Paul Chong . . . On whether the law allowed such scanning without customer's consent, Chong said nothing illegal had taken place. He said customers were not informed of the scan so as not to alarm them. "We do not want to make a mountain out of a molehill. In the end, the scan might not turn up anything. If we had informed the customers, it might cause an alarm," Chong said. (http://www.nandotimes.com, April 29, 1999)

Note: The scans were done not by the Singapore Telecom, but by the Home Affairs Ministry's IT security unit. One wonders why the customers could not be informed in advance, what the real purpose of the scans were. One must remember that Singapore is not completely a democratic state, and opposition to the ruling government has not been tolerated any more than spitting on the sidewalk is tolerated. This same technology is available to other nation-states, corporations, e.g., ISP's and the like. One wonders how many of our personal computers have been scanned without our knowledge.

Australia: Government to Hack into Personal Computers. Civil liberties campaigners hit yesterday at the Government's plan to hack into personal computers as part of the security checks for the Olympic Games. They claim new powers to be given to Australia's domestic spy agency, Asio, represent a breach of individual privacy. When a computer user goes online, Australia Security Intelligence Organization officers want the ability to read the users' files. (South China Morning Post, April 29, 1999)

Note: In the interest of security and protecting society, many violations of individual freedoms have taken place. Those in power make the rules and those in power decide who the criminals are. Those in power use security officers and intelligence professionals to carry out these tasks. Imagine what Netspionage agents who don't play by any rules but their own can do in the future as this technology improves.

United Kindom: Intercepting the Internet. A secret international organization is pushing through a law to bring in eavesdropping points for Web sites and other forms of digital communication. European commission documents obtained this week reveal plans to require manufacturers and operators to build in interception interfaces to the Internet and all future digital communications systems. The plans, drafted by a U.S.-led international organization of police and security agencies, will be proposed to EU Justice and Home Affairs at the end of May. (http://www.infowar.com)

Note: We know that many laws (we must be legal you know) are written and passed in secrecy for reasons of national security. How many such laws in how many nations are already in effect that may provide a process for "special" search warrants or maybe no need for warrants at all in the interest of "national security." Again, as with other countries, the employment of Netspionage techniques at its best.

The headlines read, "China: Foreigners Must Disclose Internet Secrets to China Soon."[4] According to the article, the Chinese government is going to require that foreign businesses advise them what encryption software they use to protect their sensitive information transmissions over the Internet, excluding foreign diplomatic offices. These foreign firms are also being told to provide the names of the employees who use the encryption software, their e-mail addresses, telephone numbers, and the location of the computers that they use. It was also reported that "no organization or individual can sell foreign commercial encryption products." That makes sense because the Chinese Netspionage agents want businesses to use the Chinese encryption software to which they probably have the keys. So, the quandary is, should foreign businesses provide that information or should they leave the country? They actually have no other choice. They will undoubtedly stall and, if forced, provide the information in order to continue to chase the one billion potential customers.

There are hundreds more of such incidents that can be cited. When analyzing what each nation is doing, and what they are doing together, the picture becomes somewhat frightening from the standpoint of individuals' freedoms and the protection of a global businesses sensitive, even encrypted, communications and databases. Such noted backdoors allegedly being placed in products by Microsoft, Intel, and others make it even easier to invite Big Brother into our societies, personal lives, and businesses.

One must remember that corporate managers, information systems security officers, the intelligence officers, and other professionals who are responsible for safeguarding their nation, business, and supposedly the nation's and business' citizens. They are the ones who are being asked to conduct such surveillance, intelligence collections, and investigations. If you recall, in the United States, employers can legally read all the e-mail of its employees that are on corporate systems.

Most do it without thinking whether it is right or wrong. It must be right because it is in the interest of national security, in the interest of the business, thus protecting my way of life, paycheck and thus my family. Sure, and back in the 1930s and 1940s there were also people in Germany with all good intentions of preserving their way of life.

Remember, those in power, to include nations, and businesses will often do whatever it takes to maintain that power and survive. As we enter the 21st century and go full-speed into the information age, one must be ever vigilant that modern technology is only used for the benefit of the human race, personal freedoms, and to ensure a level, equal, global marketplace playing field.

---

[4]Article written by Matt Forney for the *Wall Street Journal*, January 25, 2000.

Remember, as we enter this new century, the nation-state will become less important as the global communications network, Internet, and technologies of all kinds provide all of us with more information and the ability to become "The Sovereign Individual" instead of members of a "sovereign nation-state."[5] We already are seeing what the nation-state is doing to survive.

A retired U.S. military intelligence officer put it this way:

> *I am thinking globally, domestically, and individually. You say that you are not willing to give up a little freedom for security, but I ask what freedom is there without security? It is security that gives us freedom; not freedom that gives us security. Only when we have a constitution founded on sound principles and backed by a strong and powerful government is our individual right, albeit freedom, guaranteed and enjoyed by the people. I admit that our government is created by the people for the people, and it is the people's government. But, once the government is created, the individual must give up certain rights so that law and order are preserved for the benefit of the whole. It is the whole that counts. It is for the whole that our government must infringe upon certain individual rights to enable our country to be vigilante and not be vulnerable to high-tech invasion and crime. I personally would give up a little of my freedom for security. I am willing to sacrifice some of my personal freedom so that our country stays strong and give me the greater freedom of FREEDOM.*

The above is probably typical of many of the world's citizens, business managers, and security officers. So, what's wrong with that loyal and patriotic statement? Plenty! What if benefiting the whole means the majority. What about protecting the interests of the minorities, e.g., Jews in 1930s–40s Germany; Japanese-Americans in the 1940s; Blacks in the United States for decades, the students in Tien An Men Square, and today, the people in Yugoslavia? Who will it be in the new century?

What does giving up a "little" freedom mean? How much is that? Infringe on certain individual rights? Yep, as long as they are your neighbors and not yours, right? Sacrificing some personal freedoms?

We do it every time—the freedom to keep more of what we earn—the tax collector calls. Want to see Big Brother in action? Look at the abuses by the U.S. Internal Revenue Service (IRS) as documented before Congressional hearings. Now, give them the power and technology of the Internet to track every one of your financial transactions, tap your fax line, read your e-mail for indications of hiding money, etc. Send someone e-mail complaining about the IRS and automatically they may open up a "special tap and trace" on your every cyber move? Would

---

[5]*The Sovereign Individual* is an excellent book written by James Dale Davidson & Lord William Rees-Mogg, published in 1997, by Simon and Schuster, ISBN 0-684-81007-7, wherein they discuss the demise of the nation-state in favor of the individual and the conflicts that will occur in that process.

these tax agents believe they are doing anything wrong? No, just using Netspionage techniques to ensure people pay what they should.

As a corporate manager, employee, or security officer, it is easy to rationalize the need to follow orders to protect the nation, business, and family, even when individual violations of personal freedoms occur. "It is for the greater good"; "if you've done nothing wrong, you have nothing to fear." Many are willing to give up personal freedoms for security—at least until the nation-state comes knocking on their door, but by then it will be far too late.

The Future of Netspionage in Information Warfare

Information warfare (IW) is the term being used to define the concept of 21st century warfare, which will be electronic and information systems driven.

Information warfare, as defined by the U.S. Defense Information Systems Agency (DISA), is "actions taken to achieve information superiority in support of national military strategy by affecting adversary information and information systems while leveraging and protecting our information and information systems." This definition seems to be a good summary definition of all the federal government agencies' definitions.

The federal government's definition of IW can be divided into three general categories: Offensive, Defensive, and Exploitation. For example:

- Deny, corrupt, destroy, or exploit an adversary's information, or influence the adversary's perception (Offensive);
- Safeguard ourselves and allies from similar actions (Defensive) also known as "IW hardening"; and
- Exploit available information in a timely fashion, in order to enhance our decision/action cycle and disrupt the adversary's cycle (Exploitative).

Whether we are talking offensive, defensive, or exploitation, information is, as always, the key element, and the most important information will be gathered by techno-spies and Netspionage agents.

One may wonder how they can be involved in a country's information warfare activities, after all, isn't that between governments and their military forces? Nothing can be further from the truth. Remember that during World War II, the allies bombed cities and private factories of the Axis forces. Today's and tomorrow's cities and private factories are on the Internet, a nation's information infrastructure, and its Web sites. The Chinese of the People's Republic of China have the view, as do most other countries, that information warfare will include the civilian community:

. . . The rapid development of networks has turned each automated system into a potential target of invasion. The fact that information technology is increasingly relevant to people's lives determines that those who take part in information war are not all soldiers and that anybody who understands computers may become a fighter on the network. Think tanks composed of non-governmental experts may take part in decision making; rapid mobilization will not just be directed to young people; information-related industries and domains will be the first to be mobilized and enter the war . . . (The British Broadcasting Corporation Summary of World Broadcasts, August 20, 1996, translated from the *Jiefangjun Bao* newspaper, Beijing, China, June 25, 1996, p. 6)

One can look at information warfare as being a factor in information, systems, and telecommunications protection. The info-warriors, cyber-warriors, techno-spies, Internet terrorists, or whatever one wants to call them, present challenges to everyone concerned with making the Internet a free space for sharing information and learning, as well as a safe place to travel and visit. Remember that these armies of info-warriors are looking at the targets presented along the Internet, and many of these are commercial, nonmilitary. The weapons that they will use can be categorized as attack, protect, exploit, and support weapons systems. They have the funding, identification of targets, and are developing plans and sophisticated application programs to attack a nation's information infrastructure, businesses, which include those on the Internet.

As the growth of networks continues worldwide, it will bring with it more threats from sophisticated, international techno-spies. Such threats will include an increased use of jamming techniques as a denial of service, to commit electronic extortion or to adversely impact a competitor's ability to perform electronic commerce on the Internet. As more forms of public communication come to rely on the Internet, it is expected that more sophisticated eavesdropping techniques will rise, which will allow Internet techno-spies working for businesses and government agencies to invade personal privacy. The increasing use of the many Internet-based telephone and video teleconference systems, which may be vulnerable to eavesdropping, will make this more common.

From a Netspionage and techno-spy standpoint, that next roach, bee, or butterfly you see buzzing around your office and computer may be the techno-spy collecting information from the emanations of your information device. The "eyes" of the future techno-spy bug may be a camera lens which captured the video and transmits it in real time through wireless Internet links to its handling agent in another part of the world.

The 21st century will bring with it an increased use of technology by terrorists. Before discussing terrorism and techno-terrorists, let's define these terms so we can have a clearer understanding of the subject.

The Use of Netspionage by Future Terrorists

Netspionage provides intelligence information and terrorists need good intelligence information so they know where to strike, when, their target's vulnerabilities, and the like. Today's terrorists are not only using technology to communicate and technology crimes to fund their activities, they are beginning to look at the potential for using technology in the form of information warfare against their enemies. It is estimated that this will increase in the future.

Because today's technology-oriented countries rely on vulnerable computers and telecommunications systems to support their commercial and government operations, it is becoming a concern to businesses and government agencies throughout the world. The advantage to the terrorist of attacking these systems is that the techno-terrorists acts can be done with little expense by very few people and cause a great deal of damage to corporation or the economy of a country.

They can conduct such activities with little risk to themselves since these systems can be attacked and destroyed from the base of a country friendly to them. In addition, they can do so with no loss of life thus, not causing the extreme backlash against them as it would if they had destroyed targets with much loss of life.

Netspionage Through Commercial Satellites

The future techniques of Netspionage will include the use of commercial satellites. Already, the Space Imaging company has begun using 1-meter resolution with their Ikonos. Earthwatch with QuickBird-1 and Orbital Imaging with OrbView-3[6] are not far behind. With the use of such technology, corporations will be able to get through their Internet connection a birds-eye view of the competitor's new research and development, or manufacturing facilities. If the site is out in an area that is difficult to get close to—no matter—a satellite photo or two will do nicely. Based on the progress of construction, the corporation will be able to determine when this new facility with its new capacity will be ready for operation to compete with your corporation.

In the future these same satellites will use the other spy techniques now reserved for government spy satellites. In fact, they may even be able to pick up emanations coming off the competitor's computer and be able to read them as if they were standing right behind the individual using the computer. As networks become more wireless, the satellites may be able to pick up the competitor's transmissions and send them back to the satellite firm's clients via the Internet. The price for such services will be small compared to the benefits.

---

[6]*Popular Science* magazine, p. 25, January 2000.

Summary

When we look at rapid, technology-oriented growth, we find nations of haves-and-have-nots. We also see corporations who conduct business internationally and those that want to do so. The international economic competition and trade-wars are increasing. Corporations are finding increased competition and looking for every competitive edge. Their nation-states will become more willing to assist them in that endeavor because the nation-state knows that economic power is world power. As sovereign individuals, do corporations and we as individuals have the power to fight for freedom and privacy against such a force as the nation-state-global corporation?

One way to gain the advantage is through industrial and economic Netspionage. It is true that both economic and industrial espionage have been around since there has been competition. However, in this information age, competition is more time-dependent, more crucial to success, and has increased dramatically, largely due to technology. Thus, we see the increased use of technology to steal that competitive advantage and ironically, these same technology tools are also what is being stolen. In addition, we now have more sensitive information consolidated in large databases on internationally networked systems whose security is questionable but the Netspionage threats are not.

References

Drew, Christopher, Sherry Sontag, with Annette Lawrence Drew. *Blind Man's Bluff: The Untold Story of American Submarine Espionage.* New York: Harper Paperbacks, 1998.

16

Business and Government Agencies— Shared Responsibilities

Capitalism and Democracy
—Impediments to Fighting Netspionage?

For businesses and government agencies to fight Netspionage, they must work together. However, the success of such endeavors depends on the relationship between them. In some countries such as France and China, there appears to be a more supportive role by the nation-states for their nations' businesses. Their goal appears to be focused on what has been discussed throughout this book, and that is enhancing the economic power of the nation-state and its place in the world by increasing the power of a nation-state's businesses.

Other governments such as the United States are often at odds with the global corporations that can make the nation an even more powerful force in the world, for example, Microsoft. The United States is a capitalistic society and a fairly democratic one. However, the government agencies often attack the businesses in the United States in the name of the consumer.

As we embark on the road of the future, we find it is a technologically built and traveled road. U.S. global corporations such as AT&T, Intel, Microsoft, and AOL are dominant in the worlds of telecommunications, ISPs, chips, and software. Where many countries would nurture these corporations, and help support their global dominance, the U.S. government continues to examine such corporations for monopolistic tendencies, often disapproving mergers and taking them to court in order to attempt to divide the corporation into pieces. The government's interest is allegedly protecting the consumer with apparent disregard for the changes in the global marketplace that such players dominate.

Add to this the U.S. federal, state, and other investigative agencies such as the FBI. Having spent millions of dollars on computer crime centers, anti-espionage awareness briefings, and requesting that businesses report violations of such laws as the economic espionage act, the FBI, for example, often declines to help the victims because the dollar loss is not over a certain amount. They already are behind in current investigations and have no time to take some new, smaller cases; or they may decline to take the case due to political pressures.

Add to these problems the fact that fighting Netspionage in a democratic nation-state is not easy. One must always be concerned with legal searches, proper surveillance, the rights of the victims, and the Netspionage agent once apprehended. This is not to say that such requirements are wrong, but one would probably agree that attacking the Netspionage problem in a nation-state controlled by a dictator would probably be much easier. To summarize one former member of the U.S.S.R., "We now have democracy in my country. I like democracy, but I would like democracy with more control."[1]

Netspionage Has Occurred
—Call the Government for Help?

The Internet, corporate intranets, and the global information infrastructure resembles the environment of the United States in the 1800s, in the days of the cowboys, sheriffs, and desperados. In the "Wild West," when desperados ran wild, hired guns worked as bounty hunters or robbers, the sheriffs and marshals were literally out-gunned, and often citizen vigilantes took the law into their own hands to "hang 'em high." You know, perhaps not that much has really changed—maybe just the technology.

Why shouldn't businesses count on their local law enforcement—their local sheriff—to help them if they believe they are the victims of Netspionage? Let's take a look at the possible consequences. Imagine you are the CEO and have been told by your staff that someone has attacked your Web site, corporate intranet, or that there are indications that someone used the corporate computer to steal proprietary information. Now you must choose—handle it internally or call in the local sheriff.

Deciding to Make the Call

Is reporting required by law? If yes, should this incident be reported? (After all, just because you are supposed to report it doesn't mean the legal staff can't interpret the law differently to get you off the legal hook.) If not required by law to be reported but against the law, should the incident be reported?

---

[1] Of course, it is not the purpose of this book to debate the different forms of government vis-à-vis Netspionage, but to simply point out that democracies have problems that often require a democracy to fight Netspionage with one hand behind its back.

Making the Decision—Factors to Consider

Costs versus Benefits—What is the cost in terms of lost public or shareholder confidence once the word got out that "you've been robbed?" What about lost productivity due to disruption, expending hours to support the sheriff's investigation? What are the benefits to the corporation? Should a sense of duty and community service be factored into the decision?

Extent of Loss—Is the loss more than the cost of supporting the investigation and loss of pubic confidence? (Yes, one may be naïve enough to think the cost is irrelevant, the Netspionage agent must be found and prosecuted. However, business is more about profits and not justice—a sad but all too true statement.)

Probability of Identifying and Successfully Prosecuting the Suspect—Is there a good chance the agent will be found and successfully prosecuted? If not, why report it and suffer the bad public image?

Potential Lawsuits That Will Follow—If a suspect is identified, will the identified suspect sue the corporation? Probably. What will be the potential cost of defending against such a lawsuit? What is the potential financial and public confidence loss in terms of lost revenue?

Time in Supporting the Criminal Justice Process—How long will the investigation through the prosecution cycle drag on? Months? Years?

Advantages of Law Enforcement Help—They can perform investigative acts that are illegal if done by citizens. They can obtain search warrants to recover the stolen property. They have access to related information to support the case, and they can physically protect victims and witnesses under some instances.

Disadvantages of Law Enforcement Help: Loss of Control Over the Incident—The corporation is now at the mercy of the criminal justice system, which does not worry about public image of the corporation, costs to the corporation, and the like. The criminal justice process will probably be costly and time-consuming. Once started, the corporation must be willing to cooperate in prosecution.

If the matter is handled internally, you want to quickly recover and get back to business. You want to avoid any bad public relations, image problems, and any knowledge of the incident being leaked outside the inner corporate circle. You want the entire matter kept quiet. You direct that the problem be fixed: Identify the vulnerabilities, patch the holes, and hopefully put a process in place to identify other vulnerabilities and fix them before someone tries to take advantage of them. That's what many businesses and government agencies do today—and with good reason as we shall see by the scenario described below.

In this case, you as the CEO consider such an attack an outrage, and you won't stand for it! So, you want the person found and prosecuted. You direct that the local sheriff's office be notified and explain the problem. Your security officer calls and is transferred several times to various offices and at each one the incident is explained. Finally, someone says they will send someone out to take the complaint—if you're lucky. Often a complaint is taken over the phone and eventually someone may show up. In this case, you're in luck.

A deputy sheriff shows up and in trying to explain what had happened, your staff determines that this person barely has enough knowledge to turn on a computer and use it for word processing. So, an information technology (IT) person is assigned to assist, along with support from the security office. In addition, the Human Resources personnel and legal staff must be kept apprised of the matter to avoid any legal or personnel problems that may develop.

Over the next several hours, the incident is described to the deputy in detail, notes taken, and people interviewed. The deputy is shown the crime scene and proof that the crime did occur, e.g., audit trails. The deputy then says that those audit trails on your server's hard drive are evidence and must be taken as evidence. It is explained to the deputy that it is not possible because the entire network would be shut down. The deputy insists and a compromise is reached by providing the deputy the drive after installing a mirror image copy of it so as to continue the business processes—just the beginning of a long and expensive process.

The deputy sheriff leaves, and subsequent calls between the deputy and the corporation become fewer. Then the deputy explains about being extremely busy with other cases. One of several things will happen:

- The investigation will be kept open, but never solved;
- The investigation has identified a suspect, but the prosecutor decides there is not sufficient evidence to prosecute (after all, this public servant is concerned about his/her win-loss record as private practice with a highly regarded firm is the goal. He/she is just here for the practice);
- The Netspionage agent is prosecuted, found not guilty and sues for millions of dollars;

- The Netspionage agent is found guilty, pays a fine, does not go to jail and sues for millions; or
- The Netspionage agent is convicted, goes to jail, and upon release is a reformed citizen and is never heard from again, at least not until they sell their story to TV or the movies!

So, you decide—should you call the local sheriff in this "Wild Information Age West," or handle it internally by calling in a hired gun or vigilante?

The U.S. government authorities want businesses to report such incidents, whether or not they will be investigated. Is this to track in their databases for the sole purpose of using the statistics generated to support more funds from Congress, or are they really going to do something about the problem?

According to one source,[2] the 1998 federal techno-crime prosecutions resulted in 417 cases being referred; only 83 of those were prosecuted; 47 persons were convicted; and 10 were found not guilty. In comparison, federal agencies referred over 132,000 other types of cases with over 83,000 prosecutions. Consumer fraud cases resulted in 627 referrals, and 319 prosecution. So, compute the odds of success and then determine if you would call your law enforcement for help.

A True Example
—The Government Is Not Getting the Message

A firm had proposed to a U.S. government agency of teaming together in a project to determine if that firm was a target of Netspionage. The firm had already realized that it was a potential target based on its business. However, what it really wanted to know was the possibility of any active Netspionage being conducted against them, and what the possible Netspionage agent would want to steal from the firm. Of course, the agents, as is usually the case, declined to answer specific questions as to what they knew of Netspionage activities directed against the firm. And as is often the case, they cited national security considerations for not discussing the matter. Is this true or was it just a smokescreen to hide the agency's incompetence? On the one hand, the firm may be losing its "crown jewels of information" without knowing it; on the other, the government may know it but remains silent.

Discussions were held and an operations proposal plan was developed. The plan, if successful, would not only assist in determining what information the potential Netspionage agents were after, but more importantly for the federal investigators, they could learn the Netspionage techniques that were being directed against a firm. Such

---

[2]*New York Times*, "Report Questions Government Efforts Against Computer Crime," 8/20/99.

techniques, it was reasoned, would probably also be tried against other targeted businesses. The information provided would assist in educating the agents and other businesses as to what to watch out for and how to defend themselves against such threats.

The agents dutifully reported their plan to their headquarters and subsequently met with the firm once again. However, instead of discussing the implementation of the plan, the agents provided representatives of the firm copies of the U.S. Economic Espionage Act of 1996 and proceeded to advise the representatives that under federal law, they must report any attempts by anyone to commit economic espionage. The agents advised that since the matter would have to be reported, no operational plan or sting operation was necessary.

The agents then went on to suggest that the firm unofficially set itself up to a Netspionage attack and at the first sign, notify the agency that would then open an official investigation. The agents stated that during any release of information to the public, e.g., new media, they would be sure to cite the excellent cooperation given by the firm. The agents failed to take into account the adverse publicity and the inevitable questions by the media and stockholders as to how the firm could allow such Netspionage activities to occur and why management was not doing a better job to protect the assets of the corporation. The firm's representative declined the agents' offer; and the meeting and relationship was terminated.

It is unknown whether the matter was dropped by the agency or the agents decided to set up their own sting operation. If the agency did nothing, excellent opportunities to mitigate Netspionage were lost. If the agency conducted its own operation, the results were never released to the firm who could have used such information to provide better defenses against the Netspionage threat.

Such results are common when businesses seeking help and offering help are not treated as equals with government agencies in the common fight to protect the sensitive information of U.S. global corporations and thus the economic power of the nation.

One unnamed source who experienced several disappointments in dealing on such matters with U.S. federal agents, stated that the agencies need to stop treating techno-crimes (to include Netspionage), as a typical white-collar crime. A better model would be to treat such crimes as a bank robbery because that requires an immediate response with aggressive pursuit of the suspects.

Changing from Adversary to Equal Team Members

Businesses and their government agencies have a responsibility to protect and share information in this age of international business competition.

Businesses must identify what needs protection; determine the risk to their information, processes, products, etc; and develop, implement, and maintain a cost-effective sensitive information protection program.

Government agencies must understand that what national and international businesses do impacts their country. They must define and understand their responsibilities to defend against such threats, and they must formulate and implement plans that will assist their nation in the protection of its economy. As a priority, this assistance must go to helping their nation's businesses thwart the Netspionage threats.

Both business and government must work together as only through understanding, communicating, and cooperating will they be able to mutually support each other in the world of business and economic competition. Thus far, the general relationship between businesses, in the United States at least, and government agencies has been one-sided: businesses dutifully report and provide information, which then goes into some government agency's black hole, never to be seen again. When the business reporting the information asked as to what happened based on that information, national security reasons are cited for not providing an answer. Speculation, often confirmed, is that the information is placed in a database for future reference. For some information this is valid. For other reports, it is unacceptable to the business community.

This process and one-sidedness is expected to continue into the future. Some government agencies put on their public relations hat and talk about partnership, but privately, some agents confirm that nothing has fundamentally changed. The process remains the same.

The Future

There are some good signs of cooperation, but often those are because of a rapport between managers in the corporations and individual government representatives. Based on the following history of "Internet non-regulation,"[3] there are some signs of hope:

- 1934: Communications Act passed—Enhanced service providers" are not "common carriers."
- 1966: Data networks and services exempted from regulation.
- 1980: Regulatory exemption retained to spur innovation.
- 1982: AT&T modified final judgement—Distinguishes "telecom" and "information" services.
- 1987: Enhanced-services regulatory exemption preserved.
- 1996: Communications Act passed—Decreases regulation by opening sector to competition.

---

[3]*Red Herring* magazine, p. 208, February 2000.

- 1999: Cable access proceeding—FCC defers to the market initially before acting.

On the other hand, discussions, rumors, and urban legends continue to talk of state, federal, and global taxes on Internet activities. One must remember that the bureaucracies of the nation-state are fighting to maintain their control and power. Laws, regulations, and taxes backed by agents and military forces are their tools for maintaining their power, control, and very existence.

These questions require serious consideration when your information systems are being attacked, because it dictates your response. As a nation-state, would you attack a country because of what a terrorist or economic spy did to a business or government system?

In order to defend against Netspionage, businesses and government agencies must abandon old processes and with them old prejudices. Neither the nation-state nor the global corporation can deal with the problem alone. It is simply too big and too complex.

Every nation and business must begin now to prepare for these new forms of 21st century business and economic warfare, supported by Netspionage.

Summary

In some countries, there is growing cooperation between businesses and government agencies to support each other in achieving success in the global marketplace. This cooperation includes the fight against Netspionage. In other nations, such as in the United States, there continues to be almost an adversarial relationship.

Only through close government and business cooperation will there be any hope to defeat the growing Netspionage threat in the future and also achieve success in the global marketplace.

17

Epilog: We're All In This Together

Welcome to the End of the World or the Beginning of the New One—Whichever Comes First!

We in the Western civilized world think of only the Gregorian Calendar. That calendar, according to one dictionary is ". . . a corrected form of the Julian calendar, introduced by Pope Gregory XIII in 1582 . . ." However, mankind has found many ways to measure time and dates. There is the Islamic calendar. This calendar began when the prophet Mohammed (Peace be upon him) immigrated from Makkah to Madinah. Thus, October 9, 1999, in Hijri is Saturday 29 Jumaada al-THaany 1420 A.H. It is also 328 of the Dionysian Period, 6712 of the Julian Period, Asvina 17, Saka Era 1921 (India), Era of Alexandria 7492 (Coptic), Ethiopian Year 1992, Buddhist Year 2542, Kouki 2659 (Japan), 11 Heisei (Japan). (See http://www.panix.com/%7Ewlinden/calendar.shtml for some interesting calendar information.)

The main point of all this is that calendars and dates are good for marking time and dates. They give us some baseline, a reference point, for making our lives a little more organized. But that's about it. Technological developments, Netspionage, and security issues will not change because some of us mark the end of a year by a specific calendar. So, you may sell your belongings, and wait for the second coming and the end of the world as we know it, or whatever your preference. However, what if we aren't all using the same calendar? What if whoever is supposed to come has a different calendar? Who is right? Does it matter? Well, maybe, if you are one of those who sold all they owned and are camped out on a mountaintop somewhere waiting for the end of the world.

Who is "right" and what is "right" will play a major role in the 21st century, but it won't be about calendars. It will be about individual freedom, government monitoring of our communications, privacy, security, "Big Brother," Netspionage, and who will win the battle for cyberspace, the miscreants or us.

The basic answer is really very simple: If we keep doing what we're doing, we'll keep getting what we're getting. There is no magic in beginning a new year and new century by one specific calendar. The only thing of importance in January 1, 2000, on the Gregorian calendar was the Y2K issue. And when all that was said and done, we were listening to all the experts giving their opinion as to why "it wasn't so bad." One benefit of finally getting to that date is that we thought we didn't have to listen to all that hype any more—wrong. "Experts" are still explaining what happened and why. One thing is for certain though, we can buy Y2K books very cheap, but then again, who needs them? Come to think of it, did we really need them in the first place, getting little old ladies scared out of their bank accounts and all that rot?

So, what can we really expect to see in the new century? Undoubtedly the future will bring an assortment of conflicts (see Figure 17–1). We discussed it throughout this book, but let's just end with a short recap of what things may come. Let's look at two general scenarios—a kind of the glass is half full and the glass is half empty views.

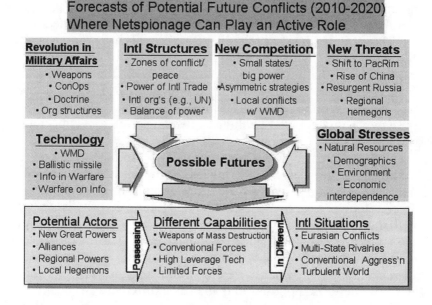

Figure 17–1 An array of possible future conflicts. Can you identify the areas where Netspionage can play a vital role?

Scenario One—The Glass Is Half Full

Well, from the technological viewpoint, changes will continue and continue more and more rapidly, even faster than they did in the last century. In fact, microcomputers will, in the information-dependent nations, be provided to citizens for free. That trend is starting, although the price in commercials online is a high price to pay for such "free" systems. There will come a day in the not too distant future when human voice to computer voice will be as easy as talking to each other. However, it will probably be more like trying to talk to one's teenager. Over time though, these systems will perform as well as they do on *Star Trek*.

Can you imagine how many millions of people that will bring into the global information age? So many are now held back because they can't afford a computer, they can't understand how to use the software, they have difficulty using keyboards, and even have difficulty understanding the basics of it all. All these people will be able to just talk to the computer in their own language and the computer will respond in kind. The "universal" translator will be developed to a sufficient state as to make learning languages meaningless, unless you just enjoy doing so.

The Internet will continue to expand throughout the world. The e-commerce phenomena will continue to grow and become as common as ordering a pizza on the telephone. The watch will also be your cell phone, your GPS, your Internet node, and basically your "all-in-one" information device. The "nano-devices" will be performing artery cleansing and technology will assist in the development of miracle cures and marvelous replacements for those who were paralyzed, lost their sight, and otherwise disabled.

Information sharing will become faster and more pervasive throughout global households. These systems will be integrated voice, video, and data systems and available for anyone to contact anyone in the world from any place in the world, in real time. There will come a time when the microprocessors containing the history of the world, all the mathematics known in the world, in fact all the knowledge of the world, could be implanted into one's body and be easily accessed and processed by the human brain. Children will go to school with that knowledge and learn how to use that knowledge to take it farther with each new generation. We will solve problems that today seem mind-boggling, like how to get Windows to work the right way every time.

By the whole of mankind communicating in a common language comes better understanding, less chances of conflicts, and a wonderful world for the generations yet to come—perhaps. Yes, all that is possible, but perhaps humanity's track record suggests otherwise.

Scenario 2—The Glass Is Half-Empty

The history of our species is one of conflict, violence, quest for power, wealth, control, and hatred towards those that are different from us in religion, nationality, race, or any other factor that we may dream up as rationale for treating people with disdain.

Yes, there will be great strides in medicine, communications, time saving devices, automation of repetitive jobs, and the like. While at the same time, the technology available for the good of mankind will also be available to those that don't share the same hopes and dreams. Terrorists, revolutionary groups, militia groups, organized crime, hackers, crackers, phreakers, info-warriors, racists, bigots, perverts, spies, and the other miscreants of society don't all just magically disappear at the stroke of 0001 hours, January 1, 2XXX as noted in the Gregorian calendar.

The techno-crimes and Netspionage will continue to increase in intensity and sophistication on a massive, global scale. More and more of the miscreants will form underground groups and coordinate their attacks on their intended victims, just as they have against the Indonesian government, Pentagon systems, furriers, political groups, just to name a few. These attacks will continue to increase, as the attackers believe they are immune and hide on the other side of the world, away from the "eyes of the law."

We believe the attacks may become so prevalent and vicious that there will be an outcry for governments to take action to stop outrageous violations of international and national laws. These demands for government action will come primarily from businesses, especially those involved in e-commerce whose businesses will be suffering major losses. The businesses have the power and the money to influence governments to take action. In addition, we'll see more businesses taking action on their own by hiring cyber "hit teams" to take out their attackers, at least in the virtual sense, because of governments' lack of swift action. Vigilantism will grow and guerilla warfare on the Net will be a continuous way of life for some time to come.

Some nations will try to stop the miscreants, while others will not because they are either too poor, too weak, or in collusion with the miscreants. Millions of people will gladly sacrifice some of their freedoms and privacy for security. "Big Brother" will be getting bigger.

The use of technology to gain the competitive advantage in the global marketplace will reach new heights of sophistication and ruthlessness. Information—computer warfare backed by Netspionage—as a tool in global economic warfare will become commonplace causing chaos in the electronic commerce arena and especially in financial circles, to include stock markets' manipulations. Billions upon billions of a nation's currency will be stolen perhaps even forcing some smaller nations to declare bankruptcy.

Throughout all this, the corporate manager, techno-crime investigator, law enforcement, and security professional will try to stem the tide but with limited effect. They will continue to lack sufficient budget and other resources to adequately do the job, although what they will be able to accomplish will be a vast improvement over what we have today.

More and more nations will fight wars through their computers. The use of infantry, aircraft, bombs, and rockets will be the exception. One good thing about that is that human casualties will be minimal. The basic exceptions will be to use the 20th century warfare methods against those nations who are not technologically dependent for their information infrastructures to support national services.

What will really happen as we go through the 21st century is anyone's guess. We imagine it is somewhere in between scenario one and scenario two. One thing is for sure: Information will be the key to success in either scenario. Sensitive information will be valued by the corporation that owns it and sought by the ones who don't. The Netspionage agents and techno-spies will play a critical role in determining who survives in the dynamic, global marketplace.

Appendix 1

The Economic Espionage Act of 1996[1]
****

By Patrick W. Kelley, J.D., LL.M., M.B.A.
****

New federal legislation strengthens protection of U.S. trade secrets and establishes clearer investigative parameters for law enforcement. Mr. Kelley is the chief of the Administrative Law Unit, Office of General Counsel, at FBI Headquarters in Washington, DC.

The development of proprietary economic information, commonly called trade secrets, is an integral part of virtually every aspect of U.S. trade, commerce, and business. Protecting trade secrets is essential to maintaining the health and competitiveness of critical segments of the U.S. economy.

The ever-increasing value of proprietary economic information in the global marketplace and the corresponding spread of technology have combined to significantly increase both the opportunities and motives for conducting economic espionage and trade secret theft. As a consequence, foreign governments, organized criminal enterprises, and rogue thieves use a variety of means to target individuals and industries to gain illicit access to valuable information, data, and technologies.

This appendix discusses new federal legislation that will assist federal, state, and local law enforcement officers in recognizing and investigating trade secret theft. New laws became necessary because prior state and federal legislation had not kept pace with the rapidly changing technological environment. For example, if an individual downloads a computer program code onto a disk without the permission of the code owner, has a theft occurred, even though the true owner never lost possession of the original code? If a theft occurred, is the value of the material taken determined by the value of the disk on which the code is now recorded or the value of the code itself?

---

[1]http://www.fbi.gov/library/leb/1997/july976.htm.

Although Congress had enacted patent and copyright protection laws, computer crime statutes, and laws designed to prevent government employees from wrongfully disclosing proprietary information obtained by virtue of their official duties,[2] no federal law protected, in a systematic, principled manner, trade secrets from theft and misappropriation. Legislation in the states varies but, in general, offers inadequate protection to victims of trade secret theft.[3]

Broadening Protection of Trade Secrets

In passing the Economic Espionage Act of 1996 (the Act),[4] Congress moved to remedy these problems by making the theft and misappropriation of trade secrets federal crimes. The Act adds a new Chapter 90 to Title 18 of the U.S. Code and employs a two-tiered approach designed specifically to combat both economic espionage and more conventional forms of trade secret theft and misappropriation. The chapter defines key terms, prescribes stiff maximum punishments, includes forfeiture provisions, provides for extraterritorial jurisdiction under certain circumstances, preserves existing state law on the subject, and protects the confidentiality of trade secrets during enforcement proceedings. Relevant sections of the Act are discussed below.

Section 1831 Economic Espionage

Economic espionage, as described in Section 1831, refers to foreign power-sponsored or coordinated intelligence activity, directed at the U.S. government or corporations, entities, or other individuals operating in the United States, for the purpose of unlawfully obtaining trade secrets. Section 1831 punishes the theft, misappropriation, wrongful alteration, and delivery of trade secrets when accused parties intended to, or knew that their misconduct would, benefit a foreign government, instrumentality, or agent. This section also makes punishable attempts

---

[2]18 U.S.C. 1905.

[3]Torren, "The Prosecution of Trade Secret Thefts Under Federal Law," Pepperdine Law Review, vol. 22, no. 59, 1994–95. Every state recognizes trade secrets as property that the law may protect from theft; however, the manner in which the states choose to protect them varies.

Thirteen states have statutes specifically coveringtheft of trade secrets; eight states include trade secrets as valuable property in their statutes governing crimes against property; two states include trade secrets in their computer crime statutes; two states list trade secrets separately from other property in their larceny statutes; and 24 states and the District of Columbia make no explicit mention of trade secrets in their penal statutes.

[4]Pub. L. No. 104–294, 110 Stat. 3488, (1996). The law's complete name is the Federal Economic Espionage and Protection of Trade Secrets Law.

and conspiracies to commit such offenses. The prescribed maximum punishment for an individual offender is 15 years' imprisonment, a $500,000 fine, or both; for an organization,[5] a fine of $10 million.

The principal purpose of this section is to prevent economic espionage, not to punish conventional commercial theft and misappropriation of trade secrets, which is the function of Section 1832. Investigators should administer Section 1831 with its principal purpose in mind and should not, therefore, attempt to apply it to misconduct by foreign corporations when there is no evidence of government-sponsored or coordinated intelligence activity. Rather, such misconduct should be pursued under Section 1832.

To prosecute an offense under Section 1831, the prosecution must show that perpetrators acted with the intent to, or had knowledge that their actions would, aid a foreign government, instrumentality, or agent. This specific-intent requirement separates conduct that is criminal from that which is innocent.

For example, the section does not proscribe legitimate economic reporting activities conducted by diplomatic, consular, and mission personnel in the United States and abroad. Thus, an economics officer assigned to a mission in the United States may gather unclassified labor statistics, gross domestic product data, import and export figures, agricultural output measurements, and similar publicly available material, without violating the Act. On the other hand, the theft of a secret formula for a newly developed pharmaceutical would be a crime under the Act whether committed by an economics officer or a common thief.

Section 1832 Theft of Trade Secrets

Section 1832 punishes the theft, misappropriation, wrongful conversion, duplication, alteration, destruction, etc., of a trade secret. The section also punishes attempts and conspiracies. The intangible nature of trade secrets required that the section be written broadly enough to cover both conventional theft, where the physical object of the crime is removed from the rightful owner's control and possession, as well as nontraditional methods of misappropriation and destruction involving electronic duplication or alteration in which the original property never leaves the dominion or control of the rightful owner.

The section does not require an intent to aid a foreign government, agent, or instrumentality; rather, it is aimed at conventional commercial trade secret theft, misappropriation, criminal conversion, and so

---

[5]Defined at 18 U.S.C. 18. In general, an organization may be held accountable for the criminal acts of its agents under a theory of respondent superior where the agents were acting, at the time of the offense, within the scope of their employment or agency.

forth. Thus, it covers purely "domestic" offenses or crimes committed on behalf of foreign corporations and individuals not affiliated with a foreign government. Because this offense is considered less serious than economic espionage, it warrants less severe maximum punishments: For individuals, 10 years' imprisonment, a fine, or both; for organizations, a fine of $5 million.

Congress did not intend for the law to apply to innocent innovators or to individuals who seek to capitalize on their lawfully developed knowledge, skills, or abilities. Thus, this section incorporates a high-threshold specific-intent element. To successfully pursue a case under this section, prosecutors must show both that the accused specifically intended to convert a trade secret to the economic benefit of someone other than the rightful owner and intended to or knew that the offense would harm or injure the rightful owner. Prosecutors also must show that the accused knowingly engaged in the misconduct charged. This high threshold of proof clearly separates conduct that is criminal from that which is innocent or simply careless.

Section 1834 Criminal Forfeiture

Section 1834 is designed to permit recapture of both the proceeds and implements of the offenses specified in the chapter. This section may prove especially telling because the proceeds of trade secret theft may be staggering in certain cases. The forfeiture provisions are meant to supplement, not replace, the authorized punishments in appropriate cases. The section provides for an in personam action against the offender, rather than one against the property itself, and preserves the rights of innocent third parties. The section incorporates, through reference, existing law to provide procedures for the detention, seizure, forfeiture, and ultimate disposition of property forfeited under the section.

Section 1835 Orders to Preserve Confidentiality

Section 1835 requires that a court preserve the confidentiality of an alleged trade secret during legal proceedings under the Act consistent with existing rules of criminal and civil procedure, evidence, and other applicable laws. This preserves the trade secret's confidential nature and, hence, its value. Without such a provision, owners may be reluctant to cooperate in cases for fear of exposing their trade secrets to public view, thereby destroying the law's value.

Section 1836 Civil Proceedings to Enjoin Violations

Section 1836 authorizes the U.S. attorney general to seek appropriate civil remedies, such as injunctions, to prevent and restrain violations of the Act. This provision is analogous to Section 1964(a) of Title 18 (part of the Racketeer Influenced and Corrupt Organizations Act). Under it, the district courts may prevent and restrain violations of the new chapter by taking such actions as 1) ordering individuals to divest themselves of any interest, direct or indirect, in any enterprise; 2) imposing reasonable restrictions on the future activities or investments of a person, including, but not limited to, prohibiting any person from engaging in the same type of endeavor as the enterprise used to perpetrate the offense; and 3) dissolving or reorganizing any organization. Thus, this section provides powerful weapons to enforcement and prosecutorial arsenals.

Section 1837 Extraterritorial Investigations

To rebut the general presumption against the extraterritorial effect of U.S. criminal laws, Section 1837 states that the Act applies to certain conduct occurring beyond U.S. borders. To ensure some nexus between the assertion of such jurisdiction and the offense, extraterritoriality is provided for 1) if the offender is a citizen, permanent resident alien, or an organization incorporated under the laws of the United States; or 2) an act in furtherance of the offense is committed in the United States.

Section 1838 State Laws

Section 1838 states that the Act does not preempt nonfederal remedies, whether civil or criminal, for dealing with the theft, misappropriation, or wrongful conversion of trade secrets. As noted above, several states have criminalized the theft of intellectual property and many have provided civil remedies as well. The Act does not supplant them.

Impact On State and Local Law Enforcement

Although the Economic Espionage Act defines federal offenses, its significance is not limited to federal law enforcement agencies alone. State and local law enforcement agencies can play important roles in administering the Act and protecting the proprietary information of business interests in their jurisdictions.

Identifying Offenses

All law enforcement personnel must learn to recognize the offenses defined by the Act. Some offenses seem obvious, but dealing with intangibles may require officers to expand their perceptions of property, value, theft, and espionage.

For example, if someone takes a computer with the intent to permanently deprive the rightful owner of its use and benefit, a larceny obviously has been committed. If, however, the same individual merely copies the formula for a newly developed chemical compound stored on that computer with an intent to use the formula for personal gain, would officers recognize that a crime has been committed? Similarly, if an exchange student at a local university is caught copying a professor's research notes on the use of ceramics in high-combustion engines, is it a matter for the dean or the police?

Recognizing Proprietary Thefts

Officers who respond to seemingly innocuous complaints involving commercial enterprises must be alert to trade secret theft possibilities because even owners may not realize the true gravity of an offense. What appears to be a simple breaking and entering with no apparent larceny may actually be a disguised or bungled trade secret theft.

Consider this case: A firm reports what appears to be a simple breaking and entering into a particular office but notes that nothing apparently had been taken. The evening before the break-in, however, a computer in that office had been used to prepare an important bid proposal on a multimillion-dollar project. Once the significance of that fact is grasped, the responding officers will realize that they may not be dealing with a petty misdemeanor but, rather, with a serious felony.

Processing Crime Scenes

Officers responding to potential proprietary thefts must ensure that their preliminary investigation and preservation of the crime "scene" is not limited by traditional crime concepts. In the above scenario, for example, preservation of the computer keyboard for possible finger-print analysis would be just as critical as securing the passageway through which the apparent thief gained entry. Similarly, ascertaining the identities of personnel who knew the computer in question was being used for preparation of the bid proposal would be vital to the investigation.

Tracking Patterns

State and local agencies should analyze trade secret crime reports and statistics to identify patterns in order to determine whether organized or systematic trade secret offenses are being committed in their juris-dictions. Seemingly random break-ins of high-tech firms in an industri-al park, for example, may be the work of sophisticated trade secret thieves. Sharing information concerning such trends with the FBI may prove beneficial.

Reporting Foreign-Sponsored Proprietary Theft

Investigators who uncover any trade secret theft or misappropriation potentially concerning an agent or instrumentality of a foreign government must immediately notify the FBI, due to the possibility that economic espionage may be involved. Of course, liaison with the FBI is appropriate in any trade secret theft case but becomes absolutely essential in economic espionage cases.

Ensuring Secrecy

State and local agencies should educate all of their personnel on the proprietary nature of trade secrets and take measures to ensure that trade secrets entrusted to their personnel by victimized owners for investigative purposes be kept secret. Innocent disclosure of such information may destroy its value as surely as would purposeful destruction.

Advising Businesses

Given the growth in technology and the increasing focus on proprietary information, businesses may be expected to ask for guidance on how to keep their trade secrets safe. While large corporations often have their own security experts to provide this type of assistance, smaller businesses, particularly sole proprietorships and partnerships, may ask for tips or training on preventing trade secret theft and economic espionage.

Detailed responses to such questions are beyond the scope of this appendix, but an excellent place to start is to emphasize that an aspect of trade secret law requires that owners exercise objectively reasonable steps to keep the secret in question secret. Owners who are careless or negligent in safeguarding their secrets will not be able to meet this requirement. Owners must take affirmative steps to mark clearly information or materials that they regard as proprietary, protect the physical property in which trade secrets are stored, limit employees' access to trade secrets to only those who truly have a need to know in connection with the performance of their duties, train all employees on the nature and value of the firm's trade secrets, and so on.

Conclusion

The Economic Espionage Act of 1996 is a powerful tool for combating trade secret theft, whether committed by agents of foreign governments or by "freelancing" thieves. Because it fills gaps in existing federal and state laws, the Act should establish a clear framework for law enforcement agencies at all levels to pursue both interstate and international trade secret offenses.

Appendix 2

About the Authors

William C. Boni, MBA, CISA

Mr. William C. Boni is a specialist in information protection in Los Angeles. He assists clients in safeguarding their key digital assets against the many threats arising from the Internet. In addition, he has pioneered the innovative application of emerging technologies including computer forensics, intrusion detection, and others, to deal with incidents directed against e-commerce systems. He has designed and implemented programs to protect critical information, intellectual property and trade secrets, and implemented programs to safeguard organizational networks and computer systems.

Mr. Boni has been quoted by leading publications such as the *Wall Street Journal, U.S. News & World Report*, and the *LA Times* and appeared on many network broadcasts, including *Prime Time Live* and CNN, discussing espionage and cyber crime. His distinguished career includes work as a U.S. Army counter-intelligence officer; federal agent, and investigator; vice president of information security for a large bank; and project security officer for "Star Wars" programs. He is a member of the American Society of Industrial Security Committee on Protecting Proprietary Information, and a Certified Information Systems Auditor (CISA). He is currently the Global Director of Information Protection for a Fortune 50 high-technology company.

Dr. Gerald L. Kovacich, CFE, CPP, CISSP

Dr. Gerald L. Kovacich graduated from the University of Maryland with a bachelor's degree in Asian history and politics; the University of Northern Colorado with a master's degree in social science (emphasis in public administration); Golden Gate University with a master's degree in telecommunications management; the DOD Language Institute (Chinese Mandarin); and August Vollmer University with a doctorate degree in criminology. He is also a Certified Fraud Examiner, Certified Protection Professional, and a Certified Information Systems Security Professional.

Dr. Kovacich has more than 37 years of security, criminal, and civil investigations, anti-fraud, information warfare, and information systems security experience in both government and business. He has worked for numerous technology-based, international corporations as a security, information warfare technologist, investigations, and anti-fraud program manager and consultant. He has developed and managed several information systems security, investigations, and anti-fraud organizations to include providing service and support for information warfare projects.

Dr. Kovacich has taught both graduate and undergraduate courses in criminal justice, technology crimes investigations, and security for Los Angeles City College, DeAnza College, Golden Gate University, and August Vollmer University. He has also lectured and presented workshops on these topics for national and international conferences as well as written numerous published articles on these subjects, both nationally and internationally.

Dr. Kovacich was the president of Information Security Management Associates, a Mission Viejo, California-based information systems protection and high-tech crime investigations consulting firm; and associate of Safetynet Services Consultant, SDN BHD, a Malaysian security and investigative consulting firm. He is an associate, responsible for computer and telecommunications protection, anti-fraud programs, business security, and investigations training and consulting for PT Citamulia Prajakonsulindo, an Indonesian banking and business-consulting firm. He is also a member of the Association of Certified Fraud Examiners' International Committee; ACFE Liaison Officer for Southeast Asian Nations; and former chairman of ACFE Computer Fraud Committee.

Dr. Kovacich is currently living on an island in Washington State where he continues to write, lecture, and conduct research relative to information systems security, information warfare defensive and offensive operations, high-technology crime, and techno-terrorism.

Index